ROBERT BROOKOVER

WISH IS MY MASTER

The Honor of War

TAMPA

Cover
Painting by Lauren McKeown
Design by Frank Weaver

ISBN 978-0-578-05766-8

For Mary Elizabeth

Dear Mother:

I suppose you have forgotten me as you do not write anymore, but I think about you all every day and wish to be there, but wish is my master.

Charles Kite

Camp Golden, Caroline County, Virginia
January 25, 1863
Company I, 10th Virginia Regiment
Killed: Battle of Chancellorsville
May 3, 1863

Wish Is My Master
The Honor of War

In Memoriam

Valerie Cole

Patti Ware

Harrison Kowiak

Who also died too young.

FOREWORD

At the suggestion of friends who read "The Honor of Love", I offer this guidance. For sixteen years, we lived in and served the people of the Shenandoah Valley of Virginia (Elkton, Woodstock, and Winchester). Later, we did the same for eleven years in Manassas, Virginia. During that time, people shared family lore, letters, and journals about the Civil War, and the impact that war had upon their heritage. Recollections of family intrigue, faith, political conspiracy, human sexuality, and love emerged.

As you read, please note that this series is a work of fiction: eighty percent is the product of real life story recounted to me, while twenty percent is fictional glue used to hold the series together.

I thank God for those descendants of the war—many long gone—who took time to tell their stories that I might weave them into this story. As our nation commemorates the sesquicentennial of The War Between The States, I wish you would take time to recount your family stories: tell them, write them, and record them. Make certain future generations know from whence you came. Maybe, someday, your stories will inspire an author to write.

Chapter 1

Amy Yardley

August 21, 1860
Atlanta

Stephanie approached exhibiting cleavage her pale-pink wedding dress afforded. Drury followed, donned in his gray uniform, sword buckled to his side, plumed hat tucked under one arm, offering George his right hand. "Congratulations," George said, patting Drury's right shoulder.

Drury smiled. "We've drained Georgia of her two most beautiful belles."

George nodded. "My sentiments exactly."

Placing her hand on my back, Stephanie guided me away. "Why the sad face?"

Swallowing hard, choking back grief, lifting my head toward heaven, preventing a flow of tears, I embraced her, whispering, "I wish Father were here."

Feeling Stephanie's arms tighten around me, hearing her sob, she nudged me, looking into my eyes. "If I had one wish—one fulfilled wish for my entire lifetime—I'd wish him here."

"Wish—wishing—that's all..."

"It is your wedding day, Stephanie," Sarah said from behind me. "Alexander would scold you both if he knew of your dismay."

A tear fell from my cheek, wetting a spot on my yellow bodice. "I'd pay a king's ransom to hear Father scold me."

Sarah embraced me. "Only God and time will tell if he ever awakes."

Chapter 2

Amy Yardley

"Wake up, Amy, wake up!"

The voice called from that dark place where dreams merge with reality. Shaking, tormented, writhing, I refused consciousness. Father lay shot a few feet away. Blood streamed from a wound above his temple. Women shrieked. Men sheltered their spouses. A second percussion split the air causing me even in my dream to lurch.

"Amy," George yelled. "Wake up."

Neither mind nor heart allowed the possibility. Horatio and Robert knelt beside Father, turning him onto his back. A commotion to the side of the front door drew my attention.

"Father," I screamed, "Father." Pushing Horatio away, kneeling, I rested his head on my lap and watched the shooting play out in reverse. The second shot echoed again. Nathaniel grabbed the assailant's hand holding the pistol. Forcing him to the porch, Nathaniel turned the barrel toward the man's head and pulled the trigger.

My hands—palms up—eased from under Father's head, as if compelling me to take their blood-smeared state into account. Not wanting to deal with reality, I wiped my hands on what I thought was my dress—trying to remove the blood—but realized I wiped them on the naked flesh of my thighs.

"Amy," George shouted, shaking me. "Wake up!"

I did. The front door opened. Sarah rushed out into the darkness. Naked, kneeling on the porch, George covered me with a quilt. The door opened again. Blinking, squinting, I tried to make sense of what I saw—make sense of the words I spoke I thought I'd never speak. "Father, you're awake."

Trying to stand, I remembered my nakedness. Wobbling, Father approached George who helped him take a seat on the settee. I sat next to him. He had remained unconscious for almost two months. Sarah had nursed him by forcing him to swallow mashed food and water, expecting him to die any moment. But now, he sat beside me, needing explanations.

"What's wrong? Why are you on the porch in the middle of the night?"

"We decided to sleep here," George said. "Amy was dreaming."

Curling up, I tried to speak. "Dreamt about the shooting—do you remember?"

"Yes—your wedding day—Nathaniel fought off the gunman. It feels like yesterday."

Sarah pushed a chair beside her brother and sat. "Alexander, two months have passed. Drury and Stephanie married yesterday."

"They did?"

"Yes," I said. "It's the end of August."

"You dreamt about the shooting?"

I nodded. "The feelings come back from time to time. In my dream, I see you lying there." I pointed to the place at the front door. "I see the blood, thinking you're dead."

Lifting me, he placed his arms around my back. The quilt fell, revealing my shoulders, but I didn't care—didn't care about nakedness, about prim and proper southern etiquette, about anything except Father's embrace—his tenderness, his strength, his love. I felt as if life might cease if I ever found myself without him.

Whatever occurred next, I know not. I awoke to the light of day to see George staring at me, listening to a cardinal chirp. Standing, making his way to my side, kissing me on the forehead, he squinted. "Do you remember your dream?"

"Vividly," I whispered, taking his hand. "Every detail." I gasped. "Is Father all right? I mean—I didn't dream his awakening, did I?"

"No—he's fine—what a miracle. After you fell asleep, Sarah and I helped him to the mattress on the dining room floor. He's slept since."

Sitting up, I placed my feet on the porch. "I want to see him."

"Wait—we need to talk," he said, taking a seat on the chair Sarah had used. "That's the third time..."

Reclining, I repositioned my head on the pillow. "It was also the last time—Father's embrace gave me peace. The dream won't recur."

"You're sure?"

Nodding, reaching up, placing my arms around his neck, I kissed his lips. "I'm certain."

Again our eyes met. "I'm going after them," George said. "The Unionists in Cherokee County and Andrew Shelton have gone too far. Enough is enough. The attempt on your father's life was the third time they tried to kill one of us."

"George, please don't. What if they *kill you*?"

"They'll have to kill Nathaniel and Drury, too."

"What?" I re-wrapped the quilt around me. "What are you talking about?"

"Honor—I'm talking about honor and revenge and standing up for what one believes. Drury and I talked during their wedding party. Men I considered neighbors place more weight on the unity of a nation than on what we mean to each other here in the same state. If they want your father dead, then they want me dead—you dead—Sarah dead—and who knows who else? One way or the other, the assassination attempts must cease."

"That's it? My feelings don't matter?"

"What honor is there in fear—living as if you have no backbone? Amy Yardley, you didn't fall in love and marry someone who runs away."

"No—no I didn't." Turning, I studied the male cardinal chirping from a low hanging pine branch. "Red—Father's red blood in my dream, bright red feathers on that bird, your face flushed red with determination. There's nothing I can do to stop you when you've made up your mind. Get yourself killed. I'll bury you next to your parents."

Chapter 3

George Yardley

September
Sunday Morning

"When will you return to Alpharetta?" Alexander asked as I helped him down the church steps. Another month had passed in which he gained strength and resolve. Amy and Sarah remained in the narthex reminiscing with Stephanie and the Sinclairs about the weddings.

"Tuesday."

"So we'll have Monday together?"

"Yes, why do you ask?"

"I want you in on a meeting tomorrow with Governor Brown, Alexander Stephens, and other aspiring Confederate leaders. It's important they hear your perspective about our militia."

"They will not want to hear what I think."

"They may not like what you think, but I will make certain they hear." He tipped his hat, greeting a woman I failed to recognize. Her smile convinced me they enjoyed more than a casual friendship. "These gentlemen conclude that because our militias train, they're ready for battle."

"I'd hate to go to war right now. I shoot straight and hit targets, but doubt my proficiency under fire."

"What are you saying?"

"I told Drury my militia can't hit what they aim at in a serene pasture. Most, if faced with returning fire, would turn-tail and run."

"Our leadership must hear that. Our officers tell a different story."

"I doubt Drury stories," I said, standing beside the carriage awaiting the ladies.

"Drury is not a senior officer. Senior officers, according to Napoleon, always paint a rosy picture. Political and military leaders need facts not illusions. If the officers training the troops told the truth regarding military preparedness, they'd lose their commands." He nodded toward Sarah's and Amy's approach.

"After her dreams," I said, "do you wonder what I'd be up against with Amy if that assassin had killed you?"

Alexander looked down, refusing eye contact. "No—I mostly wonder how Nathaniel had the presence of mind and the strength to act as he did—to save my life."

"Have you two solved the problems of birthing the Confederacy?" Sarah asked as her brother helped her into the carriage. Amy followed offering an inquiring glance.

"No," I replied. "If anything, we've clarified them."

The ride home proved peaceful. I admired Atlanta's beauty. People went about their business as if they had not a care in the world.

Chapter 4

George Yardley

Monday Morning

Our carriage clanked along the brick road, delivering Alexander and me to the armory. There, the Atlanta Grays mingled in small groups, creating an air of military superiority while exhibiting a fashionable Southern uniform. From my previous visit, I recognized a guard posted at the gate and saw others preparing for drills. None seemed attentive to our presence, though every man paid heed as Colonel John Bingham, recently assigned commander of the Grays, greeted us. After exchanging cordialities, Colonel Bingham informed Alexander the attendees had sent word of their tardiness. Unbeknownst to Mr. Stephens, Mr. Davis had arrived in town.

With time to spare, Bingham invited us to observe preliminary drills. Alexander and I eyed each other, proceeding with our host to a parade ground. At the far end, the grounds faded into a pine thicket.

"What will we see?" Alexander asked.

"Three of our finest units," Bingham replied.

With raised white eyebrows, Alexander grimaced. Three sections consisting of twenty-five soldiers marched from behind headquarters onto the grounds, each man attired in gray wool pants and jackets, every piece of equipment held in place by leather belts and shoulder straps.

Captain Price, mounted upon a black gelding, saluted the colonel. "Sir, we are ready."

"Let us see a drill. We'll repeat it when the other guests arrive."

"Yes sir," the captain replied, turning his horse and riding toward the troops. Each squad received a barked order. The center section marched in a tight two-line formation toward the woods while the other two double timed at forty-five degree angles, flanking an imaginary objective. All three sections—front row kneeling, back row standing—fired by rank, rear rank firing first followed by the front rank. Two distinct volleys cracked the air.

"Impressive," Alexander said, addressing the colonel. "What's wrong?" He asked me.

"Not one could hit the broadside of a barn at twenty yards."

The colonel stomped his right foot. "These are the best trained troops in the South."

"Then surrender before hostilities begin. Most shot high. To prove it, conduct the same drill with me as the target. Not one would hit me."

"Now George," Alexander said as he motioned toward three carriages at the gate.

Looking around, I spotted an empty barrel. Turning it on its side, rolling it out onto the field, I stood it upright. By then, the three platoons had returned to their original positions. Stretching my handkerchief out, using a rock to hold a corner on top of the barrel and splinters to hold two other corners, I formed a target. Upon my return, I found myself in the presence of Jefferson Davis, Alexander Stephens, Governor Brown and Robert Toombs. Horatio stepped from around the carriage.

"What's the purpose of the barrel?" Alexander asked.

I turned to the captain. "Perform the same drill. See how many balls hit that handkerchief." Jefferson Davis stared at the target.

"Mr. Yardley doubts the marksmanship of our troops," Bingham said.

"Fine," Mr. Davis said, "see if your men meet Mr. Yardley's test."

The colonel signaled the captain. Turning, looking at the target, he galloped off.

They repeated the drill. The left and right flank double timed to their positions, coming to rest while the center section took its place. Lieutenants and sergeants shouted commands culminating in the order to fire. This time, they shot at will. The volleys resounded through individual clouds of smoke that formed into three large clouds.

"Colonel Bingham, may I retrieve my handkerchief?"

"No," Mr. Davis said. "Let us walk together." He moved at a brisk pace toward the barrel with the others following.

Alexander and I approached. "The handkerchief is as it was," I said under my breath.

"We may experience the wrath of Mr. Davis."

"What is his position?"

"In all likelihood, you look at the president of the Confederacy."

"Is that right?"

"Yes," Alexander said, as we watched the party near the target.

Colonel Bingham took the lead. The handkerchief and barrel remained unscathed.

"Mr. Yardley," Jefferson Davis said, "what must we do to correct this atrocious marksmanship? Seventy-five balls flew—not one found the mark." He glared at Bingham.

"Give me five minutes with one platoon."

"Permission granted," Mr. Davis responded.

Selecting the middle squad, seeing their embarrassment, I sought their attention. "Any of you ever hit something you aimed at?

A silent response followed until one spoke. "Yes, I have."

Well, I need all of you to hit that target. When your sergeant gives the order to fire, aim at the ground in front of the barrel. You're shooting high. Now do it, and show your mettle." Realizing no one trusted my instruction, I approached the lieutenant, requesting his musket. "Is this loaded?"

"Yes, sir."

"Does it shoot straight?"

His head bowed. "I don't know."

Walking three paces forward, straining under the watchful gaze of the other platoons, receiving the undivided attention of the future leadership of the Confederacy, I took aim. Inwardly, I heard Father's instruction. Outwardly, I sensed a presence not seen. Slowly, I pulled the trigger. To the center left, a black hole appeared in the handkerchief. "You men do the same. Squeeze the trigger; don't pull it."

The sergeant bellowed commands. The rifles reported. Balls flew blasting the barrel to pieces. At first, a tense silence aired, followed by an excited chorus.

"Don't," I said as the shouting quieted. "You must do that under fire. If you get off the first shot, there won't be as many Yankees firing back." A loud approval of laughter sounded.

Turning, I walked toward Bingham. Mr. Davis addressed Alexander. For some reason, I stood back rather than enter the ring of conversation. When Mr. Davis finished speaking, he turned. "Young man, what are you doing over there?" With a wave of his hand, he motioned me to join them. "I understand you train with a militia in Milton County."

"Yes, sir. I am a member of the Milton Guard."

"What did you instruct those men to do?"

"Aim at the bottom of the barrel. The blast kicks the rifle barrel high. If they aim at the chest, they'll miss high. If they aim low at the knees, the ball might find the torso."

"Mr. Yardley," Colonel Bingham said, "can you remain in Atlanta to address this issue with my officers."

"Colonel, your officers will get word." I turned, giving recognition to the troops. "Besides, I've only been married a few months to Mr. Frey's daughter. It's time I get her home to Alpharetta."

"For your sake," Mr. Davis quipped, "I hope she's more attractive than Mr. Frey."

"She is. As a matter of fact, I don't know anyone who isn't more attractive than my father-in-law." Through the laughter, Alexander smiled a look of approval.

ಞಞಞಞ

"Would you like to go home or by the club for a noon meal?" Alexander asked as we departed in the carriage.

"Home—have an itch to return to Alpharetta."

"You appear deep in thought."

"Do you feel all right about Amy living on the farm?"

"Why, yes. Of course. I feel she's where God wants her. Why do you ask?"

"I've taken her away from Sarah and you. As much as I love her, I know you love her too. If someone took her from me, it would leave a hole in my heart. You must feel the same."

"We do in one sense; but in another, we are happy, because Amy is happy."

"Has Amy changed?"

"Yes, she appears more womanly and is completely devoted to you."

"She misses you. I don't want her to feel bad, but I don't know what to do except bring her to see you."

"You are always welcome. As well as you two ride the horses, you can get here lickety-split if need be. Besides, I sail for England in the middle of October. Sarah will be alone for three months. It would be nice if you visited."

"Why are you going to England?"

"Business—my last trip before war starts as well as my last trip with my friend, Captain Percival."

"What do you do in England?"

"I take in dramas and orchestra presentations. There's a game they play for leisure, called golf. Once or twice a week, I'll go out to see how many fours I can get."

"Fours?"

"Some golf courses consist of eighteen holes. It is supposed to take four shots to sink the feathery on each hole. Thus, out of eighteen different holes, you count the number of fours. Most of the time, I'll score five to six fours in a round and then have a multitude of five's and sixes."

"Whoa, I'm lost."

"I'd like to introduce the game in Georgia."

"Introduce it?"

"Well, yes. Each hole is about a hundred yards long. If I bought land that could hold eighteen holes, I could establish the first links in America."

"Links?"

"The holes are linked together—like a chain. You finish one hole and proceed to the next. Thus, they refer to the eighteen holes as links."

"We'll have to talk about this at length," I said. "Your description puzzles me."

The carriage proceeded to Wheat Street. Sarah and Amy sat on the front porch.

"Have you borrowed my husband long enough?" Amy asked.

"Why yes," Alexander replied, "but I had to coerce him to return here. He didn't seem all that interested to see you."

I smiled knowing Alexander was returning fire for my earlier comment. "It was my idea to return home," I said, staring at Amy. "Don't believe your father. If he had his way, we'd be dining at the club."

"Alexander," Sarah said, "the lies you tell. You ought to be ashamed."

"I am—sometimes."

The clanking of horse hooves drew our attention. A carriage stopped. The door opened. Drury and Stephanie stepped out. Stephanie, in a plaid gingham dress, stared at Amy as she ascended the steps alone, not speaking. Ignoring us, she embraced my wife. Amy returned the gesture.

"Thank you," Stephanie said. It seemed a word of gratitude flowing from deep inside. Without further explanation, she turned, walked down the steps to her husband, entered the carriage, and departed.

"We will return to Alpharetta tomorrow," I said, watching the carriage drive away.

"You changed your mind?" Alexander asked.

"Farm work and leather work can wait. Spending time with those we love has taken on new meaning."

As I watched Amy and Stephanie embrace, I eyed Drury. The events at the armory were one thing; but seeing Drury wait at the carriage was another. Something made me understand it was no longer if war came, but when. I felt an intense foreboding that a year from now the life we shared would not exist.

Chapter 5

Amy Yardley

Sensing a stirring in my husband, I wished us alone. Realizing he intended on remaining in Sarah and Father's company, I refused to push the issue. The journey home would provide time to pursue the matter. George had adopted my family. Whatever thoughts Stephanie's embrace precipitated, he needed time.

Approaching Sarah, placing his arm around her, George smiled. "Do you think your brother might indulge us with an afternoon batch of juleps?"

"Alexander, you heard your son-in-law. Why do you stand there as if a statue?"

"Please forgive me," he said, bowing, imitating a slave. "I'll get right to it—didn't think we accepted slavery in this house." He opened the front door, making his way to the cabinet in the dining room.

"May I help you?" George asked. "I'd like to learn to mix the concoction in case you're in England."

"Certainly," Father said, "as long as you don't mind being mastered by women."

"Alexander," Sarah said from the parlor. "I heard that comment."

"I intended such."

"I intend for you to practice Southern etiquette."

"I do on occasion; but no man can stand up to that burden every moment."

"What burden?" Sarah asked, walking into the dining room.

"The Southern belle's expectations regarding Southern etiquette."

"My, my, does the Southern gentleman apprise us of his feelings about his heritage?"

"Just one Southern gentleman's appraisal," I said. "My husband feels differently."

"I've not yet learned the art," George said. "I believe the first step is acquiring the ability to make juleps. If I mix them strong enough, most women won't care whether I'm a gentleman."

"Haven't we had this conversation?" I asked.

"Yes," Sarah said. "Seeing how your father corrupts your husband, you'll have it your entire life."

"If the truth were known," I said to George, "women would have *you* refrain from being a Southern gentleman when in their presence."

Father ceased stirring, looking at me as if astonished I understood such things. Slowly, he resumed circulating the spoon in the pitcher. "That's how most women feel about me," he said. He paused; I think waiting my response. None came forth. "Are you concerned about the other women's responses to George or George's response to them?"

"Both."

George eyed me. "Both?"

"Yes, both. Jealousy stirs a woman's heart."

"What does that mean?" George asked.

"It means when we are in public, every woman—both young and old—takes special pleasure in admiring you. It's hard to live with what I see in their eyes. The farm is wonderful. I have you to myself."

"I'm insulted you imagine I would succumb to another woman's desires."

"George," Sarah said, "you're not Jesus. Women seduce men."

Father raised the pitcher. "Juleps, anyone?"

"Amy," George said, "I love you. Women may look, but I refuse to fall into temptation."

At that moment, jealousy departed my being. He meant what he said.

Horatio appeared at the front door, not bothering to knock. He entered.

"Come in, why don't you?" Father said. "Don't mind us."

"I am in—carrying information. Jefferson Davis put the word out your son-in-law is the best damned soldier in the entire South." A brief pause ensued as we eyed George and as Horatio addressed my husband. "He's to offer you something—a commission—when circumstances birth war."

"I hope not," George said, addressing Father. "If I'm the best soldier, Amy and I will go to England with you."

Father sipped his julep. "Soldiers have been known to desert before war starts."

"May we embark for England in the morning?" I said.

Father smiled. "Did you marry a coward?"

"No, I did not."

Sarah turned to Father. "Stop bantering. This talk upsets me—war and the like."

Father turned to Horatio. "I hope you refuse; but may I prepare you a drink?"

"Certainly—I would enjoy that."

"What does this mean?" Sarah asked. "Will George get caught up in this war?"

"We will all get caught up in it," Father said.

Sarah sipped her drink. "Incredulous—the thought of fighting our own people—what has this nation come to?"

"That's the problem," Horatio said. "We're not one people. We're not one nation. We've never been one of anything.

Furthermore, statehood means more to most than our national identity. I claim residency in Georgia—not the United States."

"True," Father said. "In England, I refer to myself as a Georgian—not an American."

George came to my side and took my hand. "We talk about freeing the slaves, and that must be done. Governor Brown offered an equitable solution, and the Yankees turned it down. Something else stirs this pot."

"It does," Father said.

Horatio took his drink from Father. "True."

"Then, what is it?" Sarah asked.

Father took a seat. "Political power—who will rule the country. All this so-called compromising is political heresy. We began as an agrarian society; but the North transitioned into a shipping and industrial culture with different values. It is nothing more than old ways versus new ways. They see the South as a drain on the nation's economy. If they remove the institution of slavery, they know we will fall. Morally, they have the high ground. England abolished slavery last century. Everyone in this room agrees that one person should not own another. The war shall be fought over economics and states' rights. If we lose, the victors will impose a new rule of government. Our hope is that the North has not the resolve to fight."

"I doubt they lack resolve," Horatio said.

Father took a seat in the parlor. "I doubt it also."

"Why is it our only hope?" I asked. "Can we not win the war?"

"There are twenty million Northerners and five million Southerners," Horatio said. "We are outnumbered."

"If we know we will lose, why fight?"

"Because men are stupid," Sarah replied. "Throughout history, they've never abandoned the killing fields."

"There is no turning back," Father said. "The dye is cast. The sounds of war will fill our cities and valleys when the cold of winter passes unless we elect a president to unite us."

"I doubt Jesus could manage that," Sarah said.

"Jesus isn't running for the office," Horatio added.

I kept my eyes upon George. He appeared agitated.

"Well," George said, "let us enjoy the next eight months."

"Amen," Sarah said. "Amy, let's fix supper." She stood, inviting me to the kitchen. "Horatio, if you and Cynthia would care to join us, you are welcome."

"Thank you, Sarah. We may do that."

Father chuckled. "You've never declined an invitation. Set two more places, Sarah."

Chapter 6

George Yardley

Atlanta

A rap at the front door interrupted dinner. No one came to another's front door in the South after dark unless trouble knocked. Around the table, a silence awaiting Alexander's response posed itself. He stood, making his way through the parlor. I followed. From my vantage point, I saw a shadowy silhouette.

"Yes?" Alexander asked. "What can I do for you?"

"Mr. Frey, you don't know me. I heard two men talking in a bar. George Yardley's your son-in-law?"

"Yes."

"He's in danger—men out to get him."

With that, the man scurried down the steps, disappearing into the darkness. Alexander, seeing me, beckoned. "If you're in danger, so is Amy."

Returning to the dining room, Alexander took his seat, peering into expectant faces. "Oh, just a beggar—guess he smelled Sarah's cooking—wanted food. I gave him coins."

Emotions swirled within my chest. What happened alarmed me. Not the intruder's message, but Alexander's story that sought to protect the women from truth. The story that confirmed he would lie if the situation called for it.

Dinner proceeded with additional talk about the prospect of war, but Horatio and Cynthia turned the conversation toward Amy and me. They wanted to know about life on the farm.

"I have an idea," Alexander said. "You three should go to England with me on my next and probably last crossing."

"Alexander," Sarah said, "have you gone mad?"

"No, it would be 'smashing' to use an English phrase. Why shouldn't these young people witness the glories of the earth? And," he said after a pause, "it is high time you see a part of the world other than Atlanta."

Amy's eyes bulged. Sarah would have no part of it. "Don't get your hopes up young lady. Your father fantasizes. Before long, he may give the brothers Grimm a run for their money with his own make-believe fairy tales. Even if he thinks of you as Snow White, your prince dines at this table. For the love of God, Alexander, why put such a notion in your daughter's head?"

Alexander Frey

Very rarely had I lost a moment's sleep. The moon illuminated my bedroom, which served to make it more difficult to doze—not that I wanted to. Whatever danger George faced, I concluded, resulted from his prowess as a marksman and possibly as a leader. The question that stirred was who wanted George out of the way? Southerners jealous of George's capabilities? Or, had Northern spies infiltrated the South? Were there those who would kill George to prevent his abilities from enhancing the military efficiency of the South? After all, I thought, if the South achieved an early upper hand due to superior training and marksmanship, it could abbreviate the war. Killing George could be advantageous.

George Yardley

Too groggy to tell if the sounds I heard were raindrops or dewdrops, I turned over to a new dawn. In Atlanta, daylight awakened me; but on the farm, I always awoke before dawn.

Amy's face lay illuminated by morning light. Knowing if I caressed her cheek she would rouse, I refrained, though suddenly I felt a presence. Two ghostly figures, my parents, near the opened window, vanished from sight. Jumping up, peering into the dawn, I saw a horseman ride past the house investigating every floor, but especially the first. Slipping behind the curtain, I watched. Continuing up the street, the rider kicked his horse.

"What's wrong?" Amy asked. When I turned, she lay propped against the headboard.

"A rider—he studied the house."

She pulled a pillow to her chest. "Where is he?"

"Rode off." Lying down next to her, we curled up. "Have you ever seen anybody ride past here this early?"

"No. I never awoke at this hour until I moved to Alpharetta." She fell back to sleep.

A floorboard squeaked followed by footsteps descending the stairs. Before I knew it, I awoke, though uncertain as to whether I had dreamt the images of my parents and the rider.

After dressing, I found myself outside brushing and saddling the horses.

"What's wrong?" Sarah asked from the kitchen window.

"Nothing. I need to get back to the farm." I said. "We're not going to England, are we?"

"Doubtful—Alexander dreams."

"I feel as if I've lost control of my life. I need time at home."

"Get Amy up, have breakfast, and we'll get you on your way."

Chapter 7

Amy Yardley

Tuesday Morning

We rode at a quick pace, but not a gallop, clearing the city's outskirts within fifteen minutes. George refused to speak, which roused my anxiety. He appeared wary, searching. His eyes scanned the woodland at two-to-three second intervals. With my mind on him, the trip to Milton County went faster. Before long, we approached the Montross cabin where George had helped the Waylands.

I saw something; knew I heard something. Why am I on the ground? Why is Pearl running away? A pain filled my abdomen— filled me with a sinking, weakening, sensation. A warm, moist fluid stained my dress. Red, I thought. Red, red, red, was my last recollection except for George shouting my name.

George Yardley

Howard Montross, with breechloader in hand, ran toward me as I knelt next to Amy. "George, is that you? What happened?"

Placing my arms under Amy's neck and knees, lifting her, I carried her toward the cabin. My attention focused on Amy, though instinct made me aware someone fled through the woods. The cabin door, partly open, opened further as Mrs. Montross appeared. She directed me to place Amy in the same bed where I had placed Mr. Wayland.

"What happened?" she asked.

"Someone shot at us."

Then I spotted the blood stain. Taking a knife, I slit the dress but caught myself. "Mrs. Montross, would you please look? I can't bear to see." She separated the slit, tearing the dress and Amy's undergarment.

"A ball lodged in her lower abdomen—blood oozes," she said.

Howard Montross studied the wound. "We have to get the bullet out and cauterize the wound. Bring the kettle of water and a knife," he said to his wife. "With your permission, George, I have to do this."

He looked at me; but I had no idea why he asked permission. Rushing to the fireplace, he held the knife above yellow-red coals until the steel glowed hot. Returning to Amy's side, he plunged the blade to one side of the ball, forcing it out. A blood-bubble spurted that Mrs. Montross patted dry.

"The wound looks clean," she said. "Let's cauterize it."

Howard returned to the fire preparing the knife. "If this doesn't work, I can stitch it. She won't bleed to death."

His words comforted me, allowing my thoughts to turn to the shooter. The searing sizzle of flesh awakened my senses. He placed the knife on a table. "You want me to go with you?"

"Stay here to protect the women. Don't know who I'm dealing with."

"You're leaving your wife to traipse after the gunmen?" Mrs. Montross asked. "She may need you when she awakes."

"Take care of her till I return."

Outside, Splinter and Pearl stood near the front door.

"Look at that," Howard said pointing to Amy's horse. It took a moment, but I realized what Howard saw. The horn on Amy's saddle had been blown away by the shot. "That probably saved her life."

"I'll take both horses—may need them to chase down this bastard before I kill him."

Howard looked, shrugging his shoulders. "Whoever shot her will die by morning."

"I'll pay you for any expense," I said, riding off with Pearl's reins in my left hand.

The leaves on the ground were disturbed where the gunman mounted his horse. The trail led toward Atlanta. If the assailant returned there, he could hide his whereabouts in the city. I had a decision to make: ride cautiously, making certain I didn't ride into an ambush or fast. I opted for speed.

The tracks stood out on the dry dirt. The gunman rode at a gallop, which served to imbed the hoof prints. I kicked Splinter, pushing hard. Halfway to Atlanta, I jumped from Splinter to Pearl. After switching horses, I noticed the tracks became less intense, slowing to a trot and then to a normal pace. I pulled up on the reins not wanting to ride into a bullet and not wanting to lose my chance to kill the man who shot my wife. The trail left the road, moving into the woods. Past that point, around a bend and out of sight, I tied Pearl to a tree, and remounted Splinter.

Another horse whinnied. Raising my musket, I shouted, "Come out—I won't kill you."

A man appeared from behind a thicket walking with his hands up, leading his horse. "You said you wouldn't kill me."

"Get over here." As he reached the road, I made him lie face down with his hands flat on the ground. "Who are you?"

"Quincy Boxer."

"You have two seconds to tell me why you shot my wife."

"Aimed at you and missed."

"What's your motive?"

"What you and your wife did in Savannah with the slaves, and the fact you killed those bounty hunters. There's a thousand dollar reward on your head—placed by..."

"By who?"

"If I tell you, they'll kill me."

"You don't get it do you?"

"Percy Lee and James Cavanaugh."

"Where they from?"

"Percy is from Savannah, and James is from Cherokee County."

I drew my pistol, pointed it at the back of his neck, and pulled the trigger.

Chapter 8

Amy Yardley

Milton County

A week of recuperation passed at the Montross cabin. After convincing Sarah and Father to return to Atlanta rather than accompany us to the farm, George saddled the horses. Word about the shooting and our return home reached Alpharetta through the postal carriers. Nathaniel, resting under a willow in the town square, spotted us. Standing, he waved.

"How long have you waited?" George asked.

"As long as Mother demanded." He caught my eye. "Amy, glad you've mended."

"Glad, too," I said, sliding down off Pearl.

"Guess you have instructions to inform Lillian of our arrival?" George said.

"That's a fact—she means business."

"When's Aunt Lillian ever not meant business?"

Nathaniel nodded. "Can't say, but I'm to inform her of your presence."

Embracing Nathaniel, I thanked him again for saving Father's life. "Any chance Lillian might let us settle in before she makes an appearance?"

"None—unless Father puts his foot down."

"Nathaniel," I said, "I need time—a day or two. Hold her off until tomorrow, if not the next day."

He mounted Winsome. "I'll talk to Father first. Maybe he can restrain Mother. Glad you're back." Turning, he made a complete circle. "Did you catch the shooter?"

George nodded. In turn, Nathaniel nodded as if understanding something that needed no explanation.

"What happened?" I asked, directing my attention to George. Nathaniel looked down at me. "Amy, the shooter's dead."

"What? George, is that so?" He nodded once more. "Why didn't you tell me?"

"Haven't told anyone."

"I'm your wife."

"He doesn't talk much about killing," Nathaniel said. "He nods a lot."

֍֍֎֏

Thursday passed without Lillian's arrival. Friday morning, I heard the buckboard. Robert drove. Samantha and Leslie sat on the plank across the back. Nathaniel rode Winsome. George and I stepped outside onto the front porch. Lillian refused to take her eyes off me. George helped her down. By the time he assisted the girls, Lillian had her arms around me tight and firm.

"You all stay here until I grant permission to enter the cabin," Lillian said. Holding my hand, she guided me inside.

The fire formed a bed of coals. Taking an iron poker, she stirred the yellow-red embers, placing two split pieces of hickory in their midst. In seconds, the new wood caught. "Please sit," she said. I did so. "This is where George's mother and I sat when we talked—in front of this fireplace." She stared into the flames. "Are you all right?"

"No, I'm not." It was the first time I told the truth since the shooting. "Something's wrong, but I don't know what."

Lillian's face grew pale. "Can you explain?"

"Maybe—I've regained strength, but..." I wanted to weep—not cry—weep, as if grieving.

"What's wrong?"

"It feels like something died in me—below where the bullet lodged. It feels like I'll never have children."

Chapter 9

Alexander Frey

October, 1860

Exiting church, meandering down the steps, Horatio signaled me. We made our way to the rear of my buggy.

"Alexander, certain gentlemen require your presence at a meeting at two o'clock this afternoon in the office of Alexander Stephens."

"On the Sabbath?"

He allowed neither explanation nor opportunity for argument. Turning, Horatio lost himself in the crowd.

Atlanta's society, steeped in Christianity, spun in a whirlwind of political upheaval. Hoping to gain insight from the common sentiment as to what might prompt this urgent meeting, I remained by the carriage, listening and questioning.

Talk centered on the presidential election a month away. The Democratic convention that met in Charleston fractured into two parties, if not three, concluding with the Southern delegates walking out. With the party ruptured, two candidates emerged: John Breckenridge of Kentucky and Stephen Douglas of Illinois. To make matters worse, John Bell of Tennessee threw his hat in the ring representing the Constitutional Union Party. A divided South and a divided Democratic Party stood nary a chance against an emerging Republican Party led by an Illinois lawyer, Abraham Lincoln. Threats of secession sounded from every voice based on the prospect of a Lincoln victory. During the ride home with Sarah, I concluded that in the meeting I would hear the plan of secession from the Southern leadership.

We partook of dinner after which I napped. The walk to Alexander Stephens' office proved refreshing in the autumn air. To my surprise, Donald Thomas, Robert's brother, joined me, making his invitation to the meeting known.

"What was the talk at the Methodist Church this morning?" I asked.

"A Lincoln presidency and disgust over Douglass and Bell entering the race," he said. "Breckenridge doesn't have a chance."

"What about secession?"

"It's a matter of when and which state goes first."

"What's your guess?"

We stopped outside at the office door while I awaited his answer. "Alabama, but South Carolina seems bent on leading the charge."

"Well, we're about to find out," I said, opening the door.

Governor Brown directed us to seats near the head of Stephens' conference table. "We waited for you, Alexander," the governor said. He asked Reverend Woolridge to pray.

The governor moved to the point without introduction or comment. "Gentlemen, we are confronted by the possibility of an anti-slavery president and by a president who affirms he will preserve the Union. Thus, I asked you to assemble that we might discuss our commitment to secession."

The agenda moved rapidly; but in doing so, I failed to greet my friend, Edward Walker, seated across from me. "Edward, it is good to see you. Forgive me for not speaking. How are Mrs. Walker and your daughter, Gretchen?"

"Good afternoon, Alexander. Mrs. Walker is well, and Gretchen remains enamored with your son-in-law." Those at the table knew of George's gallant exploits at the ball. "More importantly, how is Amy?"

"Recovered from the wound—Freys heal well. She's riding her horse—a good sign."

"And George?"

"He's George—busy at farming and leather work."

"That's not all he busies himself with," Alexander Stephens said. "He has the Milton Guard in the best shape of any militia unit."

"Well, that seems to be the consensus amongst those who know little about fighting. If you asked him, he would tell you it scares him that people believe his Guard is so well trained." A silent pause allowed me to greet the others at the table. Afterwards, I turned toward Governor Brown. "If we are to discuss secession and a president who vows to fight to preserve the Union, we better talk about military preparedness."

"Interconnected issues exist," the governor said. He thought for a moment and then presented a list. "Secession, slavery, military preparedness, and states' rights." Another silence followed. "Anything to add?"

"Our families and our wealth," Jacob Goldman said.

The Jewish community chartered their synagogue in Atlanta in 1857. Mr. Goldman and his family were long-standing members, understanding their place outside the mainstream of southern culture. His presence at the meeting meant one thing. An army needs boots—boots that Jacob's factory made.

"Yes," I said. "Critical issues—our families and wealth. Thank you, Jacob, for confronting us with the reality of who and what matters." Jacob nodded.

"Politics and war always crash into family and wealth," Governor Brown said. "The issue is sacrifice, isn't it?"

"Indeed," I replied. "Sacrifice *is* always the issue. In deference to Jacob, we Christians understand sacrifice as does the Jew.

When it comes to war, neither religion prevents headstrong and heartless descent into that pit of hell." A silence followed. "A sacrifice has been made that one of us, the Jew, rejects while the other, the Christian, holds as justification for any cause. The South will fight in the name of Christ and for the sake of God as will those who seek to preserve the Union."

"Where might that leave us?" Jacob asked. "For what cause shall we fight?"

"For the cause of family and wealth, but I doubt your sons will take up the sword."

Jacob cocked his black-bearded face. "Why might that be?"

"Because Southerners won't allow it," I said, studying the faces around the table. "Enough prejudice exists that your sons would have to shave their beards and disguise their identity." Brows furrowed.

The governor broke the silence. "It seems we strayed."

"No, we have not strayed," Edward said. "Alexander drove us to the heart of the matter. Governor, you made an honest and forthright proposal concerning slavery. Congress rejected it. Everyone—Southerner and Northerner alike—knows a civil war will cost five to ten time more than your proposal to purchase and free the slaves. If slavery was the only issue, we would get off cheap and with no loss of life if congress accepted your bill. The issue is whether the constitution grants a state certain rights superseding those of the Union. In our nation's history, we have taken for granted that such rights exist. Now, Mr. Lincoln and his Republican Party hold fast to the premise that the Union of states must exist at all cost." He hesitated. "Is the sacrifice of our families and wealth worth the political conflict of states' rights?"

"Yes—unequivocally," Alexander Stephens said. "Without the right of a state to govern itself—to establish its own laws and moral standards—we will find ourselves enslaved to the impositions of ruthless masters in Washington who will deprive us of our God-given rights." A chorus of affirmations echoed around the room. "Our wealth will be taxed and our families will become impoverished. We either fight to retain our southern culture, or we lose it."

"So, what are you saying?" I asked. "We will sacrifice our families and wealth to either a brutal war or to the government of the Union. We can take our pick."

"Precisely," Stephens replied. "We fight for our heritage; or, it will fade into history."

"And if we lose the war?" I asked. "Our heritage is lost."

"Only if we lose the battle," Governor Brown said, "and that is why we meet today. Do we have the resolve to win?"

"Twenty million Northerners and five million Southerners," I said. "They have ships and an industrial infrastructure that rivals any nation in Europe." I paused, looking around the room. "We have one summer of resolve. I take it that we intend to start this war next spring. If we are not victorious by October, our cause—our culture—and our heritage are lost."

"So," Alexander Stephens said, "make it a quick, brief war—demoralize our enemy. The Pennsylvania/Maryland border must become our northern border."

"Easier said than done," Donald said. "The Northern newspapers flame the fires of a long and cruel war."

"They print fear to scare us into a lack of resolve," Governor Brown said. "One sound victory in Pennsylvania, Ohio, or Delaware, and they'll turn tail. Maryland may secede."

"Well," I said, "we can talk till Election Day. We need to prepare ourselves for a long and sacrificial war—spend resources we need to spend—to persuade Lincoln of our determination to fight. Let us prepare our militia in the hope they will never fight."

Somehow, my words turned the debate to a conclusion. We decided to build a forge to produce cannons, cannonballs, and bullets on the eastern outskirts of Atlanta next to the railroad tracks. Edward and I pledged the funds for the factory and assumed production oversight.

As the meeting ended, Jacob approached Horatio and me. "My sons will go to war. All I ask is that we prepare them." He turned to leave. "Good day, gentlemen."

"The Jew means business," Horatio said. "He won't allow us to separate his family from our cause."

Governor Brown stood. "If he is willing to sacrifice his sons, then so be it."

I approached the governor to shake hands. "In case you do not understand, we just committed ourselves to war. Once Lincoln is elected, we wait to see which state secedes first." I thought for a moment and then nerved myself to speak. "I'm not positive; but think our brothers in the Democratic Party put up two or three presidential candidates to assure a Lincoln victory. If divided as a party, then a Lincoln presidency is certain. Following that, secession is a sure thing."

"How dare you, Alexander, make an allegation such as that," Stephens said.

"Alexander is a worldly man," Horatio said. "He knows more than he lets on. Besides, we have his commitment and his money. He is with us."

"He's been shot as has his daughter," Donald said. "If he wanted, he could sail for England and leave this forthcoming ordeal behind. I well imagine Mr. Frey knows more of what he speaks than anyone else in this room."

Chapter 10

Alexander Frey

I strolled away from the meeting down a familiar and secretive path. Mrs. Beatrice Perkins, widow of Captain Rodney Perkins, and I maintained a lasting friendship. In her youth, she followed her husband from one army outpost to another until word came to Fort Smith that the Cheyenne killed him. With an air of rigid emotion, she packed their belongings and returned to Atlanta where she found her father near death and her mother a stroke victim. Within the month, her father died leaving her to care for her invalid mother. About eight years before Beatrice's arrival, my wife had died giving birth to Amy. Horatio introduced us.

It happened once or twice a month when not at sea that I called upon her. Her home, located in the business district two blocks from the railroad station, stood devoid of neighbors and convenient to my office. The window shade covering the two windowpanes on the front door provided invitation. If pulled down, I could knock.

As I approached the quaint two-story, modest structure, an errant, foreign emotion welled. Beatrice's friendship was steeped in the truest sense of the word, in the truest English fashion. For years, I marveled at how happily married English men and women maintained friendships without desecrating their marriage. Poets proclaimed the glory of these relationships. Though widow and widower, Beatrice and I found our way into such a relationship. We shared everything except sexual intimacy. At times, we shared touch through embrace and through the holding of hands.

Lost in thought, I failed to realize I had taken the final steps to the front door. My knock proved gentle. The welling emotion grew stronger creating an internal conflict—part of me wanted to flee—while part wanted to burst through the door.

"Alexander, what is wrong with you?"

Inside, closing the door, I allowed our eyes to meet. Regardless of what I wanted to do to her, a nerve restrained me. Unable to speak, I eyed her up and down. At first, she resisted my embrace and kiss. And then, I felt her release into my care. Ten years of passion unleashed itself. In the parlor where we had shared our friendship, we lay on the floor sharing each other.

"I'm afraid to ask," she said as we separated, making brief eye contact.

"I'm afraid to answer."

"But you will—won't you?"

"Yes," I said, standing, fixing myself while looking away so she might do the same. Turning, I found her seated on the sofa.

"Well?" she said. "What was that about? And, don't say you don't know."

I seated myself in the red cushioned chair where I always sat, unable to withhold the truth. "Forgive me."

"Forgiveness will play no part in this conversation."

"Sorry—but I just committed the South to war."

"To war? I doubt even the likes of you could do so by yourself."

"There were others, but they waited for me to give the word; so I gave it."

"And how might you have done that?"

"By telling them we needed to commit resources to train our militia and by committing my own resources to build a forge."

"A commitment to war in your mind," she said, searching for a word, "means a commitment to sex?"

I looked down, embarrassed. "Forgive me. Something made me hesitate outside. I almost didn't knock."

"And why might that have been?"

"I don't know." She peered at me waiting. "I felt an emotion outside that I'd never felt and didn't know its implications. While assessing my reservation, I knocked."

"The front door is not the only thing on which you knocked."

My eyes widened in recognition of her humor and truthfulness. "Would you like me to leave?"

"No. Actually, I'd like you to do to me again what you just did. Besides, if you leave, you may never return."

"Why? Why would I not return?"

"Because I know you, Alexander Frey, and I know sex distances friends. In case you don't understand, we just became lovers."

"What?" I said, standing.

"We have been the greatest of friends," Beatrice said. "Now, the challenge before us to is to become the greatest of lovers. If I allow you to leave, guilt will prevent your return."

"Well, I must return home."

"Yes, but not yet."

She rose, approaching me, taking both hands in hers. "An Indian war took my husband. I will not allow the prospect of civil war to take my friend and lover—at least not without a fight."

She stretched upward on her toes placing her arms around my neck, kissing me. Persisting, she continued until she felt my kiss.

๛๛๛๛

Darkness had not yet fallen as I walked away. Something or someone trailed behind me. In my coat pocket, I felt for my derringer, cocking it in preparation. I removed it, concealing it in my right hand. Hearing silence, my instincts confirmed a presence. If lucky, I thought, it was a ghost—maybe that of my wife. Darkness descended. Whatever lurked, I hoped lurked in my mind alone. Suddenly, I nerved myself to turn, pointing the derringer. Nothing presented itself except relief. Resuming my stride, I hurried home without uncocking the gun.

Not able to resist, I went to the dining room where I poured bourbon, drinking it straight and then poured another. This one I fondled as I seated myself in the parlor. War, sex, and alcohol, I thought, and wondered about the mixture. I believed that what I did on the Sabbath would return to haunt me as I felt haunted during my walk home.

Chapter 11

Alexander Frey

"Long meeting, yesterday?" Sarah said.

I entered the kitchen dressed for the office. Melon, bacon and biscuits awaited me.

"Do you have time for eggs?"

"No. This will do." Once seated, I bowed, offering a blessing for the food and the presence of God throughout the day.

Sarah poured coffee, setting a cup at my place. "That's the first time I remember you including Amy and George in prayer. Are they in danger?"

"Who?"

"Amy and George—why did you pray for them?"

"They face no more danger than us."

"The danger of war?" she asked.

"Yes." I paused. "If Lincoln is elected, and I believe that a foregone conclusion, we will make war by this time next year, probably by April. I committed along with Edward Walker to build a forge. The intent is to supply the army with cannon and shot, though I should have committed to building a shipyard in one of our ports. If the war takes longer than six months, we will lose without a naval force."

Taking her seat, Sarah sipped her coffee. "That is a lot to digest."

I completed breakfast, gave my sister an embrace, which I did every morning, and began my walk to the office. Even though I wanted to sail to England once more, that prospect grew more remote by the hour. Commitments—business commitments, family commitments, and in my heart, a commitment to someone I loved more than a friend—prevented the possibility.

Upon settling in at my desk, I wrote Beatrice a note, which I intended to deliver along with a bouquet of flowers at noon. Why, I wondered, had yesterday's meeting resulted in such activity?

When not thinking about her, I searched my mind for builders to construct the forge. I developed a list of architects in Atlanta while trying to sort out the factory's location. Horatio, Jacob Goldman, and Edward Walker arrived at ten o'clock, having given attention to the same details. Within the hour, we made the necessary decisions regarding the location and the approximate cost. To our surprise, Jacob pleaded to contribute a third of the funds and to share in the profits. William and I agreed to the offer making certain Jacob realized the outlook for profit appeared dim. Horatio committed to perform the necessary paperwork to incorporate *The Southern Ironworks* and to order the furnaces and forges.

Having stopped at a flower shop, I proceeded to Beatrice's home with a quick step and a quickening heart. Though feeling boyish embarrassment, I wanted to see her. Maybe, I thought, she understood I would feel this way and that precipitated her concern that I wouldn't return.

Finding an envelope wedged in her front door with my name printed thereon, I opened it, faced for the first time with her handwriting, which I admired, and read.

> *Alexander:*
> *Upon awakening this morning I found mother dead*
> *and am making funeral arrangements.*
> *L, Beatrice*

I imagined the "L" stood for love, which warmed my heart. Not able to fight the impulse, I reached for the doorknob, checking to see if it turned. It did. Entering, I gazed into the parlor almost as if inspecting a crime scene. Then, I entered the kitchen searching for a vase and finding an empty one on the windowsill. In a moment, I fitted the bouquet and poured water into the container. On a little desk in a room off the parlor, I found a pen, inkwell, and paper.

Beatrice:
Please accept my sympathy regarding your mother's
passing. I shall return this afternoon.
L, Alexander

PS: I hope not to have mistaken the meaning of the
"L".

Placing the flowers and the folded note together on the coffee table, I closed the door. As I walked away, a strange thought overcame me. Maybe, what I felt following me home last night was the ghost of Beatrice's mother. It humored me to think she died, and her spirit found us in love's embrace on the parlor floor.

Deciding to go by the club, I encountered Horatio at the entrance. "Where have you been?"

"Well," I stumbled over my words.

"Mrs. Perkins came here looking for you. Her mother died." Horatio waited for his words to sink in and then continued. "She needs to talk with you."

"Did she tell you her destination?"

"Home—she made the funeral arrangements."

"Have you eaten?"

"No."

"May we share a meal?"

Sitting in the middle of the club's dining room, I felt as if every eye glared at me. Imagining at first I appeared guilty over the previous night's affair, I concluded word spread about the forge. Maybe hungry business eyes longed for war profit.

The meal proved quick and to the point. Horatio reported no additional news since our morning meeting. We parted company.

Beatrice greeted me with a bowed head, unable to look at me and unable to speak. Trying to understand, I found my voice crippled, which led me to act. Approaching her, I placed my arms around her, embracing her. Her head and arms came to rest against my chest, through which I felt faint sobs. My arms tightened.

"Thank you for the note and flowers," she said. Her voice cracked through a stronger sob.

"I returned this morning of my own accord."

"I know." She looked upward into my eyes. "I was so happy last night that I failed to look in on Mother before I retired. I don't know when she died."

"I think she died before I left." Her eyebrow contorted. "As I walked home, I felt the strange sensation that a ghost followed me."

"Do you believe in ghosts?"

"Certainly, doesn't everyone?"

"I don't know. If it a ghost, I hope it was my mother and not my husband. He was a jealous sort. I'd hate to think he witnessed..."

"If it a ghost, I'd prefer it was your husband." We gazed at each other. Laughter emerged.

"We're a pair, aren't we?" she said. "You arrived yesterday having indulged in the business of war—to indulge in me—for which I am grateful. My mother dies, and we indulge in ghost stories." She paused. "Oh, what's the use? For the first time in my life, I feel free. I was enslaved to my husband and then enslaved to my mother. You have been my only source of joy for ten years." She looked at me with lips and eyes that smiled and kissed me.

Truly, I knew in that kiss she was free, but that I wasn't. Politics and the threat of war had mastered me.

Chapter 12

George Yardley

"You work in secret," Amy said, standing at the shed door.

Startled, I grimaced. "It's scary when someone sneaks up on me. If that happens in battle, I'll wind up dead or in an enemy prison—neither prospect suits much."

"A morbid thought I care not to address. What are you making?"

"Leather jackets for each member of the Guard." Walking to a cupboard, opening the door, I exposed six completed coats. "I have twenty-four yet to make."

"Is this something you want to do yourself?"

"Would you like to help?"

"What could I do?"

"Anything you set your mind to. You could sew the pocket flaps," I said, pointing to one on the workbench. She approached giving me her undivided attention. "You need a sharp punch and a sharper needle. Making the holes for the stitching is troublesome if you don't keep your tools honed."

"Is that so?" she asked, catching my eye with a teasing smile. "Such talk excites me. Is your needle honed?" As my fingers grasped the needle on the workbench, I caught on. "That's not the needle to which I refer," she said.

"I'll never live that down. May we work now and play later?"

On her tiptoes, she reached up, kissing my cheek. "Promise?"

"Promise."

For about twenty minutes, she studied my every movement. "May I?" she asked. The leather proved thick and tough, refusing to relent to the punch. "Why won't it penetrate?"

Holding the pocket flap, I stretched it across a brace. Selecting a tool, I held it up. "It's called a punch. You are pushing." Assessing how to get my point across, I held up my hand, palm toward her. "Take your index finger and punch my palm." Hesitating, she did so. "It's a quick motion. If you push with the punch, the leather bunches. If you punch it or poke it, the sharp point pierces the leather."

She tried again. To her amazement, it worked. She formed a new flap, punched the holes and sewed it to a jacket. By bedtime, she finished the three pockets and then, finished me.

೫ೆಲ್ಬ್ಬ್

Next day, returning to the cabin for the noon meal, Amy spotted a buckboard. It was Nathaniel. In the wagon, sacks of flour and cornmeal from the Marietta Mill lay stacked.

"If I hadn't delivered this, you'd have had nothing to eat this winter." Nathaniel said. "Or, don't the newly-married eat?"

"Funny," Amy said.

We greeted each other. Amy instructed us to put the sacks in the cellar while she fixed dinner. Obliging, Nathaniel and I went to work.

Completing the work, Nathaniel motioned toward the shed. We walked inside. "Need to tell you something." I waited. "Received word in Marietta that Andrew Shelton and others want Amy and you dead."

"How do you know?"

"Word travels. Why don't we kill the bastard?"

Moving a piece of leather on the workbench to collect myself, I spoke. "I've thought about it."

"What's his problem?"

"Wish I knew."

"You know some things. You know about the fire and the Livingstone widow dying; you know his connections in Cherokee County; and, you know his politics."

"Not sure about his politics, though I guess he sides with the anti-secessionists, those who want to preserve the Union. He doesn't own slaves. None of it adds up to reasons to kill your neighbor."

"No, it doesn't," Nathaniel said. "Unless he thinks you saw him kill that widow and start the fire."

Amy called. Strolling toward the back door, I confirmed my cousin's reasoning. "I've made certain Andrew knows I believe he killed the widow."

We entered the cabin to find the table filled with strips of dried venison, carrots, spinach, and biscuits and jam.

"Looks like you're mended?" Nathaniel said to Amy as we sat.

"Pretty much—the pain is gone."

Before anyone touched a bowl or serving spoon, I offered the blessing. As we passed the dishes, I noticed Amy staring at Nathaniel. "What are you looking at?"

"Nathaniel's leather jacket—he wears it as much as Father wears his. Do you take it off at bedtime?"

He ignored the question, turning our attention to news of Samantha and Leslie. Though no one said it, it seemed nice to enjoy a meal without talking of war or Andrew Shelton.

Nathaniel climbed up on the buckboard, placing his musket between his legs in the footwell.

"Cousin," I said, "it's time you purchase a pistol."

"Don't have the funds, but will when I'm as rich as you."

I bowed my head, embarrassed. Robert and Lillian were not rich. If farming was all a family did, inflation made it difficult to make ends meet. Farmers needed an additional trade for monetary success—that's what The Yardley's Leather Works did for my family. On the other hand, Robert seemed content. As I watched Nathaniel ride off, I committed to purchase a pistol for him the next time I visited Atlanta.

Early Sunday morning as we awakened, Amy questioned whether we needed to go to church—her mind set on the leather jackets. I made short order of her protests. "Neither Father nor Mother permitted work on the Sabbath—nor shall I."

Chapter 13

Alexander Frey

At the cemetery after the committal service, mourners greeted Beatrice. As they departed, I posed a concern. "We have a problem," I said, escorting her to the carriage. She gave me a sideways glance. "I must introduce you to my family."

Silence followed as we walked. "You see that as a problem?"

"Yes—I request permission to discuss our situation with Sarah."

"Would you define our situation?"

I didn't think posing the question would create difficulty, but I understood women enough to know they always needed more information, especially about relationships.

"Our situation—our situation is best described by your commentary last Sunday night. Our relationship transitioned from friendship to—well, at least—uh, lovers."

"Gallantly put—your artful, confident words would faint any woman into a swoon. Not sure of yourself?" she asked with a smile.

My frustration exposed itself along with a degree of curiosity. "Why do you make this so challenging?"

"Me? Have I offended?"

"You're playing me."

Beatrice's smile intensified. "You think this is playing?"

"If you're not careful, these mourners will think you have a strange way of grieving."

She turned to investigate. "I hadn't noticed."

"Hadn't noticed what?"

"My fellow mourners."

"Do you think they notice you?"

"I hope so," she said. The smile dissipated. "You have my permission to discuss our relationship with Sarah." She turned, walking around the carriage to where her driver waited.

I remained in a mental fog. My driver guided his carriage beside me. "Mr. Frey, may I take you to your office?" From inside, Horatio encouraged me to take a seat.

"Home," I said. "Take Horatio wherever he wants." I entered the carriage, seating myself across from my friend.

Horatio broke the silence. "Having female problems?"

"The answer to that obnoxious question is yes, I am."

"Would you like advice?"

"Not from you—you got me into this."

"Oh, I see, you choose to blame rather than resolve."

"You are to blame for all the problems I've had in my entire life."

The carriage swayed and clattered through the cemetery gate. An autumn breeze freshened the air.

"If that's the case," he said, "everyone should have as good a friend as I've been to you."

"Please, Beatrice plays games, and now you play."

"My advice—marry her—soon."

"Marry her? How could you pose such a thing? We just buried her mother."

"Why not? She would make a good wife, and if the truth be known, would harness your hostility toward me."

"I plan to discuss our relationship with Sarah. Have you obtained all the information you need to obtain about Beatrice and me?"

"So far, but that leaves the marriage question."

"That question will not be answered today. I must acquire Sarah's and Amy's responses to me having a woman friend."

"Friend?" Horatio said. "Your friendship with Mrs. Perkins ended as it should have ended years ago. A blind man could see that. Whatever your relationship was, it has no resemblance to the past. I'm looking out for your best interest and hers. Now that her mother died, every eligible man in Atlanta will knock at her door."

Horatio's words stung. Though I doubted his postulation, I felt jealousy. I knew she would never open her door to anyone but me. Caught up in thought, I exited the carriage without giving Horatio the time of day.

"Don't worry," he said out the window, "I'll pay the driver." I retrieved my wallet, but before I could pay, the driver, the carriage, and Horatio departed.

Walking up the stairs, not certain what to say, I stopped on the porch staring down at the bloodstain that remained from the shooting. It was, I determined, time to move on from death, from thoughts of war, from a secret relationship, to whatever my future held. For certain, Sarah knew nothing of my friendship with Beatrice. Once I informed her, we would inform Amy.

"Why are you home?" she asked as I entered the house.

"I have a personal matter to discuss. May we sit?" I said, motioning to the sofa. A wrinkled brow, squinted eyes, and pursed lips crossed her face. "Please be patient with me." I paused. "For ten years, I have enjoyed a personal friendship with Mrs. Beatrice Perkins. I doubt you know her. Her husband, Captain Perkins, was killed on the frontier by Indians. Subsequently, she returned to live here with her parents. Her father died shortly thereafter. This past Sunday, her mother died. I've come from the funeral." Catching my breath and my train of thought, I failed to comprehend how Sarah received the news. She sat emotionless. "Our relationship has grown into something more than a friendship. There, I said it."

Sarah rustled in her chair, looked out the door, and then turned to me. "Alexander, I am happy for you, and I believe Amy will be even happier. When might I meet Mrs. Perkins?"

Shocked, my anxiety subsided. "Uh, well, I've not given that a thought."

"Due to her mother's death, may we extend an invitation for dinner this Saturday night?" She stood. "And may we extend an invitation to Horatio and Abigail?"

Standing, I embraced Sarah. "I will do so this afternoon."

"Will you eat before you return to the office?"

"Why yes. Thank you for your sensitivity."

She took a few steps toward the kitchen. "I am honored you approached me regarding Mrs. Perkins."

On returning to the office, I found Horatio and Edward Walker waiting outside. Entering, Horatio reported Alexander Stephens had located a more appealing site to build the forge. The railroad had completed a track into the armory. With war looming, troops could muster and travel from one central station. Stephens, at Jacob Goldman's urging, received commitments from two landowners to build the forge on their property adjacent to the tracks outside the armory gate. Familiar with the area and in agreement with the plan, I committed to the idea.

Upon concluding the discussion, I expanded the invitation list to Saturday's supper. "Gentlemen," I said, "would you, along with your wives, do me the honor of joining Sarah and me for dinner this Saturday evening?"

"Certainly," Horatio said.

"I knew you would accept," I said and turned to Edward. "Horatio never declines a dinner invitation. Do you believe you could attend?"

"Why, yes—we can."

"Edward, please invite Gretchen."

My friend and business acquaintance appeared shaken. I discovered later that rarely had anyone included his daughter in social engagements. Though blind, she had grown into a lovely young lady. With their status in Atlanta's society, not to mention their wealth, the Walkers knew every young man in Georgia would have pursued Gretchen save for her blindness.

"Thank you, Alexander," Edward said. "Your gracious invitation is accepted." He turned, unable to hide his emotion. "I must go." Neither Horatio nor I extended farewells. The office door closed leaving us alone.

"You certainly know how to charm people," Horatio said.

"What?"

"Not many people include Gretchen in social engagements."

I thought about Amy—about how perfect she appears in my eyes and the eyes of others. For a moment, I pictured her blind. Blindness, as George offered leaving the Walkers' ball, ruined everything.

"If you see Edward before Saturday, tell him supper is at five. Mrs. Perkins will attend." Horatio smiled and departed.

After straightening my desk, I retrieved paper and pen to write Beatrice. Upon completing the note, I found a boy on the street, paying him a nickel to deliver it.

৯৯৯৫৯

Saturday afternoon created an anxiety worse than any storm through which I ever sailed. My carriage arrived home at four o'clock. Sarah presented me a bouquet of roses from our garden intended for Beatrice. Taking the flowers, I arrived at Beatrice's at 4:30, stepped from the carriage, approached the front door, and knocked. I received no answer. Peering at the driver, I repeated the knock. Twisting the door handle, it resisted. I imagined the flowers in my hand wilting along with my heart.

Returning to the driver to discuss the dilemma, I received a blank stare. Standing in the street, contemplating my predicament, I noticed the driver's eyes focus upwards. Turning, I saw Beatrice tapping on an upstairs window. In a moment, she opened the door.

"Your refusal to open the door petrified me," I said.

"You are fifteen minutes early. I refused to open the door partially dressed."

"Forgive me—I should have realized."

"Besides, you failed to inform me you would arrive with the carriage."

"I wanted to spend time with you before supper." Remembering the flowers, I offered them. "Please accept these along with my plea for mercy."

Receiving them, she went to the kitchen, filled a vase with water and returned placing the bouquet on a table in the entranceway. I watched as the pale green silk dress buttoned to her neck swayed with each step. "You look beautiful."

"Thank you."

"I have something to tell you." Our eyes met. "Other guests will dine with us." Raised eyebrows questioned me. "Horatio and his wife, Abigail, along with Edward and Ellen Walker. The Walkers have a daughter named Gretchen who is blind. She will also attend."

"Do they know of my presence and our relationship?"

"Horatio does."

"Am I to be a spectacle?"

The question took me back, causing my weight to shift. "No, well," I said thinking through my predicament, "anyone as beautiful as you is always a spectacle." A slight smile appeared, alleviating her frozen consternation. "I don't know what I thought when I invited the others. It seemed right."

"If that is the case, then I am certain it is right. We shall have a wonderful evening." Standing, she reached for her shawl draped over the back of a chair. Contemplating her beauty, I wondered how I could have ignored it for ten years. Lost in thought, I failed to move as she stood at the door waiting. "May we go? Or, would you rather gawk at me?"

Opening the door, I turned to her. "I'd gawk at you all night if you allowed the privilege."

"May we depart?" she said, gesturing toward the door. Closing it, she locked it. The coachman stood by the carriage. We rode sitting side by side.

"You will enjoy my friends. They are delightful except Horatio."

"Tell me about Gretchen."

"She was born blind into a wonderful family. She danced with George at the ball last spring."

"George danced with her?"

"Yes, splendidly."

"Interesting young man, is he not?"

"Amy finds him so."

The ride ended. Coincidentally, the Walkers and McClerkens arrived at the same time. Awkwardly, I performed introductions at the street, making certain to welcome Gretchen. Ellen took Gretchen's hand as they ascended the steps allowing Edward to follow. Sarah waited at the front door, greeting her guests. Then, before I could introduce Beatrice, Sarah embraced her.

After Sarah offered cordials and cheeses, the ladies socialized in the parlor while the men made their way to the porch. We took seats, each holding a glass.

"A decision was made this afternoon," Horatio said. "South Carolina will secede first. The state government shall demand the Federalists abandon Fort Moultrie and a new fort under construction in Charleston Harbor named Fort Sumter."

"It matters little where a war begins," I said. "What matters is where it ends."

"I dare say," Edward replied. "Let it not end in Atlanta."

"True," Horatio said. "May it end in Pennsylvania or Delaware."

"Let us pray it ends within a year," I said. "And let us not talk of war tonight. I have a more enjoyable matter in mind.'

"I see that," Edward said. "Tell me about Mrs. Perkins. She is delightful."

Horatio chortled. "It took Alexander ten years to figure that out."

I aimed a stare of fiery darts. "She is delightful—I wish a certain friend of mine would present himself as delightful."

"Edward, you ought not allow him to speak of you in that manner," Horatio said.

Edward sipped his bourbon. "I never know whether you two hate each other or love each other."

"We better go to war soon," I said. "If we don't, I will kill him. At least in war, someone might get him first."

Horatio smiled. "I'd rather fight a war than fight you."

Edward stood. "Now that you have entertained me, may we join the ladies and enjoy the evening?" Edward held the door open for Horatio and me.

"Gretchen," I asked, "are the ladies behaving?"

"Yes sir, Mr. Frey—except Mrs. Perkins."

"Gretchen," Mrs. Walker said. "Whatever do you mean? Beatrice, please excuse my daughter."

"No," I said. "Maybe I need Gretchen's insights. What did you mean?" I looked at Beatrice.

"Mr. Frey," Gretchen said, "Mrs. Perkins behaves quite well. However, she is very much in love with you."

"Gretchen Walker, please apologize this instant." Mrs. Walker said.

"No need," I said. "Gretchen, most women fall very much in love with me when they meet me."

"Now who's misbehaving?" Gretchen asked.

"Your observation, Gretchen, is very true. Mrs. Perkins loves me and I love her. You are charming to see what everyone else sees, but refuses to address. You honor me with your forthrightness." I stepped toward Beatrice, took her hand, nudging her to stand.

Looking into her eyes, I said, "If Mrs. Perkins ever honors me with marriage, I would like you, Gretchen, to be her attendant."

Beatrice approached Gretchen, bent over and hugged her. "I would like that also."

"Did I hear affirmation of Alexander's proposal?" Horatio asked.

Beatrice demurred. "Yes, as long as Alexander agrees."

"Strange marriage proposal," Edward said.

Placing my arm around Beatrice, I held up my glass. "Gretchen, you saw the obvious. Thank you for making my proposal so easy."

"Thank you," Beatrice said, lifting her glass as the others followed.

"It's hard to believe that last Saturday night I had no thought of marriage."

"It's hard to believe that last Saturday night you had no thought of starting a war," Beatrice added.

"Shall we dine?" Sarah asked, directing us to the dining room.

Standing at the head of the table, I noticed Sarah nodding toward me, indicating I should take charge. "Proper southern etiquette often eludes me," I said. "I offer the following seating arrangement with everyone's permission. Forgive me if I misplace anyone. First, Horatio, would you take your normal seat on the front porch?"

At the foot of the table, Sarah slapped the top of her chair. "Alexander, Gretchen may not know how to take you. Apologize for your rude behavior."

"Miss Frey," Gretchen said, "I would take Mr. Frey in no other way. He brings joy and frivolity to our lives."

As we dined and made small talk, an important matter dawned. "Ladies and gentlemen," I said. "May I ask you to refrain from discussing the matter of our pending marriage with anyone until I have the opportunity to inform Amy?" I paused. "I am sure, if I did not make that request, Horatio would place an engagement announcement in the newspaper tomorrow."

"I was thinking of doing just that," he said.

"Possibly, Sarah and I can ride to Alpharetta tomorrow in time for church."

Chapter 14

Alexander Frey

October — Sunday Morning

Sarah and I slipped through the door of the Alpharetta church searching for Amy and George, spotting them in the third row. With that bench full, we sat in the back until the service ended.

"There's your father," Samantha said.

Amy scanned the rear of the church until she saw us. A smile as radiant as the sun illuminated her face.

"Nothing is wrong," Sarah said as Amy and George made their way up the side aisle, approaching and embracing us. "We wanted to surprise you."

Stepping back, Amy grinned. "I am surprised and happy."

Robert and Lillian welcomed us. "What brings you city folks to the country?" Robert asked.

Sarah and I looked at each other emitting joy, giving away the fact we carried good news. "Let's go outside," I said. "Sarah brought food left over from a dinner party last night."

"All right," Amy said as we neared the carriage. "I can stand it no longer. You two act as if they cancelled the war."

Studying the town square, I decided to first share my news with Amy. "If you all would excuse us, I'd like to take my daughter for a walk." Reaching for her arm, I guided her in the direction of the church.

"What?" she asked. "I know something good happened."

Smiling, I looked down into the depths of her brown eyes. "Yes, it did. Something good for me, and I hope for you." She waited, beauty pouring from her. "I have kept a secret from you and Sarah. I am not sure why, but I did. In late 1850, Horatio introduced me to a young widow whose husband was killed by Cheyenne Indians. She had returned to Atlanta to care for her parents. We became friends, often sharing each other's company in private. Let me assure you, our relationship remained honorable." As those words emerged, I felt a desperate pang to explain; but Amy interrupted.

"You kept her a secret? How could you?"

My head tilted in recognition of Amy's hurt. "During the last week, our relationship turned in the direction of marriage." Amy fainted, collapsed before I could break her fall. "Sarah, George," I called. They came running.

"What's wrong?" Sarah gasped.

"She's fainted," I said, removing my hat, fanning her. In an instant, she regained consciousness, bewildered and weak.

"I'm sorry, Father. Would someone fetch me water? My mouth is dry." Lillian ran to the buckboard, returning with a canteen. After taking a sip, Amy insisted on standing.

George placed his arm around her. "Would someone tell us what is going on?"

"Father has a secret female friend he desires to marry." She paused as we gained eye contact. "I don't know whether it was the secret he kept or the fact he plans to marry that made me faint. Do you have other secrets?"

"None," I said. "And for that remark I will accept your apology when you are prepared to offer it."

WISH IS MY MASTER

She broke down, first placing her head in her hands and then rushing toward me, reaching to embrace me. "I'm sorry. Please forgive me. I am happy for you."

Amy Yardley

For the second time in my life, I didn't want to let go. I didn't want the moment to end. There was not, I felt, enough strength within me to express how much I loved Father and how sorrowful I felt over hurting him. I held him as tightly as he held me, cherishing the moment—a moment I cherished then and during the next four years.

"Come," he said, pulling me away. I could neither look at him nor he at me as we walked. When out of earshot, he stopped and turned placing his hands on my upper arms. "Amy, I would never do anything to separate us."

My eyes refused to look up. "I know."

"If you prefer I didn't marry, I won't."

"Stop," I said. My eyes found his. "I would no more rob you of your joy than you would have robbed me of mine when I met George. You caught me unaware. I want you to be happy. Do you hear me?"

"Yes, Sweetheart, I hear you." He took me in his arms for one last embrace. "We'd better get back."

"Does Sarah like her?"

"Sarah loves her, or I wouldn't be here."

"She does?"

"Yes."

"That makes me feel better. When may I meet Mrs. Perkins?"

"Well, uh..."

"This afternoon—we have our horses. George and I will follow you to Atlanta."

Sarah had filled the others in with the details. Before anyone offered congratulations, I spoke. "George, we are going to Atlanta with my parents. Let's eat and depart."

Stopping his fork halfway to his mouth, he stammered. "All right, we're going to Atlanta."

Chapter 15

Amy Yardley

Arriving in Atlanta, I went inside to freshen up. Wasting little time, I descended the front steps to the carriage. Father gave the driver Mrs. Perkins' address. In order to maintain decorum, Father decided he and I should make the visit.

Riding in silence, I pondered the impending threat of war. How could life in a matter of six months take such turns? Marriage proved more joyous than I imagined except for the matter of pregnancy. Lillian comforted me by explaining that sometimes women facing emotional strain find it difficult to conceive. She put the lack of conception off to the two months in which I helped Sarah care for Father. If I awoke during the night, I'd wonder if what I felt as a result of my own bullet wound caused something to die within me. My time came early that month and then had not come for these past seven weeks. Mother presented Father with a baby girl and died. Sadness and tears welled-up when I thought of never presenting George with a child. But, this carriage ride should steer us into Father's future. I felt the carriage stop.

"We've arrived," the driver said, opening the carriage door. We stepped down, proceeding to the front door.

"Beatrice is not expecting you—please be considerate."

"If she is as Sarah described, I'll wager everything in my purse she expects me."

"Women," he said, "they know each other better than men know them."

His knock drew an immediate response. "Beatrice Perkins, please meet Amy Frey Yardley."

I extended my right hand. "Pleased to make your acquaintance."

Beatrice smiled at Father then at me. "I prayed in church this morning Alexander would arrive with you."

"May we come in?" Father asked.

"Please," she said, guiding us to the parlor.

Before taking a seat, I embraced Beatrice, kissing her cheek. "Thank you for making Father so happy. It pleases me God has led you to marry."

A tear welled, rolling down Beatrice's cheek, which she wiped with her fingertips. "It would seem God and the threat of war has led us to wed."

Beatrice and Father exchanged a glance I chose to ignore. "Now that I've met Mrs. Perkins, I am mildly upset you kept her a secret. We will discuss the matter later." I laughed as I completed that thought, doing so to give Beatrice more time to compose herself.

"Thank you both," she said, "for being so gracious and understanding. Amy, your father has been my sole companion since my husband's death." She hesitated. "He gave me happiness for ten years, and now he gives me joy."

"He might have shared that happiness with Sarah and me if he had had the courtesy to share you with us," I said, raising my eyebrows.

"Possibly, we should return home," he said. "This has been a long day."

Standing, taking matters into my own hands, I addressed Beatrice. "We may return home if Mrs. Perkins agrees to share a noon meal with us tomorrow."

Chapter 16

George Yardley

Monday's dinner went well. Beatrice communicated an interest in Alpharetta. Being Methodist, she knew of those who settled the area including the Yanceys. My father's leatherwork turned the conversation. On three occasions, she had bought gifts from us, one being a belt for Alexander.

"Father," Amy said, "I remember the belt. What became of it?"

"Oh, I wore it out. That was five years ago."

Sarah smiled. "In the last five years your father's girth expanded. There's a greater chance he couldn't stretch it out, than that he wore it out."

"Thank you, Sarah, for reminding me of my spent youth." Standing, approaching him, Beatrice whispered something in his ear. "Well, one person here thinks I have youthful qualities." Mrs. Perkins smiled as did Amy.

I went to saddle the horses giving Amy time to talk with Beatrice and Sarah. Alexander followed. "Well, what do you think?" he asked.

"I think she is a fortunate woman."

Chapter 17

Alexander Frey

"If war comes," I said, accompanying Beatrice home in the carriage, "George and Amy may pay the price. Committing the South to war haunts me regarding them." Cocking my head in denial of the despair I felt, my heart raced. The carriage came to a stop. Paying the driver, I sent him away. "Funny," I said, walking Beatrice to the door, "no one inquired about a wedding date."

A small bench sat along the walk leading to her house. "Would you like to sit for a moment?" she asked. "This business about war and your business concern me. You mentioned one last trip to England. If I recall, such voyages take three months?"

"Yes."

"May we wed before...?" She paused. "I would like to see England."

I understood the planet spins on an axis, that time measures days and weeks, but suddenly, time and the axis sped out of control like a toy top spinning into oblivion. "If that happened, we would have to depart soon—the Sea Lion arrives late this week. We'd have to marry immediately."

"Alexander, we enjoyed a ten-year friendship—may we enjoy a marriage?" She waited. "I am thirty-five and have never been married to my best friend."

"Nor have I."

"Please consider my offer. I would love to wed and sail for England."

Chapter 18

George Yardley

A whirlwind of church, guard training, chores, and sewing jackets ensued. By the end of October, we had completed twenty-eight. Throughout, I insisted Amy practice her marksmanship with a pistol. She held the weapon with both hands, but in so doing, shot straight at about ten feet. I took pleasure in her progress, having her practice in the clearing on the other side of my parents' graves so Andrew Shelton could see.

"The Guard consists of how many soldiers?" Amy asked one evening as we sat on the front porch.

"Thirty—you know that."

"Yes I do. I also know two members own jackets—one Nathaniel Thomas and one George Yardley."

Ignorance embarrassed me. Sitting in silence, I castigated myself, alarmed by things I failed to contemplate.

Amy took my hand. "Are you all right?"

"Yes—no."

She laughed, shaking her head. "Confusion reigns."

"There's so much to think about—at times I fail to see the obvious. If that occurs in the midst of battle, I'll become a casualty."

"George Yardley, don't put yourself down. You saw me, didn't you?"

"If I missed anyone as pretty as you, I'd have been blind."

"You've said there could never be anyone as pretty as me."

"Well, I've changed my mind."

"Changed your mind?"

"Yes—Leslie and Samantha are as beautiful as you."

"Anyone else?"

"Not that I can think of—but give me time."

"I'll give you time. I'll give you two months of sleeping by yourself in the loft."

She stormed inside. I chased her to bed. We laughed and loved each other.

In the middle of the night, I awoke to weeping. "George, I think I'm barren." She sobbed, wrenching sobs, turning her back to me, hiding her face in the pillow.

Reaching, nudging her to me, she resisted. "Amy Yardley, if that's what God intends, then so be it. With the threat of war, we'd be foolish to bring a child into this world. Whether or not we have children doesn't matter."

"It matters to me."

"What matters?"

"That I can't give you children."

"How do you know it's you? Maybe I'm at fault."

"How could anything be wrong with someone as strong as you?"

She continued to withhold herself. In that moment, God convinced me of the significance of silence. Snuggling up to her, I placed my arm around her waist, wishing with all my heart to comfort her.

A letter arrived from Alexander. Beatrice and he would meet us at church on Sunday. It was the day I decided to present the leather jackets to the Guard.

Saturday morning brought the first autumn chill to North Georgia. As good as the chill felt and as good as Amy felt lying next to me, I rose from bed. Deciding to instill competition in the Guard, I devised a shooting match for the day's drills with the winner receiving a leather jacket. I'd award the prize after church on Sunday. Then, once we applauded the winner, I'd give the remaining jackets.

After dressing, I walked outside to relieve myself. As I did, I heard riders. Finishing, I rushed around front. In the early dawn, I saw them heading toward Alpharetta.

"Who was that?" Amy asked from the front door, holding a carbine.

"Don't know. Did you see anything?"

"No—heard horses but when I looked they were gone."

Through the pines, I saw a lantern flicker at the Sheltons' place. Maybe Andrew had tried to catch a glimpse of the riders, I thought.

"Come in here," Amy said. "You make me nervous, and besides, breakfast waits."

I blessed the food and offered a prayer for a good day. Amy cast sarcasm upon my petition, doubting God would grant a good day to a soldier training to kill other soldiers.

"Well, I hope He does. If war comes, we'll fight for God and state."

Sipping coffee, she returned her cup to the saucer. "If war comes, I wish you'd fight to stay alive."

Taking a bite of bacon, nodding, I stood. "That's sobering. Good soldiers keep good friends alive in battle. I better get to Alpharetta before my friends shoot each other. Tomorrow, we'll take the jackets to church and hand them out after worship. I want you to be a part of that. You helped make them—you deserve credit."

She smiled the first smile since confessing her fear. I collected my gear, firearms, lead and powder. "I'll return early afternoon," I said, kissing her good-bye.

"You always return after dinner."

Stepping outside, I whistled for Splinter. He stood next to Pearl at the gate. Mounted, riding toward Andrew's, I noticed tracks that went no farther than the Sheltons'. Something's wrong, I thought. Horses don't fly. The riders either slipped off the road or slipped into Andrew's. Either way, I doubted I should leave Amy.

Torn, I continued a few hundred yards, discerning a place to spy on the Shelton farm. For more than an hour, I waited; but nothing happened. Heading to town, arriving late, I endured one barb after another concerning my marital status and my inability to leave Amy.

"What's the matter, George?" Sergeant Hanlin called out as I dismounted. "You'd think after four months, she'd have tired of you."

A roar of laughter went up to which I smiled. "She'd have gotten tired of you after four seconds. Besides, you all are jealous and ugly."

Having had enough, I proposed the shooting match. Pulling the jacket from my saddlebag, I held it up. "The first one to hit three targets wins this prize. You have to be present in church tomorrow to claim it. I expect all of you to be here."

Placing three rocks on three fence posts, I ordered them to load their muskets. Each was to take his shot. If he missed, that eliminated him. Those who hit the first target would move on to the second and then to the third.

After twenty-eight shots, sixteen militiamen remained. Little Finn McDougall, our drummer boy, ran and replaced the rock each time someone knocked it off. Nathaniel stepped up, preparing to shoot.

"Cousin, what are you doing? You have a jacket."

He glared at me sideways. "Shooting. If I win, I'll sell the jacket to the highest bidder."

"This isn't a moneymaking proposition." Nathaniel aimed. As he fired, I pushed his musket upward. "See, you missed anyway."

"Not fair," he said.

"When you have something worthwhile to give, you can devise the contest and the rules. Until then, this is my contest and my rules."

I ordered the remaining guardsmen to commence firing at the second target about twenty yards away. Six shots found the mark, leaving Sergeant Hanlin to shoot. The third target was about four feet to the right of the second and about two feet higher. When Tom fired, the third target fell, resulting in stunned silence and then, laughter.

"Sort of got ahead of yourself, didn't you?" I asked.

"Wish I could explain it," he said, "but I can't.

"You know how to instill confidence in your men, Sergeant Hanlin," a voice called from behind us. It was Drury.

"How are you?" I asked.

"I'm well, Mr. Yardley," Drury said in a way that felt strange. Without another word, he continued. "I have news." A silence fell over the troop. "The governor wants you to take a position in the Atlanta Grays—that of lieutenant—and train those troops."

"No sir," I said. "It is with these men I will serve, and that's final. I won't train troops in Atlanta when I have these ne'er-do-wells to whip into shape."

"You would deny the governor?" Drury asked.

"Yes, sir."

"The governor won't appreciate your response."

"Let's see," I replied. "Drury, can you hit those stones?" He scanned the two targets Little Finn had replaced. "If you do, I'll reconsider the offer."

The captain walked forward, taking up the challenge. Drawing his pistol, he shot once leaving the first target unscathed, and then, fired again. "I believe," Drury said, "if someone looks, you will find two small bullet holes in the top of each fencepost."

"Nathaniel, go see," I said. He jogged off. Returning, he confirmed Drury's claim.

"That's some shooting. If the Grays have you, they don't need me. I'll remain here; but do what I can for you when we visit Atlanta. "Men," I continued, "we've forgone our manners. Please be introduced to Captain Drury Stith."

Most greeted him with casual words of welcome except Sergeant Hanlin. Approaching from the side, he turned to face Drury, stood at attention, and saluted. Drury returned the gesture. "Would you be so kind as to remain here until we complete our contest?"

"Certainly, though I'd enjoy my stay more if George's pretty wife were around."

"She's home tending to the things a country girl tends to," I said. "Let's see who wins the jacket." Four shooters remained.

"What jacket?" Drury asked.

"One of my leathers."

"May I participate? I've hit two targets."

I looked around considering the consequences. "What do you think, men?"

"Let him shoot," Tom Hanlin shouted.

"You don't have a dog in this fight—seeing how you missed the second target by a mile," Nathaniel said.

I agreed to the challenge thinking it good for the men. Bobby Paul Green stepped up, blowing the rock away. The next three shooters failed leaving Drury, who also knocked the rock off the post.

"What's fair is fair," I said. "You men be here tomorrow after church. Bobby won the original contest. I'll present the jacket to him. Drury, Amy and I will make a jacket for you."

"Amy?" Drury asked. "Since when is she a leatherworker?"

I shook his hand. "Amy can do anything she sets her mind to."

Amy Yardley

I held the carbine at my side, hidden in the folds of my skirt. "May I help you?" I called from the front door. Three unkempt strangers waited on horseback.

"We're looking for George Yardley," one said.

"He's not here. He's in Alpharetta training with the Milton Guard."

"That's what we thought," the same man said, starting to dismount.

"I wouldn't get down off that horse," I said, stepping outside, pointing the weapon.

"What's a pretty little thing like you going to do with that?" another asked.

"Blow one of you to kingdom come, if you don't leave."

"It's probably not loaded," the other said.

"She's pretty enough that it would be worth finding out," the first man said. "We might like to try you out."

He twitched, as if to dismount. My left hand grasped the pistol along with the right; aiming, pulling the trigger, I lodged the ball in the right side of his chest. One of the other horses reared giving me time to run inside and bar the door. From the window, I saw the man I shot slumped over in his saddle. The others had drawn their pistols, cocking them.

"Let's get out of here," one said. "Greely, can you ride?"

I detected no response but saw the third man maneuver his horse, taking the reins of the wounded man's horse. In an instant, they were gone, headed toward Cherokee County.

George Yardley

"I wouldn't mind seeing Amy," Drury said.

"Do you have time?" I asked, standing next to Splinter.

"Always."

"Let's go." I turned to the troops. "See you tomorrow, and I mean everyone. You slackers show up."

Nathaniel laughed. "He has something up his sleeve. We'd better be here or face the consequences." Some scratched their heads, while others mumbled. Drury and I rode off.

◈◈◈◈◈

"I didn't come out here to get shot," Drury said as he dismounted, seeing the pistol in Amy's hand.

"What's wrong?" I asked. "Who was here?"

"Three men," she said as I approached the porch.

"Who were they?" Drury asked.

"I don't know; but I shot one."

"Did they hurt you? Did they do anything to you?" I asked, hoping she'd not been raped.

"I'm fine. When they rode up, I questioned them. They made accusations about what they wanted to do; so, I shot one." She spoke as if in a daze, but made sense.

"How long ago?" I asked.

"About an hour."

"You're certain you hit one?"

"Certain. They rode off with him slumped over his horse. I heard one call the man I shot, Greely."

"Maybe I can catch them," I said to Drury. "Which way did they go?"

"Toward Cherokee."

"You shouldn't go alone," Drury said.

"Stay here with Amy."

"You won't change his mind," Amy said. "He has that look in his eyes—he's going to do what he's going to do."

In a moment, I remounted Splinter and departed.

Amy Yardley

"Amy," Drury said, taking a seat at the table. "What do you think is going on? If I'm not mistaken, you and George are the most shot at couple in Georgia." He laughed.

I approached the rocker, standing behind it. "We have theories—some point to our neighbor, Andrew Shelton. George thinks Andrew set the Livingstones' cabin on fire killing her and two children. He's confronted Andrew. Andrew rides to Cherokee County once a week. We think he convinced his friends we should be dead. George followed him one morning and found eight ruffians along with Andrew."

Drury leaned forward, resting his elbows on the table. "What did George do?"

"He did what George would do—a skirmish resulted."

"There's a bad bunch intent on assassinating our leadership."

"How do you know that?"

"Rumor and gossip; but rumor and gossip carry truth."

"Wish George hadn't gone alone."

"I tried..."

"He wouldn't allow you to go because of Stephanie. It's all right for him to run off and get killed; but it's not all right to make Stephanie a widow."

"If George doesn't get to the bottom of this today, he'll move you back to Atlanta. He's not taking any chances at losing you—I saw it in his eyes."

"That's all I thought about while waiting for his return. It's a sin to think they'll drive us from our home we love."

"You do love it, don't you?"

"More than you know. I feel like the freest woman on earth working here with George."

"You helped him make the leather jackets."

"Did he tell you?"

"What?"

"That we made a leather jacket for each man in the Guard." As soon as I spoke, the surprise on Drury's face made me realize I'd overstepped.

"No, he didn't. He made up a story that whoever won the shooting contest today would receive a jacket after church tomorrow. Now, you tell me you made a jacket for everyone in the Guard. How hard does he make you work?"

"Please don't ruin the surprise."

"I won't as long as you fulfill the bargain he made." I waited. "He promised to make me a jacket, because I won the shooting contest."

"His word is his word. If he told you that, you'll have a jacket."

"I know," he said. Standing, he proceeded out the front door. "Be back in a few moments." Mounting, he made his way toward Andrew Shelton's.

From the porch, I watched him ride away and about twenty minutes later, I watched him return. "What was that about?"

"Asked Mr. Shelton if he heard shooting earlier."

"And?"

"He did—so I asked him why he didn't see about it. Told me you two shoot all the time—that George gives you lessons."

"And?"

"Asked him if he knew where George went Saturday mornings."

"Did he say?'

"He did—to militia drills. Then I asked him if George went this morning. He got belligerent—shooed me away."

"He knew I was alone?"

"Yes. When I confronted him about that, he grew silent. I told him the details of the shooting. Then, I told him if George finds the men, they'd be dead by nightfall."

"And?"

"And nothing. He's a coward." Drury said, stepping onto the porch, taking a seat while I leaned against a post. "What other theories have you two cooked up?"

"Savannah—plenty believe what we did an abomination. What we did there—caring for the slaves—riled folks. Maybe when they found those slave hunters dead along that creek, they put two and two together—realized George was responsible."

"You think some want you dead because you are anti-slavery."

"We are anti-slavery, but showed our colors when we washed those slaves feet."

"I see. Truth is—whether it's the widow's death or the slavery issue, Shelton could be involved."

"There's one more thing. George thinks Andrew wanted this parcel of land—that George's father beat him to the claim."

George rode to the cabin, proceeding around back without speaking. Drury and I followed. After he unsaddled Splinter, he joined us on the back porch.

"I gave up. This eye-for-an-eye stuff must stop. Amy, after church tomorrow, you're going to Atlanta with your father and Beatrice."

Every part of me wanted to protest, but knew it useless. "All right," I said. "Drury and I figured that."

"What are you going to do?" Drury asked.

"Sit here and wait. I need time."

"You're married," Drury said. "You're supposed to think together."

"Forget that," George said. "I'm not moving to Atlanta to train the Grays."

"Thought I'd mention it."

"What's that about?" I asked.

"The governor sent me to offer your husband a commission in the Georgia Militia as a lieutenant. He turned it down."

"George, why? We could be together."

Drury laughed. "Doesn't matter to him."

"She won't be alone. Her father will keep her safe."

"For the love of God, she shot a man. Maybe she could keep you safe."

"You'll stop at nothing. Why don't you two hog-tie me and take me to Atlanta?"

"Cause when we untied you, you'd do as you damn well pleased," I said.

"First time I've heard you cuss."

"Won't be the last if you keep ordering my life."

"Listen," George said, "we'll give the jacket out tomorrow."

Drury interrupted. "You mean jackets."

"He got it out of me. I swore him to secrecy."

"Sworn to secrecy," Drury said, "as long as you keep your end of the bargain and make me one."

"I'll make one," George said. "Then, I'll shoot a hole through it to remind you how you hornswoggled my wife the day she shot that bastard."

"Now, now," Drury said. "Language here on the farm— how demeaning." He paused. "You wouldn't ruin my jacket, would you?"

"I need time," George said. "Amy, please give me a week. I'll come to Atlanta next Sunday. By then, I'll have decided about the farm."

"Yes, master," I said. "You make the decisions. I'll obey."

"With that, I'll be going," Drury said. "Amy, I do enjoy being with Stephanie."

George grinned. "Sounds like you enjoyed being with my wife."

"I did," he said, mounting his horse. "It's a downright shame you returned so soon."

I stomped my foot. "Drury, take that back."

"I would; but I'd be lying."

George turned to me. "Amy, get me a gun. I'll put a hole through him. That way, we won't have to make his jacket."

Drury tipped his hat. "Mrs. Yardley, thank you for the pleasure of your company. I do not know when I ever enjoyed an afternoon more with a married woman." Kicking his horse, he rode off. "Don't forget my jacket."

"All right," I said turning to my husband, "what happened out there?" Having gestured toward Cherokee, I waited for his response.

"The man you shot died." He waited for a sign of remorse. None was forthcoming. "I caught them about four miles away. First, I saw their horses, and then I saw the others digging a grave. As they finished, they spoke threats against us. Part of me wanted to end their lives right there and part of me wanted to get back to you."

"Did you recognize them?"

"One was at the cabin that Saturday I caught up with Andrew. The other I've never seen."

"Anything else?"

"No—thought there'd been enough killing for one day. I rode home." He looked over his shoulder toward Cherokee. "There's something evil out there."

"There's something evil over there," I said, gesturing toward the Sheltons'. "Seems like evil's all around us."

"We can do something about that by removing you and me to Atlanta. I need a week to straighten things up."

There was no sense arguing. His mind was made up. Our future was in Atlanta.

Chapter 19

George Yardley

Sunday Morning

I loaded the buckboard with the twenty-eight jackets, covering them with the canvas tarp Father used to protect his leather goods from rain. "Nothing ruins good leatherwork like a surprise thunderstorm," he would say.

As worship began, Reverend Woolridge acknowledged his surprise at the overflowing congregation. Alexander and Beatrice arrived at 11:00 o'clock. One pulley at White's Ferry malfunctioned delaying them, not to mention both mule drivers needed sobering up.

"There's been a killing," the preacher said to a congregational gasp. Waiting to regain his flock's attention, he went on. "Assailants attacked three men on the road to Cherokee yesterday—shooting and killing one."

He continued until I couldn't bear the lie. "That's not true," I said rising from my bench. Another congregational gasp erupted. "My wife, Amy, shot the man who died." More commotion and murmuring ensued. "If you'll listen, I'll tell you what happened." Reverend Woolridge gave his consent. "Three men rode to our cabin yesterday while I attended Guard training. They made comments to Amy about raping her. She shot one, and then barred herself in the cabin. When I arrived home, she recounted the story. Tracking them, I came upon the other two burying the man Amy shot. I don't know where you derived your information, Reverend; but it is false." A stir occurred as all eyes turned toward the minister.

Robert stood to my left. "Reverend Woolridge, where did you get your information?"

The preacher stared at his daughter and son-in-law, Andrew and Hester Shelton. "Andrew told me," he said pointing in their direction. Another commotion followed.

"Andrew, where'd you get your information?" Robert asked.

His wife nudged him. "I can't say."

Robert glared. "That's not good enough, Andrew."

Andrew stood. "Two men came by my house last evening. They told me what happened. That's all I know."

"Who were they?" Alexander asked.

"Men from Cherokee—I don't know their names."

Turning back to the pastor, I'd had enough. "Reverend, I apologize for interrupting. I couldn't allow the truth to remain unspoken in church." Bowing my head, I took my seat.

Robert refused to allow the issue to pass. "I doubt we've heard the truth."

"I doubt we've heard it also," Alexander said. "However, we are in the House of the Lord. Let us worship Him and hear His Word."

Robert sat, followed by Alexander, who gave me a look I can only describe as, *Thanks for marrying my daughter and teaching her to defend herself.* Beatrice appeared troubled—no, distraught.

Outside, after worship, people milled about talking and listening. I untied the tarp, but didn't remove it. "Men of the Milton Guard," I shouted. They approached one and two at a time.

"Where's Sarah?" Amy asked her father.

"Home—she felt Beatrice and I should have time to ourselves. I tried to convince her otherwise; but she refused."

"Amy, please stand with me," I said. She made her way to my side. I took her hand, holding a jacket in my other hand. "Yesterday Bobby Paul won the shooting contest. This is your prize."

I held up the jacket. As Bobby came forward, applause and cheers erupted.

"If we go to battle, I'm fighting next to you," Curly Rankin shouted. "It's nice to know one of us can hit what we aim at."

A good laugh sounded giving me time to compose my thoughts. "Amy and I have a gift for all of you. Would the Guard please approach the wagon?" I removed the tarp. "Bobby Paul, we burned your name on the inside of your jacket. However—we made a jacket for everyone. She'll call your name, and present your gift."

She held up the first coat reading the name, "Tom Hanlin." As she called each name, the guardsman stepped forward, receiving his jacket and a kiss and hug from my wife.

Something happened I can't forget. As Amy performed the task, a reverent, holy hush fell over the square. It seemed the women, mothers and grandmothers, wanted to cry. Some did. Men fought back tears. Maybe they wondered how many would survive the war. My parents' absence haunted me.

As Amy concluded, Sergeant Hanlin ordered the men to assemble, which they did in three rows of nine. Nathaniel stood next to me, while Tom spoke. "Yesterday, the governor offered George a commission in the Militia. He refused it in order to remain with us. Yesterday, cowards threatened Amy's life and honor. Through preparation offered by her husband, she defended herself. Let it be known that we, the soldiers of the Milton Guards, know we are the best trained and now best dressed soldiers in the South. We stand together in peace and war, prepared to defend our rights as Americans and above all, to defend our honor. Thank you, George and Amy, for this honor you bestow."

Amy and I stood with our arms around each other. I saw Alexander take Beatrice's hand. Mr. Yancey stepped forward. "George, I have no part in this and shouldn't speak; but all in Milton County are thankful for you and Amy. We thank God she was not hurt yesterday."

"And whoever confronted you," Tom Hanlin shouted, "will have to deal with us." The first true battle cry of the Milton Guards roared through the square. Goosebumps chilled the nape of my neck.

Reverend Woolridge approached Amy and me expressing his appreciation. Alexander nudged Beatrice in our direction. "Reverend, I have a favor to ask. Would you be so kind as to perform our wedding?"

The minister's jaw dropped. "When?"

"Now," Alexander said. "May we return to the sanctuary? I love this place. There's nowhere else I'd rather be wed."

He turned to Beatrice. "Young lady, are you in agreement?"

She smiled. "Are you addressing me or Amy? I fail to remember the last time someone referred to me as a young lady."

"Forgive me," Reverend Woolridge said. "Meet me in fifteen minutes. You need two witnesses." He walked away toward the church.

Alexander took a deep breath, stared at Beatrice and then Amy. "We asked Gretchen Walker to witness our wedding. I will explain to her how carried away I became. Would anyone care to volunteer as witnesses?" Before receiving a response, he turned to Lillian. "Would you allow Samantha and Leslie to perform the duty?"

Chapter 20

Amy Yardley

After the ceremony, Father retrieved my bag from the buckboard. From the carriage, I saw George and Nathaniel talking with Sergeant Hanlin. Some sense within me knew they plotted revenge against the conspirators in Cherokee County.

George stuck his head inside the carriage. "I'll see you next Sunday."

He tried to kiss me. I refused the gesture. "That's if you don't get yourself killed going after the assailants."

Stepping back, he eyed me. "You understand more than you should."

Beatrice stood by the carriage. He turned to her. "Sorry, you won't get to see our cabin today. I hope *you* understand."

"Oh," she replied, "I understand. You remember my first husband lost his life in an Indian war? I understand men who smell battle and blood. They lose all sense of reason as you have." Father helped her into the carriage. "Amy," she said, "before your first anniversary, George will be as dead as my first husband."

I leaned out the window. "Did you hear her, George?"

"Yes, I heard." He kissed me on the lips, a kiss I didn't refuse.

"Maybe we can finish the kiss next Sunday, if you're still alive," I said.

Father took his seat. "Don't do anything stupid. That's one thing I admire about you. You know which lines not to cross."

Chapter 21

George Yardley

Tom Hanlin and I decided we would train the Guard at my farm the next Saturday. Each man arrived Friday night prepared to camp and spend the next day on a march. They gathered across the Alpharetta Road. Most walked, while six rode horses. Excitement illuminated the conversation. Lugging my gear to the site, I pitched a lean-to using Father's tarp. Every man wore his jacket.

By dusk, a huge campfire brightened the darkness. An octet sang songs, sprinkling a hymn in from time to time. Others sat in groups of four or five telling stories.

"Put that fire out," I ordered with Sergeant Hanlin standing beside me.

"What are we doing?" Jeremy Glass asked.

"Following orders," Tom shouted. "Good soldiers don't ask questions. Pack your bed rolls."

The last ray of gray light surrounded them as they stood in a semi-circle illuminated by the fire's dying embers. Sergeant Hanlin stepped forward. "All right men, we're taking our first night march. There'll be no lanterns or torches. In about thirty minutes the moon will rise. Walk two by two. Help each other. Your eyes will adjust."

With our bedrolls strapped to our backs, muskets over our shoulders, we set out. Nathaniel marched beside me. "What are we doing?"

"Five hour night-march—make camp in the darkness— sleep and then find out who shows up at that cabin—enough information?"

"Guess so. You're in a mood."

"Pay attention," I said. "This training could save our lives someday."

"Or some night," he said.

For four hours we marched and thought. No one expressed fear or exhaustion. It appeared each man understood the purpose, realizing in the future we could make marches in Virginia or Maryland. The rigors of war and duty proved dire.

At two o'clock, we reached the creek where I left the bounty hunters to die. In the same clearing, we made camp, pitched lean-tos, and built a fire to combat the autumn chill. By a fallen tree, Nathaniel and I lay near each other listening to a chorus of snores, grunts and other night sounds.

"We might as well shoot a cannon," Nathaniel said. "Anyone within five miles could hear this racket. Everybody in Cherokee County knows we're here."

I laughed. "Amy doesn't make this much noise."

"What?" He turned toward me. "Oh, go to sleep."

Before first light, Sergeant Hanlin and I awakened the men. "What's for breakfast?" Nathaniel asked.

"No vittles," I said. "When we reach our objective, we'll eat."

Moving through the morning haze, we surrounded the cabin, placing each man where I wanted him. "Any movement will give your position away," I said, encouraging stillness. If we learn any lesson today, I thought, we will learn patience.

Nathaniel and I sat about ten feet into the woods—he on the west side of the road leading to the cabin—I on the right. A bird sang in the distance. An occasional breeze blew, rustling leaves.

Thirty minutes passed. The haze lifted. We made eye contact with our nearest comrades; most lay hidden about twenty feet apart. Loneliness swept over me. Instinctively, I knew any sound or motion would warn an approaching adversary, but the need for companionship increased. When war came, I thought, I will position men in groups of two or three.

Dampness sank through my clothing, penetrating muscles and joints. The need to scratch an itch overwhelmed. Gnats and flies swarmed, buzzed, and bit. Stillness accentuated every ache and pain.

I had the best view of the road leading to the cabin and the best chance of being seen if anyone approached. With my carbine holstered and my musket laying across my lap, I waited, but as I did, I grew impatient. Stealing a glance at my watch, it showed eight o'clock. I didn't know what I wanted more: a revengeful fight with the men who threatened Amy or to discover why Amy and I were targets. By nine o'clock, I gave up. As I called an end to the watch, a horse snarled on the main road and clomped away. The sounds diminished, leaving me frustrated.

"Give it up," I shouted. "They're not coming."

One by one each man twisted, stretched, and gathered his firearms. In a moment, they gathered near Tom and me, mumbling to each other. "We have a five-hour march back to my place. Let's go." They joined together in groups of two, side-by-side, stepping slowly at first.

Nathaniel and I took up the rear. Reaching the main road, we walked a few hundred yards. "What did you learn?" he asked.

"Not much. What did you learn?"

"I learned this—at first I was caught up in who might approach and from what direction."

"Yeah?"

"Then, I studied the cabin."

"And?"

"Eight armed men waited inside."

Chapter 22

Alexander Frey

November & December, 1860

Election Day, November 6, 1860, arrived with little fanfare. It was a foregone conclusion Lincoln would win the presidency. Talk surfaced that the Northern faction of the Democratic Party had nominated Senator Douglas to fan the flames of division, causing the Southern faction to nominate the current vice-president, John Breckenridge. With the party divided and with a third Democratic nominee, Senator John Bell of Tennessee tossing his hat in the ring, the Republican candidate became a shoe-in.

Lincoln received one hundred and eighty electoral votes to Breckinridge's seventy-two. For the first time in our nation's history, more individual Americans voted against the president-elect than voted for him. In the popular election, Lincoln garnered one million eight hundred and sixty-six thousand popular votes while his opponents collected two million eight hundred and nineteen thousand.

One week before Christmas, on December 20, 1860, South Carolina issued its Ordinance of Secession declaring, in its view, the Union dissolved. Four days later, the state voted to approve the Ordinance. The United States of America ceased to exist as the founding fathers had designed.

By then, George had trained with the Atlanta Grays for a month. Though enlisted, Drury treated George as an equal, creating consternation among some officers. Colonel Bingham kept the dissension under control, realizing the day approached when George would receive his commission.

With South Carolina's secession, we waited for the first act of hostility. Their militia initiated plans to engage the Union forces at Fort Moultrie and to occupy the newly erected Fort Sumter in Charleston Harbor.

The day after Christmas, Colonel Bingham received word to assign two officers in the Georgia Militia as observers in Charleston. He selected Drury as one and waited assignment of the other until George received his commission. If all went as planned, they would depart by rail on February 13th. Whoever made the request wanted the observers from other states in place before Lincoln's inauguration.

Chapter 23

Alexander Frey

Milledgeville, Georgia
January 16, 1861

Horatio and I made the trip from Atlanta to Milledgeville by carriage. Nestled in the middle of the state, the journey to the capital lasted two days.

A popular vote on January 2, 1861, elected me a delegate from Atlanta to the convention. Riding south, deep in thought, I wished my presence anywhere else on earth.

Stepping from the carriage, I came face to face with the delegates from Milton County: Mr. Yancey and Reverend Woolridge. We made small talk until Alexander Stephens approached, directing a question their way.

"You gentlemen know Mr. Frey?"

"Yes, we do," the Reverend replied.

"Maybe you can persuade him to vote against secession."

My eyebrows raised. I stared into resolute eyes. "Reverend? Mr. Yancey? You oppose secession?"

"We do," Mr. Yancey said. "We plan to vote against any act that would further sever the Union. After considering Mr. Stephens' position, we agree with him, and he with us."

"Is that so?" I asked.

"It is," Stephens said. "If Georgia, standing in the heart of Dixie, remains loyal to the Union, we might prevent war—prevent an absurd loss of life."

"Strange talk," I said to Mr. Stephens, "for someone who would seek political office in the new Confederacy."

He stared downward, shuffling his feet. "If secession fails, I need not seek political office."

"And if we vote to secede?"

"Time will tell," he said. "I shall neither abandon my state nor my nation—regardless of the nation in which I find myself."

Tipping my hat, I excused myself. Horatio followed. "What was that about?" he asked.

"Politicians—where would we be without them?"

After days of positioning, the delegates voted secession. Much was made over the popular vote of January 2nd—over the cruel weather that limited turnout and over the number of ballots cast, exceeding the recent presidential election. Nothing made sense. I feared secessionists had stuffed the ballot boxes to gain control of the conference. Nevertheless, I voted with the majority, again feeling the pang of committing the South to war.

Chapter 24

Amy Yardley

Milton County

"Well, this is a pleasant surprise," Lillian said as she embraced me, and then George. Leslie and Samantha raced through the back door.

"Gosh," George said, "you two get cuter and cuter. You're prettier than Amy."

Smiling at the tease, I gave him a mean look. Robert and Nathaniel joined us.

"What are you two doing?" George asked. "You look like the wrath of God."

Nathaniel feigned punching me. "Waiting for you to have someone order us around." They shook hands before Nathaniel and Robert hugged me, after which the men went to the barn.

"You girls run along," Lillian said. Their protest went for naught. As soon as they left, Lillian turned to me. "What's wrong?"

My head bowed. "What do you mean?"

"Why did you return to Alpharetta?"

"George and Drury received assignment to Fort Johnson in Charleston—they depart February 13th. I decided to spend time on the farm."

Lillian stirred a bowl of cornbread batter. "Are you all right?"

"No." We made eye contact before I pulled a chair from the table, banging its legs against the floor. Seated, I stared into the fire. "I'm not pregnant—scared I can't give George children." I didn't weep, but wanted to.

Lillian stopped stirring, leaving the spoon in the bowl. "Here's the truth. Barrenness becomes a woman's worse nightmare. Good-intentioned people whisper behind your back—marking you as infertile. I'll not give you false hope. Whatever God intends He intends—when He's ready to give you a child He will—not much you can do but pray and have sex."

Standing, I walked to the back door. "Sex isn't any trouble. My desire for George is the joy of my life." I hesitated wondering if I should have said that, but went on. "I pray for a child—but not without ceasing. George contends we shouldn't have children with the threat of war—in a bit he's off to Charleston."

Walking toward me, placing her arms around me, she hugged me. "Let's find the girls. They love you and miss you."

As we made our way outside, a rope-swing Robert and Nathaniel looped over an oak branch drew our attention. Samantha tried to push Leslie, who stood on a large knot tied at the end of the rope.

"May I play with the girls?"

"Yes," Lillian said. "I'll finish the cornbread."

For the next hour, we laughed and frolicked, not having a care in the world. First, it was the rope swing, then the see-saw, and then a game of ring around the rosy. Never during my childhood had I played—having neither sisters nor friends. The girls grew tired except for a race to where the men worked. I laughed so hard, Samantha and Leslie beat me to the barn.

"Playing is more exhausting than bringing in a harvest," I said, bending over to catch my breath. Before anyone responded, Lillian called for supper.

Before starting home, I asked Lillian if the girls and Nathaniel could spend time with us before George's departure. The hesitation and anxiety in Lillian's eyes answered my request. "We'll see," she whispered.

Nodding, my heart sank. "I understand. I never know what danger lurks."

ꝏꝋꝏꝋ

On the night before we returned to Atlanta, George asked me to join him on the front porch. Sitting under the winter sky, stars shone as a million droplets of light. Reaching into his shirt pocket, unraveling a paper, he presented me a gold cross, tied on a leather strip. He placed it over my head and around my neck. "I like writing poems, but not reciting them."

"Please read to me—please."

He cleared his throat and spoke.

> *The love by which I've loved thy heart,*
> *And you in turn, loved mine,*
> *Is love that weeps as I depart,*
> *And hopes in love sublime.*
>
> *Would you for me please keep this cross,*
> *Near to the heart I love?*
> *For if thou art to suffer loss,*
> *I'll love thee from above.*

I felt his presence in every part of me. Standing, taking his hand, we went inside.

Chapter 25

George Yardley

February 12, 1860

After supper, I leaned back in my chair, realizing the roast lamb and sweet potatoes I enjoyed would be my last home-cooked meal for months. Beatrice sat to Alexander's left, while Amy sat to his right. Sarah and I sat across from each other.

Beatrice stared at my wife. "Amy, I went with my husband to war. Winds howled across the grasslands sounding like the ghost of some wild Indian. Coyotes and wolves barked and called all night long. I spent my time scared to death. Rain pelted our tent as did hail louder than a thousand drummers. Why was I there? I couldn't live without him. One April morning he rode off—uniformed, gallant, leading two columns of horse-soldiers. They brought his horse back, but not his body—buried him where he fell, butchered, and scalped. Remaining here waiting for your husband to return or waiting for the news he won't rankles the soul. Nothing relieves the fear and anxiety—nothing—prayer, friends, chores—nothing."

Staring at Amy, watching her eyes sadden, I returned my coffee cup to its saucer with a slight clink. "I'll survive—no matter what."

"Bullets and cannon blasts are indiscriminate," Beatrice said. "Don't make promises you can't keep. The last thing my husband always said before he left—was—'I will see you later,' but a day came when I never saw him again." She leaned forward toward Amy. "All that matters is love. Speak love to each other in every letter. That is what sees you through."

"Thank you, Beatrice," Amy said. "Love is all that matters. I wish love was the master of everything."

"That's what God intended; but it's not our way," Sarah said. "We hate. We fight. We kill. What love is there in that? Do you think Benjamin Franklin or Thomas Jefferson ever thought we would come to this?"

Alexander leaned forward. "We disgrace what heritage remains of our forefathers. Enough is enough. At times, circumstances overshadow love."

Chapter 26

Amy Yardley

February 13, 1861
The Atlanta Armory

Colonel Bingham greeted George and me as we arrived at the armory. Not having ever met, George introduced us, after which the colonel escorted us to his office. A Negro offered coffee, which I accepted.

Standing behind his desk, Colonel Bingham touched three books resting on a blotter. "George," he said, "please read these. Two reflect upon military tactics employed during the Napoleonic Wars and *The Last of the Mohicans,* a novel by James Fenimore Cooper, portrays the necessity of sacrifice in love and war. When I study military tactics, I need something else to read that educates and entertains. Read the first two diligently."

"Thank you," George said. "Mother and I read the novel. In consideration of your guidance, I will again as I read the other two."

Bingham grasped the three books, presenting them to George. "I forget at times how you Methodists emphasize reading and education."

George nodded, accepting the books then handing them to me. "What else is happening here today? Seems like a lot of commotion."

"A fulfillment of a promise." Bingham said.

A lieutenant ushered Father into the office followed by Drury and Stephanie. After proper greetings, Amy stood by my side, holding my hand. Another officer knocked, opened the door, signaled Bingham and left. The colonel asked us to follow him. Outside, a military honor guard met us. In turn, the second officer ushered us to seats on a wooden platform. Stephanie's parents, Mr. & Mrs. Sinclair, sat with Sarah and Beatrice. Men who I concluded were state and city dignitaries took seats on the front row. To one side, I spotted Donald Thomas taking notes.

The lieutenant approached the podium. "Ladies and gentlemen, would you please rise?" He waited until all stood. "Please greet the Governor of the state of Georgia, Joseph Brown." From the side, two officers escorted him to the platform. The lieutenant requested we remain standing for an invocation, which Reverend Houff offered. Following the prayer, the governor approached the podium, directing all to be seated. Clearing his throat, he spoke.

"A first step leads to many steps, and today we take a first step. We send two sons of Georgia to Fort Johnson in Charleston, South Carolina, as military observers. They will demonstrate the qualities of Georgian culture while learning military readiness. We thank God and their families, especially, their wives, that they accepted this duty. In keeping with my word, I ask Mr. George Yardley to approach the podium accompanied by his wife, Amy. Captain and Mrs. Stith, would you please join us?" We stood, escorted to the governor's side by the two officers. "Mr. Yardley," the governor continued, "some time ago I asked Captain Stith to approach you about training the Atlanta Grays. It is my understanding you refused out of loyalty to the Milton Guards. My offer carried a commission as a lieutenant in the Georgia Militia." The governor paused, signaling a sergeant who approached carrying a small box. Taking the box, he opened it, presenting me with two metal insignias. "Mrs. Yardley," he said, "would you please join me in pinning these bars on your husband's collar?" Upon completing that task, the governor returned to the podium. "Mr. George Washington Yardley, I commission you a lieutenant in the Georgia Militia. May God's blessings protect you and keep you." He stepped aside, leading applause. The Atlanta Grays, standing in formation, erupted in cheers.

For the moment, I forgot my sadness over George's departure; but as the ceremony ended, loneliness overcame me. I took George's hand. A tear emanated from each eye. The crowd mingled. Colonel Bingham congratulated George as did Drury and Stephanie.

The train was scheduled to depart at eleven thirty, which gave us an hour to make our way to the station. Along with the Stiths, George and I found ourselves in a carriage, moving toward the center of Atlanta.

"Can you believe we married these two fools?" Stephanie said. "Before our first anniversaries, they're headed to war."

"I keep telling her," Drury said, "that war has not been declared. Why do you not understand?"

"Drury," George said, "behave or Stephanie will declare war on you." She shrugged, I think affirming George understood her feelings.

The carriage pulled up to the train station. Militia stood ready to assist, and assist they did. One opened the carriage door allowing the officers to step out. Each in turn helped Stephanie and me. By the time we gathered ourselves, Alexander, Beatrice and Sarah arrived. Drury and Stephanie's parents stood with us.

"I'll write every day," George said, as we walked through the station toward the platform.

"I'll write, too," I said, wiping away tears with a hankie. "I wish I had thought to have a letter waiting upon your arrival in Charleston." The conductors announced the call to board.

Hurried, George kissed Sarah and Beatrice, shaking hands with Father.

For one last time, George hugged me. "I love you," we said to each other at the same moment.

Chapter 27

George Yardley

Fort Johnson, South Carolina

The train traveled to Savannah where it off-loaded cargo, continuing to Charleston. We arrived in the early morning on February fourteenth. Once there, a sergeant with the South Carolina Militia escorted us to Fort Johnson.

After reporting to General Pierre Beauregard, the commanding officer, we received our assigned quarters near the officers' mess. Having no responsibilities that day, I wrote my first letter to Amy.

The days went by with the speed of a tortoise. Here, I experienced firsthand the tedium of soldiering. At least twice a week, an officer from South Carolina guided Drury and me around the fort pointing out the cannon placements, the size of the balls each cannon shot and the means by which they calculated the distance over water to Fort Sumter. Some days we observed cannoneers lob balls into the harbor, practicing accuracy.

The newspapers reported that Lincoln departed Springfield, Illinois, by train under a heavy guard. Articles made headlines out of his farewell speech.

"What does he mean by this?" Drury asked.

We lay on our bunks after supper. "What?"

"That he has 'a task before me greater than that which rested upon Washington.' What a pompous, egotistical bastard. He desires to make a name for himself. He knows states have a right to secede."

"Just because he knows, doesn't mean he'll allow it without retribution," I replied. "That's why we're here. Somebody will fire a shot either at Lincoln or someone else, and the war will start."

"Sooner than later," Drury said, throwing the paper on the floor. "Have you seen those dignitary types and rich plantation owners arriving from Virginia and North Carolina? Something is up."

"Yep, they'll start the war here."

"Why wait?"

"For Lincoln's inauguration—our southern leadership will not embarrass President Buchanan. Even though from Pennsylvania, he did everything possible to prevent war. Vice-president Breckenridge influenced Buchanan."

"That makes sense," Drury said. "Who told you that?"

"No one—have a mind of my own."

༜༚༜༚

Major Robert Anderson, commanding office of the Union garrison at Fort Moultrie, moved his troops from Fort Moultrie to Fort Sumter the day after Christmas, 1860, deciding he could defend Sumter and receive supplies if stationed in the harbor. He carried out the military exercise in secrecy, diversion, and a full moon, wounding the pride of the Southern officers' who failed to see the maneuver. Anderson and his meager garrison, along with their wives remained fortified at Sumter in what they considered the strongest and safest fort on earth.

Abraham Lincoln became the sixteenth president of the United States on March 4, 1861. By then, six southern states had seceded. Matters grew desperate at Sumter. Food and provisions diminished. The Confederacy made it clear they would not allow the fort resupplied. At the insistence of President Jefferson Davis, General Pierre Beauregard demanded the evacuation of Fort Sumter. Anderson refused the conditions. At 4:30 AM on April 12th a cannon fired a ball from Fort Johnson at Fort Sumter.

Drury and I watched through spyglasses as Confederate cannon pulverized Sumter, never once thinking the walls could protect its inhabitants; but they did. The pounding continued for two days. On April 14, 1861, Major Anderson surrendered the fort and evacuated. Not one soldier under Anderson's command experienced wound or scratch.

About an hour after the surrender, I ascended an earthworks embankment to look at Sumter. A celebration erupted among our garrison. Shots rang out amidst the jubilee. Something smashed into my leg above my knee. Crippled, I rolled down the incline. Drury rushed to my side summoning militia to assist. Blood stained my pant leg. "I've been shot."

"You have," he said.

They carried me to the hospital. Two surgeons removed the ball and tended the wound, informing me an amputation remained a possibility.

Drury waited until the surgeons dismissed themselves. "You're going to live."

"Believe so—dumb luck, isn't it?" I nodded toward my leg. "Least it isn't broken."

Sitting on a chair next to my cot, Drury peered around as if to assure no one listened. "George, I saw it with my own eyes. A soldier in the midst of the celebration aimed at you."

"Are you sure?"

"Certain."

"Did you get a look at him?"

"Yes—saw him for a second. If I saw him again, I'd recognize him."

"Bring me quill and paper. I want to write Amy."

"Will you tell her what I said?"

"No. I'll tell her that she and I have something in common. We've both been shot."

Drury glared. "You better inform her, under no circumstances, is she to travel here. Whoever shot her in Georgia is here after you."

"I'll write Alexander and tell him the truth. He'll stop her. I'll tell Amy it was an accident." As I said those words, I realized for the first time in my life I compromised my honor. "On second thought, I refuse to lie to either Amy or anyone else. If I don't tell her the truth, it'll make it easier to story later."

In my letter to Amy, I recounted what Drury stated, concluding with an order for her to remain in Atlanta. I also wrote Alexander.

Chapter 28

George Yardley's Journal

Fort Johnson

Ten days passed without a letter from Amy. An infection at the wound caused pain and fever. If the fever broke, I awoke in a pool of sweat. If clearheaded, I worried about Amy. On the tenth night, delirious with pain, the fever broke for the last time, but not before I saw Mother and Father. They sat by the stream on the farm, beckoning me, but only so far. It was clear I was not to cross over.

"George," Mother said, "Amy loves you. Go to her."

The next morning at dawn the infection departed. I tried to stand, but my muscles refused. A surgeon, Captain Drummond, examined me.

"I'm returning to Atlanta," I said.

"When your strength returns." He changed the bandages. "You may limp the rest of your life—you're lucky you didn't lose the leg." I felt relief. "I understand you haven't received mail from your wife."

"I fear something terrible happened."

"I'll look into it." He walked away, taking a seat at a small pine desk, and wrote. Standing, he ordered a soldier to get me food.

Drury Stith
(As recounted by him to George Yardley)

Having dressed, my attention turned to the door as Captain Drummond, George's surgeon, entered. "Good morning," he said. "Your friend made it through the night—he'll survive."

"That's good news."

A man of slender build, no more than five and a half feet tall, his jaw rose as he addressed me. "What do you make of the fact Mrs. Yardley failed to write her husband?"

"Something's wrong—I worry she's been shot."

"A woman? Why?"

"She's been shot as has her father, Alexander Frey. Both survived. It was touch and go with Mr. Frey."

I recounted the details of each shooting. After hesitating, I told him what I saw when George was shot.

"Come with me," he said. We exited my quarters, making our way to the fort's post office. Entering the small one room brick building, a stout Scotsman, Sergeant MacMillan, greeted us.

"What time does the mail arrive?" Dr. Drummond asked.

"Within the hour. Private White went to the train station to retrieve it."

"Is he alone?"

"Yes—wouldn't send two soldiers for one mailbag."

"Yardley hasn't received correspondence from his wife. That seems peculiar. She wrote every day before Sumter fell."

"Sure he has," MacMillan said. "I've seen four or five letters."

"He hasn't received them," Drummond said. "Something's wrong."

"Indeed, something is wrong," MacMillan said.

Drummond turned to me and then back to MacMillan. "How does Yardley's mail get from here to the infirmary?"

"Private White delivers it."

"The same White you sent to the station?"

"Yes."

"We'll wait," Drummond said. We sat on a bench outside the front door. In a moment, we saw a soldier driving a buckboard. "Private White," Drummond called.

His head turned. "Yes, Captain?"

"Where is...?"

"That's who shot George," I shouted.

"Are you sure?" Drummond asked.

"I'm sure—that's him."

"Sergeant MacMillan, go to the brig and return with an armed detachment to arrest this man. Private White, don't move." I drew my carbine, pointing it at the assailant. "Where is Yardley's mail?"

White stared down into the well of the buckboard. "Stuffed under my mattress."

"Tell Captain Stith the location of your quarters. He will retrieve the mail." As I holstered my weapon, the doctor drew a derringer from a holster strapped around his ankle, pointing it at White. "Private, do you admit to shooting Lieutenant Yardley?" A guilty silence ensued. The next morning, without a stated confession, we hanged Private White.

Chapter 29

George Yardley

Food strengthened me. Reading and re-reading Amy's letters enhanced the healing process. After three days, I walked on my own and on the fifth day, Drury and I rode in a carriage to the train station.

"How's your limp?" he asked as we took our seats on the train.

"Painful."

A seamstress in Charleston stitched the bullet hole in my pant leg. "I'm glad that shot didn't penetrate your jacket," Drury said.

"I'm glad we're homeward bound."

"Where will you make your home?"

"That's up to Amy. I'd feel safer in Atlanta."

"That would be nice for Stephanie and me and the Grays. You could train at the armory."

"My allegiance is to the Milton Guards. Even if we stay with Sarah, I will return to Alpharetta on Saturdays. It is springtime. I'll plant a crop."

Drury turned from the window. "If you need help, I volunteer. Even though I grew up on a farm, I never farmed it." He paused. "My family owns slaves. They do our farming. When I see what you have, jealousy sets in. I would love to farm, but my father would disown me. That work is for coloreds as far as he's concerned."

"Now that the war has started, who knows where we'll wind up? Come to Alpharetta. We'll sow a crop." Drury nodded, settling back for a nap.

Anxiety rushed through my veins as the train rushed through the countryside. My need to protect Amy, to be strong for her, and to provide for her, made me neglect my emotions. Retribution warped my thoughts. I decided to ask the Guard to return to Cherokee County. If we killed every man who conspired against us, who conspired to save the Union, or conspired to assassinate the Confederate leadership, the threat might diminish. From that moment, spilling blood infiltrated my being.

Standing at the front of the car, the conductor announced we had entered Georgia. I never slept—but contemplated vengeance—vengeance that would be mine and not the Lord's.

As the train slowed into the station, Drury awakened, staring at the platform. "No one waits for us. Did you send a telegram?"

"Thought you did."

"Guess we're on our own."

A Negro stood next to our luggage inside the station. "Nigger," Drury said, "take our bags and hire a carriage. We'll follow in a moment."

Watching the slave, I shook my head. "Why can't we carry our bags?"

Drury laughed. "Why should we?"

Rushing toward the slave, heading him off, I relieved him of my bag. "I'll take this."

"Yes sir, Master," the slave said. "What should I do with this one?" Drury approached. "He'll tell you."

Drury eyed me. "Keep that up and you'll ruin our way of life. If you had your way, you'd free the slaves and still fight for states' rights."

"True," I said, motioning to a carriage driver. "If I could, I'd fight to free the slaves and keep each state sovereign."

"Maybe the Union will let you fight on their side for six months each year, and maybe the Confederacy will let you fight for us six months."

The driver opened the carriage door, proceeding to the rear with the baggage. "Amusing," I said. "Why don't we find our wives before you rub off on me?"

We sat across from each other. Drury smiled. "The feeling is mutual."

Fifteen minutes later, having paid the driver, we walked up the steps to an opened front door. Before we entered, two blood-curdling screams sounded. Amy and Stephanie rushed outside.

Chapter 30

Alexander Frey

After a noon meal with Sarah, I walked to my office. Turning the corner, I eyed three men in earnest conversation at the front door. Drawing nearer, I identified Horatio and Alexander Stephens. Squinting, I recognized Robert Toombs. Seeing me, their attention turned. We greeted each other, I feeling an urgency invading the moment. Unlocking the door, I offered them seats in the parlor. Toombs spoke first.

"Alexander, a group calling itself *The Association* formed in North Georgia, making its headquarters in Cherokee County. This *Association* consists of men involved in the political decisions regarding the admission of Kansas into the Union. Some traveled to Kansas, joining up with anti-slavery forces from the Free States, wreaking havoc and killing pro-slavery families—even entire communities—who sympathized with the Confederacy. Their aim is to admit Kansas to the Union as a Free State.

Listening, my thoughts turned to George and Amy, to their safety, to George's pledge of vengeance. Lost in a maze of concern, I realized Mr. Toombs had ceased speaking. "Go on," I said.

"They perceive your daughter and son-in-law a threat and, vow to kill both. Someone—we don't know who—offered a two thousand dollar bounty to murder George and Amy."

"Go on," I said again.

"Mr. Frey, your children face grave danger. It is by the grace of God they have escaped to this point."

"Possibly, they escaped due to George's natural instincts and your daughter's tenacity," Horatio said.

"Granted." Toombs said. "Regardless, it would cause me grave consternation if Amy and George became the first casualties of war."

"Thank you for your concern," I said, my voice a whisper.

Stephens cleared his throat. "We prefer your children remain here in Atlanta where we can protect them."

"How do you know George returned from Charleston?"

Toombs turned to me. "General Beauregard sent a telegraph noting Lieutenant Yardley and Captain Stith had boarded the train to Atlanta."

"I must return to Sarah's. Thank you for this information."

The political differences between Toombs and Stephens emerged for a moment. Toombs believed the Union should be dissolved and secession honored. Stephens, on the other hand, decried dissolution while seeking means to protect slave owners. Not wanting to hear their debate, I interrupted. "I will discuss this matter with George and inform you of his decision. Knowing my daughter, she already decided to return to Alpharetta." As they stood, I asked their opinion as to which state would secede next. Stephens offered his opinion.

"As you know, Alexander, South Carolina, Mississippi, Florida, Alabama, Georgia, and Louisiana passed articles of secession. Virginia adopted a resolution and will vote on the issue in May. We expect other states to do the same. Arkansas, North Carolina, Tennessee, Missouri and Kentucky should follow, though with the diverse political positions in the latter two states, it could take till the end of the year for the entire Confederacy to form."

"Hope not. If Virginians vote overwhelming for secession, I believe the others will vote by June."

"Doubtful," Toombs said. "There is strong Union sentiment in Kentucky and Missouri. A great deal of work remains to create our Confederacy."

"Newspapers already report skirmishes including some in North Georgia," I said. "When will the first battle be fought?"

"As soon as Virginia secedes," Toombs said.

"Why then?"

"Please understand that secession creates an international issue. The formation of the Confederate States of America establishes a foreign nation on the Union's border. When Virginia secedes, the home state of Washington, Jefferson, and Monroe will border the Union's capitol. Lincoln and his cronies won't allow it. They abhor the thought."

Satisfied with Toombs' response, I remembered how much I wanted to see George. Horatio requested a ride home. We shared a carriage. Toombs and Stephens with their conflicted political views rode away together. Maybe, I thought, there is hope in the birthing of the Confederacy.

"Alexander," Horatio said, "we must discuss an issue."

"Money?"

"Correct—remember you made a commitment of your wealth to this endeavor. When will you make your funds available?"

"Who wants it and how much?"

The horses and the carriage clanked along. "Five hundred thousand dollars in the state coffers for munitions and militia training."

"And, to line someone's pocket as is often the case with Georgian politics?"

Horatio muttered, unprepared for the indictment. "What might you suggest?"

"Do you remember I used my own money to build the forge?"

"Yes."

"I choose to spend my money to defend Georgia and the Confederacy. Depositing it in the state coffers is out of the question. Inform Governor Brown that I require accounting of the state's financial needs. Then, I will make financial decisions based on the merits."

"That will disappoint him."

"Be that as it may, he won't be the first politician disappointed by the response of a private citizen. As George often says, 'Tell him to take a nap and get over it.'"

"As usual, you place me in a difficult position."

"That's why I pay you."

"How far along is the forge?" Horatio asked.

"The structure is completed. Production of cannon balls and cannons will commence next week."

"What is our greatest material need as a state and as a Confederacy?"

"Boots."

"Boots?"

"Yes, boots. Read any book on military preparation and the first thing mentioned is footwear. An army lasts as long as its boots."

"What shall we do about that?"

"Enlarge Jacob's business to produce quality boots."

"What if he won't?"

"That old Jew will build anything that makes money, as I would. War makes rich people richer. They serve as the backbone of the economy."

"Jacob's a close friend of yours?"

"Yes. There's nothing better in business and in life than a Jew who is a good friend."

The carriage stopped at Horatio's home. Anxious about *The Association*, I dismissed my friend. Arriving at Sarah's, I found Beatrice, Sarah, Amy and George on the front porch.

"If you ladies would permit, may I take Mr. Yardley for a walk to exercise his leg?"

Amy squirmed. "Certainly, if upon your return you reveal the true purpose of your walk to the three women in your life."

"Do I sense a lack of trust?"

Beatrice stood. "Why would your daughter trust you after she discovered you kept me a secret for ten years?"

"Once I had two women with whom to contend. Now, I have three."

George and I made our way to the street. Though limping, he refused the cane.

"I've come from a meeting with Robert Toombs, Alexander Stephens, and Horatio. They informed me of danger lurking in Cherokee County." I explained in detail.

"Why do they seek our lives?"

"The Union at all costs—that's their motto. Look at what they see. You let slave-hunters die in the creek. Your father-in-law finances secession. And, myth has it you're the finest soldier in Georgia. *The Association* sees you as a threat."

"Does *The Association* count Andrew Shelton as a member?"

"I'm certain."

"What are your plans for Alpharetta?"

"I'm resting till next Sunday. Then, we'll return to the farm. Drury and Stephanie may join us. He desires to plow fields and sow seed."

"Drury? I can't imagine he'd perform slave labor. Besides, after Stephanie has her way with him, he'll reconsider." I chuckled. "Oh, to be young again." We turned around to head home. "Any chance Amy might stay in Atlanta?"

"Up to her," George said. "Now that we know about *The Association*, she might reconsider.

My mind wandered, mulling George's intent to take the battle to Cherokee. "Has Drury ever fought—I mean—shot at someone or even fisticuffs?"

"Doubtful; but I'd rather he gain experience here than in the heat of battle."

"If I had my druthers, I'd rather Nathaniel with you than Drury."

"Nice compliment, but Aunt Lillian won't allow him near the farm after she hears about this gang in Cherokee."

It was the last day of April. Gnats and mosquitoes buzzed as dusk settled. Our walk produced a lack of resolution. For the moment, we enjoyed the spring breeze. I lit a cigar causing the insects to seek victims elsewhere.

The ladies waited on the porch. Beatrice stood as we climbed the steps. "Did you forget you no longer live here?"

"Forgive me."

"I forgot, too," George said, turning to me. "How will you get home tonight?"

"For old time's sake, why don't we have a drink?" I said. "Maybe reality..."

Amy took George's hand. "My husband isn't drinking anything. If you will excuse us, we will retire." She gave him a look that refused any options.

"Guess I'm going upstairs," George said.

"That's better than on the front porch," Sarah replied.

Amy opened the door. "With regard to our privacy, it would be nice if the three of you spent the night on the front porch."

Chapter 31

George Yardley's Journal

Atlanta

When Amy saw my wound, she almost fainted, referring to it as a "red-hot ember." The walk with Alexander did my leg good, but also tired me.

Being alone gave us the opportunity to talk about her pregnancy. As she disrobed, I noticed her breasts had enlarged though her abdomen seemed flat and firm. In her letters, Amy informed me she had told no one about the pregnancy and that I must keep it a secret. At best, she was three months along. We talked about becoming parents and about the information I had received from Alexander. That combination subdued our lovemaking.

During the night, I awakened to Amy's crying. Feeling for her in the bed proved futile. Lighting a candle, I moved to where she sat by the bedroom door, her gown stained red. The reality of what she felt produced a wailing I describe as the wail of death. Kneeling, placing my arms around her shoulders, pulling her toward me, she remained inconsolable. Beatrice opened the door to the candlelight and to her stepdaughter's despair.

Sarah followed. Hearing her brother in the hall, she turned her attention to him, telling him not to enter.

"We'll tend to her," Sarah said. "Join Alexander downstairs." Before leaving, I helped them lift Amy to bed, her sobs subsiding a bit. Laying her down, Sarah removed the gown. "I'll get warm water. Come with me." I left the room leaving Beatrice to comfort Amy.

✎✎✎✎

"What's wrong?" Alexander asked as I descended the steps.

"Miscarriage."

The concern on Alexander's face changed to despair. "I won't survive if Amy dies. I can't live without her. God," he prayed, "please don't take her. Please."

✎✎✎✎

"George," Sarah said from the top of the stairs. "Amy wants you." I leaped up, taking two steps at a time, stopping at Sarah's insistence. "She's had a miscarriage."

"That's what I thought."

"We'll be downstairs if you need us," Beatrice said.

Entering the room, I found Amy lying under a linen sheet with a wet cloth on her head. Seeing me, she wept, but not as hard as before.

"I'm sorry, George. I'm so sorry." Turning on her side, arms extended, fingers outstretched, she reached for me. In that moment, I knew what it meant to be needed, not loved—but needed. I knew what it meant to feel oneness; oneness that creates deep, sincere dependence; oneness that refuses to let go of the one in need.

Embraced, searching for words, I whispered in her ear. "It's all right. I have all I want and need in you."

Lying next to her on top of the linen, adjusting my position, I placed my arm around her. She fell asleep. Inching my way out of bed, then out of the room, I went downstairs to the kitchen. "She's sleeping," I said. Sarah and Beatrice returned to their bedrooms.

Alexander remained seated at the table; tears trickled down his cheeks, one finding its way into his moustache. "She wants to give you a child more than anything."

Seated across from him, my head bowed. "I'm not certain God wants me to have a child. It feels like He's either punishing me or hardening me for war. Those boys in Charleston—bombing a defenseless fort—think they won the war. During my convalescence, I read and re-read a poem by Tennyson, titled *In Memoriam*. He wrote of nature that is "red in tooth and claw." Something compelled me to look up. Alexander stared at me through candlelight, speechless. "When those boys start getting legs and arms shot off, their skulls shattered, they'll find war *red—blood red—flowing fast and deep like the Chattahoochee during a thunderstorm*. Losing a baby like we did will seem like one of Lillian's Sunday picnics in the town square."

Alexander's eyes narrowed. His tears ceased. "I met Tennyson a few years ago. A friend and I had played *fours*—golf. Afterwards, we dined in a club where the poet spent holidays. He appeared a beaten man—still aggrieved years later over the loss of his friend. How many? How many fathers and mothers will suffer what Amy and you suffered? How many *friends* will bury their friends? I wish I could sail us to England to live happily thereafter."

Returning to the bedroom, carrying a candle, I held it so as to see Amy's face. She appeared as if the peace of God had come over her.

❧❧❧❧

She awoke at dawn; my arm draped over her abdomen. Shaking me awake, she sought eye contact. "It wasn't a nightmare, was it?"

"Does it hurt?"

"In my heart and in my flesh—yes, it hurts."

We stood. I helped her with her robe. In the basin next to the door, we washed our faces and hands, cleaned our teeth, embraced, and walked downstairs.

Alexander met us. "Are you all right?"

Though fighting back tears, she nodded. "I need to go outside. Let's sit on the porch." Alexander helped her through the door to the settee. "I wanted to be pregnant more than anything," she said. "I want to give George a child." Bringing both hands to her face, she wept. Alexander sat next to her with his arm around her shoulder. "I know I'll never have a child. Nothing feels right inside me."

I had made my way into the parlor able to hear their conversation. The loneliness of not having my own father overcame me. From what I perceived, it was my lot in life to be parentless and childless. In what darkness remained, I took a seat on the high back chair next to the fireplace, allowing my tears to flow. A verse emerged.

These tears I weep for thee and thine,
Thee whom I knew in former time,
My mother, father, parents proud,
Who loved me then and love me now.

These tears I weep for thee and thine,
Thine in whose life was hers and mine,
Your mother, father, parents grieve,
Our God has now, your soul received.

Most of the time, I didn't know from whence the poetry derived. It somehow materialized to measure my emotion. And so it was, I sat grieving without parents, without hope of a child, and for the moment, with my wife nestled in her father's arms. I wanted to kill whoever wanted to kill us. *Association* or no *Association*, I decided to kill anyone and everyone involved.

I awoke to Amy's hand shaking my arm. "You've been crying."

"I have." Moisture on my cheeks moistened my fingers. She tried to turn and sit on my lap, putting her arms around my neck, but a pain struck her belly, causing a jolt.

"Oh," she cried, "something still hurts."

Chapter 32

George Yardley

Atlanta

"Decide what you want to do," I said, dressing for the day. The grandfather clock in the parlor chimed nine times. Still feeling ill from the miscarriage, Amy opted for bed. "I'm off to the armory to see Drury."

Amy turned on her side issuing a groan. "How does one grieve for an unborn child?"

"Place her in God's hands, and go on."

She turned, lifting her head. "Her?"

"That's what Sarah said—guess she could tell."

Twisting into the pillow, she spoke. "Please don't tell me anymore."

Reaching for the door handle, I turned it. "Going to the livery for Pearl—be back by noon."

"Will you tell Drury what happened?"

"Yes. It's best they know."

"All right," she said. "Hope this doesn't cause you more pain and tears."

"I hope the same for you. I love you."

Closing the door, I tiptoed downstairs. Everyone remained asleep. I charged out the door, down the steps, limping toward the livery. Feeling compelled by some outside force, I reached for my handgun, making certain it was holstered by my side. I wished someone, anyone, would take a shot at me. The desire to kill consumed me. With my parents dead, I contended with the death of my unborn daughter.

Recognizing me, Pearl pranced in her stall. The slave boy saddled her, giving us time to reacquaint as I brushed her neck.

Atlanta's streets seemed unusually busy near the train station. Not in uniform, I felt less conspicuous. Once in a while someone gestured, apparently recognizing me. At one point, I tipped my hat to two women I recognized from church. Something compelled me onward toward the armory.

At the armory, a commotion outside the offices where I received my commission presented itself. Kicking Pearl, I approached and saw Drury circling a combatant. Both threw right hooks, missing their targets. Removing my revolver from its holster, I shot twice into the air. Drury turned his attention toward me, enabling his foe to land a punch. My friend stumbled backwards falling to the ground unconscious.

"What's the meaning of this?" I asked, staring at the soldier who smashed Drury. His face and nose oozed blood. A grimace displayed a missing front tooth.

"He accused me of taking liberties with his wife while he was in Charleston," the man said. Onlookers gathered around encircling the soldier.

"Did you?" I asked. "Before he answers, one of you get a bucket of water and pour it over the captain." A soldier grabbed a basin sitting on the porch, making his way to the well. "Now, answer my question," I said, pointing my gun at him.

He hesitated holding his hands out toward me. "You don't have to point that gun."

"I'll shoot you if you don't answer. Did you or didn't you?"

"I went to see her to make sure she was all right. I didn't take liberties."

"That the end of the story?"

"She gave me the impression she'd like me to imbibe of her; so I obliged. Before I knew it, she whacked me over the head with a frying pan—near bled to death."

"Captain Stith have a different version of that story?"

"Yes."

"You men," I said pointing to three soldiers, "take this man to the lockup until we sort this out."

"I'm not going," he said.

"Go peacefully, or I'll blow a hole through you. Then, they can drag you," I said pointing and cocking the pistol. "I'll ride behind to make sure he obeys."

The soldier returned with the water bucket and drenched Drury. "Take care of the captain until I return." Two men bent over Drury shaking him.

"Lieutenant Yardley, please join me in my office." It was Colonel Bingham.

I turned Pearl, heading first toward Drury. Dismounting, I stooped next to him. "Next time you're in a fist fight and you hear a shot, throw one more punch."

Knocking on the door, I heard Bingham entreat me to enter, which I did. "Yes sir—what might I do for you?"

"Where's Captain Stith?"

"Indisposed at present."

"George, I received word about our assignment. We fight with the Army of Northern Virginia. It appears General Robert E. Lee will command the brigade. Our political leadership determined that one militia unit from each Confederate state serve under Lee. I chose the Milton Guards. Muster and depart Atlanta by rail May 26th for Richmond." A long pause ensued. "The proper response, Lieutenant, is 'Yes sir, Colonel Bingham.'"

"Yes sir, though I wish to remind you of my inexperience."

"Your capabilities outshine all others under my command. Carry out your orders."

I saluted and went to find Captain Stith. As I turned the corner, a soldier tossed a second bucket of water at Drury. He stood, swinging his fist. Three men wrestled him to his seat.

"Drury," I said, "the fight's over—relax. We need to talk." A mixture of blood and water trickled from his nose. "You men put him in a buckboard and take him home."

"Where does he live?" one asked. I gave directions and mounted Pearl. "Drury, I'll visit you later."

❧❦❧❦

I rode Pearl past the side of the house, unsaddled, her and headed in the back door where Sarah met me. "Your wife needs you upstairs."

"Is she all right?"

"Fine physically—her heart is broken."

"Where's Alexander?"

"He took Beatrice home and went to his office. Go to your wife."

At the urgency of her order, I climbed the stairs. Opening the bedroom door, I found Amy in bed staring out the window, unresponsive to my presence.

Approaching the bedside, I knelt in front of her. "Amy, I need your help." She refused to respond. "I need your help and I mean it. I'm faced with something I can't do without you." She stared without blinking. "Please, Amy, I received orders to take the Milton Guards to Richmond where we shall join the Army of Northern Virginia. We depart in three weeks—May 26th. Please come out of this. I can't leave you in this condition."

Tears streaked her cheeks. She reached, taking my hand. "I'm sorry, George. I love you. I'm sorry I lost the baby."

Holding her, I whispered. "Amy, if God intends for us to have children, we'll have them. Right now, you are the one I love and the one I need."

"When do you leave?" she asked, separating from the embrace.

"In three weeks—I've never mustered a militia. I'm not sure they trust me."

"Is Drury going?"

"Don't think so. What do you know about Stephanie whacking some soldier over the head with a frying pan?"

"Forgot to tell you—someone from the armory went to her house. He made advances. When he refused to stop, she grabbed a skillet. I'm surprised he isn't dead."

"If I had known that, I would have shot him dead today."

"What? Why?"

"At the armory, I found Drury in a fist-fight. Drury got the worst of it. As I heard the other man's story, I sensed a lie. I wanted to kill him."

"But you didn't?"

"Locked him in the brig."

"Where's Drury?"

"In the back of a buckboard heading home."

"Oh, the poor fellow."

"Plan to see him this afternoon." Amy stared formulating a question. "What?" I asked.

"Could you take me with you?"

Chapter 33

Amy Yardley

Arriving at the Stiths' in a carriage, we heard Stephanie yell for help. George jumped down and ran to the door. Stephanie met him, pounding her fists into George's chest. "Why did you do that to Drury?"

George backed away. "Do what?"

"Beat him," Stephanie said.

"I didn't do that. The man who made the advances toward you did."

"He told me you fought him."

Staring her down, George pointed his right index finger. "Well, I didn't."

The carriage driver helped me to the front door. "Stephanie, why would you think George did such a thing?"

"Let's ask Drury," George said.

We went inside. Drury lay on the parlor sofa conscious, too sore to move. "Why did you blame me?" George asked.

"I didn't—told her you shot your gun, and I got sucker-punched."

"That's what happened," George said. "Tried to break up the fight, fired my gun, and the guy clobbered Drury. If it makes you feel better, I locked him in the brig. If I knew then what I know now, I'd have killed him, no questions asked."

"Sorry," Stephanie said. "I misunderstood."

"That's all right," George said, pointing to Drury. "He'll live." He made eye contact with Drury. "By the way, Bingham assigned the Milton Guards to the Army of Northern Virginia and ordered me to get them there."

"What?" Drury said.

Stephanie approached me. "This is terrible."

"No," I said. "What is terrible is what happened last night." Stephanie eyed me pleading for an explanation. "I was pregnant and lost the baby."

Two tears rolled down Stephanie's cheeks. "Oh, my God." I found myself comforting Stephanie. "This is the worst day of our lives. You lost a baby, my husband got mauled, and your husband received orders to Virginia."

"May 7th," I said. "It seems a day of reckoning."

Drury sat up. "I'm going with you, George."

"Don't remember inviting you—besides you should stay here to protect the women."

"I'm going," Drury repeated. "I'll see to it."

"My men won't cotton to an outsider."

"I have a jacket—that makes me a part of them, and I outshot them."

"No, you didn't," George said. "You didn't outshoot me."

"Colonel Bingham will send me. I'm going."

"Just a minute, you two," Stephanie said. "Your wife, George Yardley, had a miscarriage. It would do you well to quit this jabber and pay attention to Amy. And, Mr. Stith, one more word and I'll beat you bloodier than you were beaten this morning."

Chapter 34

Amy Yardley

Father paid for a carriage to take us to Alpharetta. Drury, Stephanie, George and I rode along with Pearl tied to the back.

"What's the news?" Howard Montross hollered from his cabin door as we slowed for the descent to the river.

"The Guard's been assigned to the Army of Northern Virginia," George said. "We leave May 26th."

"Do they know it?" Howard asked.

"No," George said. "I'll break it to them tomorrow."

"Heard any gossip?" George asked.

"Yeah—talk about what Andrew Shelton and his Cherokee friends intend to do—next chance they get."

"We'll take care of them," Drury said.

"Hope better than you took care of that soldier," George said.

"Don't start," Stephanie said. "You two find a better way to release your tension than these jabs."

"I have an idea," George said, "but we can't do it in this carriage."

"You'll never do it again if you keep making light of it," I said.

Howard scratched his head, then his beard. "Damnedest conversation I've ever heard—won't try to make sense of it." He looked at his wife. "If you ladies need the privy, you know where it is." Stephanie and I eyed each other deciding to refrain.

"Be careful," Howard said as we rode away. "Been enough trouble around here."

His warning gave George a start. "Funny Howard didn't mention the wound I received at Sumter."

The ferry waited at the landing. Mr. White asked one question after another about the coming war and events in Charleston.

The Chattahoochee drifted around the raft. George stood at the stern. "Did you hear someone shot me?"

"Guess we'll hear the rest of our lives," Drury said. "Before long, you'll convince everyone you took Sumter by yourself."

George laughed. "For the rest of your life, you'll hear about the licking you took."

The barge eased alongside the dock. George stared at Pearl tied to the carriage. "Let's go to Uncle Robert's. I need to get Splinter."

❧❦❧❦

Alpharetta looked the same. A peaceful stillness floated amongst the willows and oaks, which the Guard's assignment to Virginia would shatter. In three weeks, husbands, sons and brothers would march to war.

Robert, standing at the well, saw us first. A tenuous wave of his hand portrayed a foreboding. He called for Lillian who emerged from the cabin followed by the girls. The greetings felt cool and stilted except for Samantha, who couldn't contain her excitement over seeing George.

"What's wrong?" I asked.

"A lot," Lillian replied.

George looked around. "Where's Nathaniel?"

"Not here," Robert said. "Let's go to the cabin." Everyone, including Samantha and Leslie, followed. Entering the rear door,

George and I remained standing, waiting. "I don't know if you heard, but Andrew Shelton is alive."

"We heard," George said. "Howard told us at the river."

"That's where I think Nathaniel is."

George slammed the butcher block. "You think he's at Andrew's?"

"No—I think he's in Cherokee scouting around."

George peered through the back window toward the horse pen. "Where's Splinter?"

"Nathaniel took him."

"How long has he been gone?"

"Three days. Word spread you got shot at Sumter by one of your own men. His name was White, wasn't it?"

"Yes," Drury said. "We hanged him."

"Well, he has an uncle in north Cherokee livid over the loss of his nephew—put a bounty on George's head. The man who kills you gets a thousand dollars."

"Who has that kind of money in Cherokee?" I asked.

Robert took a seat at the table. "Who knows? Plenty of slave owners do."

"*The Association*," Drury said.

Lillian turned toward him. "What do you mean?"

"*The Association* with roots out west in Kansas tried to make Kansas a slave state. Some of their kin live in Cherokee," George said. "They want no part of secession but desire a confederacy where people can own slaves. They've sworn to kill anyone who stands in their way. They see me as a threat."

"Oh, God," Lillian said. "My son is in their midst."

"Uncle Robert, why didn't you go after Nathaniel?" I asked.

"I did but couldn't find him—returned this morning."

"Did you pass our cabin?"

"Yes."

"Everything all right?"

"Yes—looked inside—nothing disturbed."

"Thank God," I said.

George approached Drury. "Amy, you and Stephanie stay here till I return. Drury and I will ride Pearl to the cabin."

Every part of me cringed with fear. Protest was out of the question. Drury fetched luggage from the carriage, sending the driver away. In a moment, George and he rode off without kissing their wives.

Chapter 35

George Yardley

At my cabin, I retrieved provisions from the cellar and closed the door. Drury appeared aimless. "Leaving tonight?" he asked.

"Tracks don't improve with age."

He peered west toward the Smokies. "Can't be two hours of light left."

Preparing for the ride, I remained unresponsive. After checking my powder and lead, I mounted Pearl while Drury climbed on a horse I had taken from the bounty hunters.

After a mile, we spotted a horseman. Pulling my pistol, I cocked it.

"You boys lost?" Nathaniel asked.

"Where you been?" I said.

"Harvesting information. Let's get to your cabin."

By the time we set the horses to pasture, darkness surrounded us on the front porch. I retrieved cigars and pipes. The gnats and mosquitoes swarmed until we lit up.

I exhaled two puffs of smoke. "All right—enough. What did you find out?"

"That cabin in Cherokee is a busy place," Nathaniel said. "Twenty-four different men darkened its door the past two days and nights."

"Know any of them?"

"Not a one. All strangers and strange looking—ungroomed beards and long hair."

Drury faced me. "That White fellow who shot you had long hair and a scraggly beard."

"I crept up outside a window each night and listened. In case you don't know, one put a thousand dollars on your head and Amy's. He'd prefer you be delivered alive. Don't think he plans to throw you a party."

"How can I go to Virginia and leave Amy in this danger?"

"Virginia?"

I blew another puff. "You're going, too. The Guard's assigned to the Army of Northern Virginia. We depart Atlanta May 26th."

"What if I don't want to go?"

"You a coward?"

Drury relit his cigar. "Hardly believe his actions the past two nights would merit him a coward." Nathaniel nodded.

"Creeping around in the dark doesn't compare to facing an enemy on a battlefield," I said.

Nathaniel leaned forward in his chair. "Hate the thought of leaving Georgia."

"You hate the thought of leaving your momma."

"That makes it easier for you since you don't have a momma to leave."

Drury jumped, wrestling me to the porch before I could tackle Nathaniel. "Hold up," he said. "We don't need you two fighting."

"Keep my mother out of this," I said pointing at my cousin, surprised at Drury's strength.

"Keep mine out of it," Nathaniel said. "This the thanks I get for what I did for you?"

"I apologize—thought I'd find you dead." Pausing, I held my emotions in check. "Amy's been shot. I've been shot. It seems our world falls apart chunk by chunk—day by day. This war's only a month old."

"When did you get shot?" Nathaniel asked.

Drury recounted the events at Sumter. Hearing the tale, I hatched a plan. In the morning, Nathaniel would return home to alleviate his parents' fears along with Amy's and Stephanie's. Second, we'd muster the guard to inform them of their assignment.

"They're mean," Nathaniel said before going to bed. "I heard three tell they were in the cabin the morning we surrounded it. If given a clear shot, they'd have killed you."

"Maybe they'll grow soft thinking we don't know what we're doing."

"Truth is, we don't know," Nathaniel said. "We're off to war. No one has fought. It's going to be a bloody mess."

"Do you mean before we leave or afterwards?" I asked.

Drury stood. "What do you have in mind?"

"He's fixing to go to that cabin," Nathaniel said. "Can't you see it in his eyes?"

"That *Association* will get what's coming to them even if I fight them alone."

"See?" Nathaniel said. "We'll fight before we go north to fight."

Chapter 36

George Yardley

At dawn, a driving thunderstorm erupted. Nathaniel insisted he return home. Drury talked him out of such foolishness. Darkened skies grew darker as morning turned to afternoon. Every time we thought we'd heard the loudest of the thunderclaps, lightning poured from the sky in wide liquid bolts producing stronger thunder. Rain teemed—winds blew it sideways. At mid afternoon, it stopped.

Drury stepped onto the front porch. "Glad that's over."

"Me too," I said. "It'll take days for that amount of water to soak in and run off."

Nathaniel joined us. "Heading home—can't worry Mother any longer."

Turning toward him, I scoffed. "Shouldn't have traipsed off in the first place."

"Don't you two start," Drury said. "Your arguing bores me."

I nodded to Nathaniel. "Spread the word in town that the Guard will meet tonight in the square. Let's find out who will go into Cherokee County this Saturday."

"Sounds good," Captain Stith replied.

I made certain Nathaniel understood my instructions; then I sent him away. Unable to work in the mud, Drury and I returned to the front porch. We sat in silence until I noticed him deep in thought. "What's wrong?"

He shifted in his seat, peering at the mountains. "Wondering which one of us—Nathaniel, you, or me—has the best chance of surviving till next May."

Chapter 37

George Yardley

"Don't know if it's possible. I want each member of the Guard mounted." We rode the buckboard to Alpharetta. "In Virginia, I'd rather be horse soldiers than foot soldiers. When we leave on May 26th, we'll need a railroad car to transport the horses."

"That's a lot to ask," Drury said.

"Colonel Bingham will arrange the transportation if I make the request."

"I didn't mean that." He waited for eye contact. "I meant asking the Guard to buy their own horses. That's quite an expense."

"Five own horses."

"Does that include me?"

"Still opposed to you tagging along, but I relent."

Ten minutes later we rode into the square. Members of the Guard milled about. Our wives had not arrived. I turned my attention to the militia.

"You men anxious to fight? Get behind that willow—I'll shoot at you to give you a taste of war."

"Just because you got shot by one of your own men at Sumter doesn't give you a right to shoot us," Curly Rankin shouted, initiating laughter. "Besides, with that fake limp of yours, you couldn't hit us if you tried."

"You want to be my first target?"

Curly shook his head. To the west, I caught sight of a buckboard. After Amy and Stephanie greeted us, I went to work.

Word spread that I had an important announcement. The ladies stepped aside, giving me access to a semi-circle of militia. "Men of the Milton Guards, I hereby inform you that higher-ups assigned us to fight with the Army of Northern Virginia. We depart Milton County May 25th to muster in State Square that night. On the 26th, we depart Atlanta by rail for Richmond. Bring the clothes on your back, your jackets, the best boots you own, and your weapons and ammunition along with a change of socks and long johns. Is that clear?"

Most stood with folded arms, nodding affirmation. "Men, how many of you can ride a horse?" All raised their hands. "How many own a horse sturdy enough to make a battle charge?" Twelve hands went up. "I propose—if I can acquire the horses—we go to Virginia as cavalry." Excited commotion broke out. "I'd rather charge into battle than walk into it." A cheer went up. "Give me a week to see what I can arrange." Pausing, I stared at Nathaniel. "Last, be at my farm Friday night ready for battle."

Chapter 38

Amy Frey

"Lieutenant Yardley," Drury said sitting next to George on the front seat of the buckboard. Stephanie and I sat behind them. "If you're determined to have a Milton Cavalry, there's one thing missing."

"What's that?"

"Swords."

"Swords?"

Drury nodded. "A cavalry charge demands slashing sabers."

George swallowed hard. "How much for a sword?"

"Cost is irrelevant if one remains ignorant of how to use it."

"More to soldiering than I thought."

"There is," Drury said, "but you're thinking and that's what's important."

"Don't know if I could do that."

"What?"

"I can shoot a man; but could I 'run him through' as the saying goes?"

Drury interrupted. "Never been in battle, but if attacked, I'd use whatever means at hand—gun or sword."

"Stop," Stephanie said. "You scare us with such talk. We don't want to hear about war."

George turned. "Deal—if we talk war, we'll do so in private."

"Thank you," I said.

Passing Andrew's, I saw the cabin. "Be glad to sleep in my own bed."

George laughed. "Your friend's husband expects us to give up our bedroom for the benefit of their lovemaking."

Stephanie came out of her seat, slapping Drury's shoulder with the back of her hand. "How dare you talk about such things to anyone other than me?" She sat, folding her arms.

George turned to Stephanie. "Wish Amy knew how to do the things Drury says you do. He brags on you all the time."

Her eyes widened like saucers. "He best not brag on himself— I've taught him everything he knows."

ᴪ❧❦❧

The cabin appeared serene and beautiful. Whether George believed me, I know not. I considered the farm my home. Though danger prowled, I loved what we owned.

Darkness surrounded us except for the dim light shining over the mountains. The men unhitched the horses, putting them to pasture. Pearl and Splinter peered over the fence as if asking why they couldn't join us. Once I understood Drury and Stephanie would sleep in the loft, we all retired to the front porch. George saw it first.

"That's the last full moon we'll share until Drury and I return from Virginia." Sitting next to George on the bench, I interlocked my husband's fingers with mine.

"The moon and sun are all we'll share while you're gone," Stephanie said. "Let's vow that when we see either orb, we'll pray for each other."

"Let's do," I said, "but let us pray now." I reached taking Drury's hand. Stephanie completed the circle taking her husband's and George's. We bowed. "God, please be with our husbands, and keep them safe. Please give them courage in the midst of battle to know what to do and when to do it. And, God, bring them safely home. I ask this through the blessed name of your Son, Jesus Christ. Amen."

Squeezing my hand, Drury kissed me on the cheek. "Thank you. I can't express what your prayer meant and how wonderful it felt."

Stephanie stood, leaned over, and embraced me. "You never cease to amaze me."

Smoke from Drury's cigar and George's pipe scented the air and repelled the insects. We sat in silence. I allowed the depth of my love for George and Stephanie to penetrate my soul, realizing I cared for Drury, but not in the same way. In the past year, God granted me the gift of a husband and a friend. I sat in silence, afraid—afraid He would take them from me as rapidly as He presented them. War, damnable war, I thought. Sarah lost her fiancé. Beatrice lost her husband. What did God and war have in mind for Stephanie and me?

Chapter 39

George Yardley

The next morning, sitting on the front porch, an idea surfaced. "Hey, you all," I shouted, "we're going on an adventure. Enough of farm work; talk of war, and fear of Cherokee County." They gathered. "Count—four of us and four horses. We're riding into the mountains and picnicking," I said, pointing to the Smokies. "Anyone ever "skinny-dipped" in a stream?"

"No," Stephanie said, "and I won't in front of you."

"Neither shall I," Amy said. "I mean, neither shall I display myself to Drury."

"Darn," Drury said. "This was getting exciting."

Stephanie grabbed his shoulders. "The only excitement you'll ever get is in this dress."

"And that goes for you, too, George Yardley," Amy said, realizing her blunder and pointing to herself, "I mean in this dress."

Laughing, I turned to Stephanie. "Plenty of mountain streams up there where we can find privacy—seeing we've heard this outpouring of modesty." Pausing, I looked at Drury. "You and I better get accustomed to bathing in streams—doubt we'll find bathhouses in Virginia."

The ladies packed the picnic. Drury and I saddled the horses. My watch showed nine o'clock as we rode away.

Crossing the Alpharetta Road, we headed for the mountains. Entering the forest, I sensed someone following. Directing Drury to lead, I lagged behind, stealing glances to no avail.

We rode toward a waterfall Father and I had visited on occasion. Below the falls, a stand of pines shaded a sandy area just right for a picnic and private enough for a swim. Drawing near, I still felt someone's presence.

We heard rushing water. With the rains, the stream gushed. Past the pines, we dismounted. Usually, a two to three feet spread of water spilled over the rocks. Today a span twelve feet wide fell. Sunshine warmed the air.

"Who's first?" I hollered over the noise.

"You two go," Amy said. "Stephanie and I will prepare the picnic."

Disappearing around the bend, we stripped, hanging our clothes on branches. Wading naked, I dipped into the cold water. More cautious, Drury nerved himself to the task. Suddenly, the unexpected happened. As I floated, the current rushed me around the bend past the women where I came to rest in a shallow eddy. Drury followed, fighting to remain submerged. Refusing to expose ourselves, we sat in two feet of water.

"Oh, my gosh," Stephanie said.

Amy turned. "George—Drury—you're not funny."

"The current took us," I said. "You two turn around. We'll go back upstream."

Amy Yardley

"They're gone," Stephanie said.

"How do you know? Did you look?"

"Sort of—checked to see if they were gone; but they weren't."

"Did you see George?"

Stephanie smiled. "I did—maybe more than you've seen."

WISH IS MY MASTER

"Unlike you, I wouldn't look on purpose."

Stephanie stepped around the blanket we placed on the sand, embracing me. "I love you—amazing God brought us together."

"I love you, too," I said. "Never had a friend—but you're the best friend I could ever have." Our husbands approached, buttoning their shirts. "Too bad you're dressed, George. Stephanie liked the view she saw when you ran away."

Stephanie gasped. "Amy, some things are secrets."

"Too late," George shouted. "Turnabout is fair play, as the saying goes. Get undressed and allow the current to float you downstream. We'll hide our eyes."

My hands found my hips. "George Yardley, I'll do no such thing—behave yourself or I'll..."

"What?" Drury said.

"I'll not swim naked. That's all the reason he brought me here. Let's eat."

When finished, George grabbed my hand pulling me off the blanket as I feigned resistance. Around the bend, we stripped. He entered the water first and turned. "The sun never shone on anyone's nakedness more beautiful than yours."

Admired, adored, I entered the water feeling refreshed as the stream rushed over me. George held his place refusing to allow the current to carry me away. As we came together in an embrace, I realized what might happen. "Are you ready?" I asked, afraid to hear his answer.

"No ma'am—that's impossible in water this cold."

Relieved, I enjoyed the stream's caress and the melding together of our flesh. "How do you feel about Stephanie seeing you naked?"

"She saw my back."

"That was too much."

"How would you feel if Drury saw your back?"

"Mortified—and I mean it. God intended certain things for the sanctity of marriage."

"You would frown upon me sneaking a peak at Stephanie?"

Straddling him, I grabbed both his ears, shoving his head under the water and back up. "No one will ever see me naked, except you."

George Yardley

Having packed the blankets and food, we mounted the horses. As we came up and around to the top of the falls, I saw the signs. Ruffled leaves exposed the forest floor. Whoever followed, rode off in a hurry. Drury noticed, giving me a questioning eye. Searching, I tried to capture movement in the distance. Stephanie and Amy rode chatting.

"There's one rider," I whispered to Drury as he trotted beside me. "He's in a hurry." We scanned the trees, but for naught.

"Who was it?"

"At this rate, we'll never know. I've seen a couple good tracks."

We looked for movement, but saw none. Whoever it was headed toward the cabin.

"You ladies ride with Drury," I said. "I want to give Splinter a run."

Racing away out of sight, I stopped seeing the tracks stretch to the far hill. If I reached the pasture fast enough, I might catch a glimpse of the intruder. It didn't happen. At the cabin, I found no one. Doubling back, I waited for the others to emerge from the woods. Before they did, I saw another fresh track. Dismounting, studying it, recognizing an indentation on the left rear shoe, I determined it was Andrew Shelton. Rankled he'd seen Amy barebreasted—naked—I desired all the more to kill him. Deceit, I thought, he's a man of deceit—a man without honor.

Chapter 40

George Yardley

For a few days, we worked the farm. Friday afternoon, Nathaniel arrived on Winsome. One question penetrated his every word. "Figured out a way to buy thirty swords and twenty-four horses yet?"

"Horses, saddles and swords," I said. "Alexander."

"Interesting," Drury said. "Do you think that possible?"

"He placed stipulations on his financial commitment to the Confederacy. From what I understand, he considers Sumter an act of aggression perpetrated by the North. He's refused funds for anything except the forge and boot factory. If a Union army crosses the Potomac into Virginia, he will make his fortune available. He opposes the federal government coercing any state. His main concern is preparation. He will abide my request, sending the Guard to Virginia armed and mounted."

Nathaniel kicked the ground. "When will you ask?"

"Drury, Nathaniel, when the boys show up tonight, muster them for an early morning march into Cherokee. I'm off to obtain Alexander's consent."

"Right now?" Nathaniel said.

"Saddle Splinter—I'll explain to Amy and Stephanie."

ৰ৹৶৹৶৹ৰ

I found Alexander and Beatrice eating supper. Their shock at seeing me receded as I assured them all was well. For a half-hour over coffee and peach pie, I presented my proposal.

"How can I make this happen?" Alexander asked.

"We need twenty-four horses and saddles along with thirty swords." Beatrice excused herself, walking upstairs. "I'll buy horses in Milton County and saddles in Atlanta—don't know where to buy swords."

"Swords—do you need them?"

"Drury said, 'When horse soldiers charge into battle after expending their shot, war becomes a matter of swords.'"

"Thirty swords—have my work cut out for me."

"You do," I affirmed, "because I'm going home to your daughter."

"Tonight?"

"Tonight."

Alexander stood. "I'll check with Stephanie's father about horses in case you don't come up with enough."

Footsteps drew my attention to the staircase. "I would like you to have this," Beatrice said. I stood. She held a sheathed sword. "George, this belonged to my husband. I believe he would want you to have it. It is a weapon of honor."

Holding it in my hands, I spoke. "Wish I knew something appropriate to say. You honor me with this gift."

"Wear it with honor—use it with honor," she said, kissing me on the cheek.

"You still miss him, don't you?" I said.

Her head bowed. "You always miss your first love." She took Alexander's arm. "I pray neither you nor Amy ever experience that loss."

The sword dangled from the saddle-horn. Darkness, moonless darkness, surrounded me, but more so, silence—silence conflicted with each step Splinter made. Riding this familiar road in my homeland felt eerie enough compared to riding unfamiliar roads in the midst of war. What if I were on foot? Splinter's presence comforted me. How do soldiers identify their own men in darkness? How do you not shoot at anything you hear—anything that moves? How can I answer my men's questions when I can't answer mine?

Passing Howard's cabin, I began the descent to the Chattahoochee realizing I'd have to cross down river. With the river swelled, the current invaded the silence. "All right Splinter," I said, leaning forward, patting his neck, "we have to do this." I remembered the sword. Raising it from the saddle-horn, I belted it diagonally across my back; the grip extending above my right shoulder. *Huh, that feels better than having it around my waist.* Splinter stepped into the water, never hesitating, carrying me up onto the far bank. I wondered what he saw, what he felt, what made him proceed into the darkness—into the river. It seemed he knew I needed him to get me home—so he did what I needed him to do. I'd read about a horse and rider being one—but now I felt it.

At dawn, I rode into the camp the Guard had made on the cabin side of the road. One set of eyes after another noticed. Men straightened up, stood up, stared. Amy stood frozen on the porch as if aware this was no time for a wife—no place for a woman. I'm not certain how I came to this conclusion; but, in that moment—maybe it was my appearance—I knew the men looked to me as their leader, and I knew they were my responsibility.

"Where'd you get that sticker?" Nathaniel asked.

"Beatrice—belonged to her husband." Reaching back with my right hand, removing it from the sheath, I reinforced the moment. "Belonged to her husband—no telling how many Cheyenne Indians died by it." Silence—the silence of wonderment—of courage—of honor—showed itself as the sun rose. "When we leave for Virginia, each of you will own a horse, a saddle and a sword. Alexander will see to it." Expecting a cheer, silence confronted me. "Men of the Milton Guards—we go to fight and defend our homeland—the heritage of our forefathers. We shall do so with honor—the honor others knew who fought for freedom—for God and country."

"You got your wish," Drury said. "The Milton Guards in Virginia mounted with swords." I nodded.

Approaching, Nathaniel took Splinter's reins. "Be careful when you wish—wishing can master you. Wish too much—you'll reap the consequences."

Chapter 41

Amy Yardley

"Anyone seen Stephanie?" I asked.

Dismounted, George shrugged. "Lost your best friend?"

Drury looked to George, then to me. "I've not seen her since last night."

George pointed at me. "Amy, search the cabin—the loft. Nathaniel, look in the shed."

Returning, Nathaniel and I reported Stephanie's absence. "Give me your attention," George hollered. "Anyone seen Mrs Stith?"

"Last night," Kinchen said.

"Where and what time?"

"When she and Amy went inside."

"Amy?"

"I used the privy. Stephanie stepped out the back door as I returned. I went to bed." Staring into George's eyes, I knew. "Oh God, they have her. *The Association* has her."

Chapter 42

George Yardley

"You men muster," I said. "Be ready to march in fifteen minutes."

They scurried like I'd never seen. In two minutes, they stood in three rows of nine, muskets raised over their right shoulders, heads up, eyes narrowed, and determined. "Lieutenant Yardley," Sergeant Hanlin said, "the Milton Guard is ready for battle."

Battle, I thought. Battle—what did these men—these boys—understand? An enemy of neighbors waited. An enemy who spied on us and, kidnapped a woman, the wife of an officer—an enemy prepared for our approach—an enemy preparing an ambush between here and the Cherokee cabin.

Remounting Splinter, I rode to where the Guard stood in formation. "Kinchen, stay here with Amy. I need you to do that."

"Yes, sir, Lieutenant Yardley."

I expected a protest. Kinchen's unconditional obedience gave me pause. He marched toward the porch, taking a position beside Amy.

"Guardsmen, we move toward an enemy certain of our approach. We face an ambush. Keep your eyes open, your ears perked. Don't wait for a command. If you see or hear anything, shoot. Do you understand?"

"Yes, sir," they replied.

"Sergeant Hanlin, give the order to march."

Granting Amy one last look, I kicked Splinter, riding to the head of three columns. Drury followed.

"Worried?" I asked.

"Angered. What breed of men would abduct a woman? After the threats Amy has received, I can't help but think about what they've done to Stephanie."

"We'll know soon enough. I tend to believe they've not harmed her."

"Riding here in front, one might take the first ball."

"We're called to lead, Captain. Doesn't make sense to bring up the rear like cowards."

He nodded. Hanlin ran up beside me. "Lieutenant, the men request permission to run a hundred paces—then march a hundred. Time is of the essence."

"Permission granted."

I dismounted. As the men approached, I dropped Splinter's reins and ran with them. Splinter followed. Drury continued riding. We counted steps out loud until I realized our voices could warn the enemy. From that time and for the rest of the war, we counted in silence.

Nearing the fork in the road, realizing the triangulation provided a perfect place from which our enemy could attack, I ordered the Guard to halt. This, also, was something I would remember: if the enemy took a position under cover in the trees on the right side of the road before the fork, once we passed we would provide clear aim at our backs. And, if another contingent flanked from either side of the road past the fork, we'd stand caught in a cross fire. And, I thought, what if the enemy took positions on both sides of the road past the fork? If so, the Milton Guards would never see Virginia.

"Sergeant Hanlin, take the left column into the woods. Fan out, leaving about ten yards between each man. Head at an angle toward the left side of the road beyond the fork. If you encounter enemy, fire. Nathaniel, do the same with the right column on that side of the road. Once you make it beyond the fork, cross the road, enter the woods, and make certain we are not flanked."

Under each man's command, the left and right columns proceeded. I watched as they spread out. "Tim Eagan, take four men, and proceed on the right side of the road. The rest follow me on the left. If shooting starts, find cover."

In awe at how each man did as ordered without question, I questioned myself. Did they trust me? Or, did they know not what else to do except what I said? Noises penetrated the air—footsteps crunching grit on the dirt road and breaking twigs in the woods. We might as well have beaten drums and sounded bugles. It felt as if anyone within miles could hear us.

My column made its way around the bend to the left. In a moment, Nathaniel's emerged onto the road from the right. Drury rode up. "Where's Hanlin?"

"Don't know—doubtful ten men got lost in that short distance."

Stepping through scrub pines, I entered the woods, seeing no one. My first instincts told me to holler Hanlin's name. My second instincts urged silence. My eyes searched for movement, but found none. How could the entire column disappear? One answer surfaced: they walked into a trap. Crouching, I stepped from the woods onto the road.

"What's wrong?" Drury asked, still mounted.

Motioning my militia down on one knee, I pointed across the road at Nathaniel surrounded by his men. Bending over, he made his way to me. "What?"

"Hanlin's nowhere to be seen."

He cowered down and crept into the woods. Minutes passed.

"Where is he?" Drury asked. Though I understood his apprehension over Stephanie, it was a question I didn't want to answer. "What if they captured your cousin?" More time passed.

"It's me—don't shoot," Nathaniel said. He had nothing to worry about. Looking around, I saw no one—including me—had the hammer on his rifle cocked. Unprepared, I thought. A small contingent of armed men could massacre us in a surprise attack. It made me think about what I needed to do if on the other side of such a skirmish—if we stood ready to ambush an enemy. First thing, I'd determine how prepared the enemy stood. My cousin stepped into the open, followed by Stephanie.

Thoughts swirled like a swarm of hornets. "Where the others?"

"Don't know—looks like someone marched them off toward the cabin."

"Where'd you find her?"

"Tied and hanging upside down from a tree limb with this note pinned to her dress."

Nathaniel approached handing me the paper. I read. *Yardley, hope you find her dead like I found my brother you killed.*

Something—I know not what—drew my attention toward Drury. Stephanie made her way to him. He acted as if he wanted nothing to do with her. A shot rang out from the trees at the fork in the road. Drury groaned. The entire column Nathaniel had led into the woods—still standing beyond the for—fired their weapons. Four or five reports sounded from the trees. Drury collapsed falling upon Stephanie, forcing her to the ground. Blood spurted from his neck splattering Stephanie's dress and face. Nathaniel dashed into the woods. I ordered my men to follow him. They disappeared through the pines.

Stephanie sat up cradling Drury's head in her arms. I knelt beside them. "Did they do anything to you?" I asked. Shaking her head, she squeezed him against her breast. The blood stopped spurting as did his gasping.

"Drury, Drury, don't leave me—please don't leave me."

In what manner she could, still holding her husband, Stephanie rocked back and forth, sobs convulsing her chest. Placing my arm around her back, I tried to support her, comfort her.

"Why didn't he get off his horse?" I asked. Strange as it sounds, that too, became a lesson. With all the emphasis I'd placed on being well mounted in war, I concluded it best to march beside our horses when in the vicinity of the enemy.

"He's dead, isn't he?" she asked. I nodded. "I won't bury him here." Sliding out from under him, she stood, fists clenched, beside herself with anger. "Drury, why didn't you get off your horse? You've left me a widow."

God, I thought, how many women will feel that pain in the coming months?

Chapter 43

George Yardley

At a loss, I struggled to lift Drury's body, placing him face down over the saddle on his horse, covering his body with a blanket. Stephanie stood helpless as if in a trance.

The crackle of multiple rifle shots echoed. Grabbing Splinter's reins and saddle-horn, I remounted.

"George, George," Stephanie screamed. "What are you doing?"

"Going to help." More shots resounded.

"Get down off that horse. Do you want to get killed like Drury?"

Unsheathing my rifle, I did as she ordered. How could I forget? Caught in the emotion of the moment, I lost my senses and would have ridden straight into whatever fight—ambush—awaited me. Worse, a woman warned me of my folly.

The gunshots grew intermittent but persisted. "Stephanie, go. Walk Drury's body to my cabin." As I embraced her, she backed away.

"No—I won't. I won't return to Amy without you. I won't worry her that you lay dead like my husband. I'll be here when you or whoever returns."

Taking a look at Drury's covered body, at his horse, at Splinter, I turned to Stephanie. "If I don't survive—return in a couple hours, ride Splinter, and take Drury with you." She nodded, but I knew it the nod of a lie. She wouldn't leave. She wouldn't face the reality of grief and death with Amy. I decided to ask. "Did they rape you?"

She nodded again. "What do you think men like that want from a woman? Yes, they raped me—four of them—all night long."

"I'm sorry."

"Don't be sorry—be smart. Don't get killed."

∽≈≈≈≈∾

Running through the woods—not on the road—toward the powder bursts, my eyes searched for movement. As the shots grew louder, they grew more frequent. About fifty yards ahead, a volley rang out. Then, silence—until I heard Nathaniel's voice. Other voices joined together in reporting their well-being, though not everyone proved well.

Nathaniel saw me first, raising his rifle. "Little late to the party, aren't you?"

"Drury's dead. How goes it?"

"Court Stonebridge is dead. Hanlin is badly wounded."

Tim Egan ran at us. "They killed Sergeant Hanlin."

"What happened?"

Nathaniel pointed toward the cabin. "They took refuge there. One by one, we picked them off."

"How many?"

Tim stared at Nathaniel. "He got them all. Told us to stay out here and shoot anything that moved. We did. He circled around and stood at the cabin's west corner on the porch. One by one they showed themselves—shooting at us through that window— Nathaniel let them have it."

"That so?"

"Think the boys got a few of them," Nathaniel said, scuffing the ground with his boot. "Tim, I saw horses in the woods behind the cabin. Get them—we'll tie Hanlin's and Stonebridge's bodies on them and head home."

"Yes, sir," he said and ran off.

Most of the Guard had gathered round Nathaniel and me. "You men help Tim," I said, turning to Nathaniel. "Stephanie's waiting. I'll see her to the cabin. Get there quick as you can."

"What should I do with the bodies in the cabin?"

"Nothing—on second thought burn it down. The remains can stand as a monument to what happens when you fight Nathaniel Thomas."

Chapter 44

Amy Yardley

Kinchen and I waited all day into the darkness of night. Unable to sleep, I joined him on the porch. Sitting in silence, we stared east toward Cherokee. A half-moon provided light. Crickets chirped, annoying our solitude.

Pondering death, widowhood, aloneness, I feared living my life as Sarah lived and as Beatrice had until Father and she met. I wondered how the torments swirling in my mind created heaviness in my heart—heaviness that squeezed and pushed downward—that made me want to cry tears that refused to well.

"He's not dead," Kinchen said.

How I wanted to believe him, wanted to embrace his thought, his kindness, his understanding of what I felt. "Thank you," I said.

He stood. "Here they come."

Examining the moment, the line of men as each appeared, I wished and prayed. Nathaniel led two riderless horses, neither of which was Splinter. Then, I saw neither horse was riderless. Both carried bodies. Feeling my knees buckle, grabbing the porch post, my fingernails dug into the pine as if scratching like a cat sharpening her claws.

Unable to speak, Kinchen spoke for me. "Who's dead?"

Nathaniel cleared his throat. "Sergeant Hanlin and Court."

The Guard surrounded the porch. I thanked God I had not heard Nathaniel say George's name, but neither did I see my husband.

"Where's George?" Kinchen asked.

"A ways back—he's bringing Stephanie and Drury. Drury's dead, too."

My grasp of the post intensified, certain if I let go, I'd collapse. It happened to my friend, I thought. She's the widow—not me—at least not me for the time being.

"Amy," a voice said. It was George. He stood before me cradling Stephanie in his arms. "You need to gather yourself—gather your strength—take care of Stephanie. Follow me."

Nathaniel unlatched the cabin door allowing George to enter. I followed him into our bedroom, where he laid her on our bed. Standing at the foot, I stared, wondering why he wouldn't hug me, wondering how distant he seemed.

"George..."

"Amy, tend to Stephanie while I tend to matters outside."

She lay there asleep, unconscious, covered in blood—blood I assumed that bled her husband to death. Walking around, I sat on the edge of the bed, reaching, touching her shoulder, shaking her shoulder, calling her name, receiving no response. Leaning over, I kissed her cheek.

Whatever came over me came gently and lovingly. One by one, I undid each button on the front of her dress. The smell of sweat and dried blood and dirt filled the room. Standing, I went to the fireplace, fetching a basin of warm water, returning with towels and soap and scissors. I also returned with a thought I determined never to raise unless Stephanie raised it: had she been raped?

Cutting the sleeves and then the waist, I removed that portion of the dress, baring her chest. Likewise, I did the same with the skirt. For the moment, I covered her with a quilt, returning to the fireplace, burning the garment.

In the bedroom, I dampened a cloth and washed her—washed every part of her starting with her face. It was something I never fathomed until that second—what it meant to care for someone's personal needs, much less the needs of one who was helpless. Father had shared an account of a Florence Nightingale, an English woman, who had nursed soldiers during a recent war. Though what I did for Stephanie seemed loving, the thought of performing such an act for a man, especially a wounded or unconscious man, seemed repulsive, crude, or immoral.

When I completed the task, she lay naked, her beautiful face surrounded by tangled hair. I wanted to brush it, but didn't. Covering her, I extinguished the candles, removed the basin and towels, and went to sit by the fire. Something told me not to interfere with the task George performed outside.

Chapter 45

George Yardley

"Stephanie told me she wanted Drury buried here on my farm," I said to the Guard. "We'll do that in the morning."

Twenty-eight militia had survived their first battle. Standing around me in the middle of the night, they appeared aimless. "Tim Egan, Court's parents live on the way to your place. I want a few men to go with Tim and the others with Kinchen to take Sergeant Hanlin's body to his wife. Stand by their families and help with the burials. Pray we never have to bury any of you."

Nathaniel stepped forward. "What do you want me to do?"

"Stay here—help me with Drury's burial."

My cousin turned, addressing the Guard. "You men fought well today. That last volley saved my life. I didn't see those last three coming at me. Thank you, and my mother thanks you. We leave for Virginia in a couple weeks. After doing your duty in the morning, go home; spend time with your families, and make certain they know you love them. George and I will get word to you about our departure."

"Nathaniel," a voice said, "we fought well today because you showed us courage. It was an honor to fight with you."

Tim took the reins of the horse carrying Court. Kinchen did the same for Sergeant Hanlin. Men said their good-byes, patted each other on the back, and divided into two groups. Nathaniel and I stood on the porch watching them disappear into the night.

"Been a long day and a longer night," he said.

I peered inside seeing Amy in the rocker asleep. "Sit for a minute." He took a seat on the porch step. I sat on the bench. "What did you learn today?"

"Not much—except—don't let men shooting at you know your whereabouts."

"Why would they shoot if they don't see you?"

"Strange as it seems—those *Association* fellows kept shooting out the window—and had no idea I was five feet away."

"That is strange."

"The lesson is—don't shoot unless you see your target."

"You sound like Father."

"That was the highest compliment you could pay me. What did you learn?"

"To get off my horse when the shooting starts."

Chapter 46

Amy Yardley

Deciding to sleep outside, Nathaniel pitched a lean-to. Drury's covered body lay a few feet from where Nathaniel sat beside a fire. The last I saw him before retiring, he held a metal cup in his hand staring into the flames. George and I slept in the loft.

At dawn, I crept down the ladder leaving my husband asleep. From the cook stove, I saw the quilt with which I covered Stephanie thrown aside and our bed empty. Hearing a board creek on the front porch, I stepped outside to find my friend peering westward, though she peered not at the Smokies but at Nathaniel waist deep digging a grave next to George's parents.

"He saved my life," she said. "Now, he buries my husband." Taking a seat next to her on the bench, I tried to hold her hand. She resisted, continuing to stare. "It was as if he swooped in like an eagle, grabbed me, and carried me off before my captors knew it."

"He carried you?"

"Like a sack of cornmeal."

"Sounds like he pretty much shot and killed the entire *Association* at the cabin."

"So, he was the big, brave hero."

I gave Stephanie a sideways glance wondering what thoughts swirled, hoping she'd refrain from involving herself with Nathaniel. "Your husband..."

"Don't worry," she said, "just wondering what makes certain men act in certain ways. What makes some men—men of honor and courage and others dishonorable and indecent? No man will want me after what they did to me yesterday."

I couldn't speak, couldn't ask, and couldn't cry. We watched Nathaniel lift Drury's body, placing it in the grave. We watched and heard each shovel of dirt thump against the blanket covering the corpse. When finished, he stomped on the loose soil compacting it. Then he waved, beckoning us to join him.

Walking, Stephanie took my hand until we stood by Nathaniel. He reached down, picked up a cross and hammered it into the head of the grave. "I'm sorry for your loss," he said. "Would you like to say anything?"

She stared downward. "Thank you for doing this. Thank you for saving my life. Drury loved this place. He said last week he wished it were his home. Now it is—forever."

Holding the shovel in his right hand, his right foot resting on the blade, Nathaniel appeared to struggle. "Not that I know much scripture; but I'd like to try. I lift up my eyes to the hills from whence cometh my strength. My help is in the name of the Lord, who made heaven and earth. Thanks be to God who gives us the victory over death in Jesus. Amen."

"Amen," George said from behind us.

Nathaniel shook his head. "Woke up, did you?"

"Sorry."

"Never thought of you as lazy—but you showed up late after I did all the work the past two days."

"Sorry," he said, turning to me. "Wish you had awakened me."

Stephanie paid George and Nathaniel no mind but instead put her arm around me.

"Before we leave these graves, I'd like Amy to pray."

Taken aback, I collected my thoughts. The men removed their hats. "Father, as Jesus said upon the cross, 'Into Thy hands I commend my spirit,' so we commend the spirit of our brother and husband into your hands. Receive Drury as we give him up to you. Amen."

Chapter 47

George Yardley

While Amy and Stephanie tidied the cabin, I went to the shed. Standing at the workbench, leaning against it, with head bowed, I questioned my abilities. Three men died in what I considered a skirmish. At that rate, a major battle would take the entire Guard. Death, my death, Nathaniel's death, felt near. How to stay alive—to lead my men without folly—to prepare them against the emotional foolishness of battle—to live with myself if I survived—to know I'd done my best—those thoughts tore through me. The door opened.

"Anguishing yourself won't help," Amy said. She stepped inside. "Stephanie told me Nathaniel proved a hero yesterday; but those men fought for you."

Refusing to look at her, I wished to talk about anything else. "Why did you come out here?"

"Because, George Yardley, I know you. I know the man I love, and I know the man I love could not endure the losses of yesterday without anguish. Hold your head up."

"Yesterday, Stephanie had the good sense to tell me to get down off Splinter. Today, you tell me to hold my head up. How will I survive this war without you two telling me what to do?"

"Stephanie and I have decided to go to Atlanta. She needs to tell her parents about Drury; but then, she and I will move in with Sarah. Accompany us—then return here—get the Guard ready for Virginia. We leave in the morning."

"I hate to leave this place, and I hate to leave you."

"It's all right to cry."

"Have no problem with that."

She approached, refusing my embrace, taking my hands, looking into my eyes. "This place smells wonderful. The leather and the tobacco smoke, it reminds me of you. While you're gone, we'll ride here from time to time so I can breathe in these aromas."

"Who will accompany you?"

"Father, Sarah, Beatrice, and Stephanie."

"I would like that. The thought of you looking over things, even for a day, comforts me."

She released my hands. Busying herself, she layered four tanned hides on the floor, rolling one into the form of a pillow.

"What are you doing?"

"We're spending our last night here." Turning, she unbuttoned her dress allowing it to fall to the floor.

Chapter 48

Amy Yardley

We awoke wrapped in hides and stiff from the floor's hardness. Upon dressing, I made my way to the outhouse and then the cabin. George met me inside. Though certain the armory would supply ammunition, he gathered his powder and balls. His currency, still that of the Union, consisted of eight hundred dollars. He tucked it into the inside pocket of his jacket.

Fixing breakfast, I called for Stephanie, who emerged from the bedroom dressed in one of my riding outfits: brown pants and a light tan shirt. "Did you plan to wear this?"

"Yes."

"Too bad—couldn't find any other clean clothes that fit."

George smiled. "Best be careful. Dressed like that I could mistake you for Amy and..."

I slammed the egg turner into the frying pan. "And what?"

Seeing my jealousy, Stephanie approached George. "You can mistake me for Amy anytime you like."

"I'll mistake the two of you. I'll mistake you for a lard jar and pour this hot grease over you."

"George, she ruins our fun."

He groaned. "It would ruin me if I betrayed her. I'd have nothing to live for." Staring at Stephanie, he nodded. "It's good to see you tease and smile."

∾❧❦❧∾

"Ready?" I said, mounting Pearl. "Let's go. We have a long day ahead. I can't leave without seeing Lillian and the girls."

Stephanie rode Drury's horse. George walked the remaining four horses to the road. Dropping the reins, he walked to his parents' graves, kneeling before the crosses. I guided Pearl to within earshot.

"Don't feel much like a soldier," he said. "I feel like a little boy who wants his mother to hold him." He took out a kerchief, wiping his eyes. "Thank you for being my mother and father—thank you for teaching me." Looking up as if to God, he added, "And, thank you for giving me Amy. Keep her safe."

Unable to control myself, I dismounted, knelt beside him, and held him, placing my head on his shoulder. "God," I cried, "why is this happening?"

He slipped his arm around me. After crying it out, regaining our composure, we remounted. Stephanie joined us.

"Hope we don't go through this with Lillian," George said. "Nathaniel is off to war—every mother's nightmare."

"I can't take it again," he said.

"You'll have to, because it's coming."

We rode off with George holding the reins of the team horses while I held the reins of the remaining horse from the slave hunters.

"We're a mile away. I smell Lillian's bacon cooking," George said.

"It smells good in the morning air," Stephanie said.

As we road to the cabin, Lillian saw us first, greeting us on the porch.

George hugged her. "You must have cooked a whole side of bacon."

She smiled, releasing the embrace. "No, but if I knew you were coming, I'd have cooked enough to keep you here through the entire war." Stephanie and I walked up the steps. Lillian hugged her, whispering in her ear. "I'm sorry for your loss."

"Thank you," Stephanie said.

Robert emerged from the cabin. "Mrs. Stith, Nathaniel told us about your husband. Please accept my condolences." She nodded.

"George, we heard you single-handedly fought and killed the entire *Association*."

"Who said?

"Nathaniel."

"Nathaniel's a liar."

"George," Aunt Lillian said, "you shouldn't speak that way."

"Shouldn't speak that way unless it's the truth. Your son single-handedly did in *The Association*."

"Nathaniel," Lillian hollered toward the barn. Stephanie and Leslie appeared at the horse pen. "Where's your brother?"

Leslie cupped her hands to her mouth. "Not here."

"Where is he?"

"Gone to Atlanta," Samantha said.

Lillian's hands clenched at her side. "Robert, this war turned your children into liars, and the shooting hasn't started." She turned to Stephanie. "I'm sorry. Please forgive me."

Stephanie nodded. "Your son saved my life. I wouldn't be here if he hadn't."

Out of the corner of my eye, I saw Nathaniel and the girls approaching. Lillian saw them, too. "Returned from Atlanta so soon?"

Nathaniel stood at the bottom of the steps as if the distance might protect him from Lillian's wrath. "Don't know what got into my sisters that they'd fib like that. You girls ought to be ashamed."

Samantha's mouth dropped open. Leslie's hands found her hips. Lillian would have none of it. "Nathaniel Thomas, get up these steps."

"Stop!" Tears welled in Stephanie's eyes. "Please stop. They abducted me and raped me all night long." She sobbed; her shoulders heaved. "Until Nathaniel rescued me, I thought..." Her knees buckled. George caught her as she collapsed.

I'm not certain what happened next. My attention turned to the girls. They stood at the foot of the steps holding hands, crying, tears running down their cheeks, unable to speak. A vision flashed. I saw that man holding me to the floor in my parlor threatening my life. On that day, I lost my innocence— not my virginity—but my innocence. Somehow, it seemed in that moment—hearing what Stephanie said and—seeing George cradle her—Samantha and Leslie lost theirs—lost any sense of life's purity that a child harbors in her heart. Going to them, holding their hands, I walked them to the barn.

Chapter 49

George Yardley

"Time to eat," Robert said, his hands dripping from washing. Grabbing a towel, he dried them and sat down at his place. "I've waited all morning for this breakfast." We attempted laughter, except Lillian, who had grown melancholy.

Samantha and Leslie placed food on the table one bowl at a time until they ran out of space. "At this rate," I said, "Nathaniel and I won't have to eat until we return from Virginia."

"That's if you return," Lillian said.

"I'll ask the blessing," Robert said, stretching out his arms. We held hands. "Dear God, please be with us now as we partake of this meal. Please be with these young men as they go off to fulfill their duty to their country. For those who remain behind, may you comfort our fears. Grant unto each the courage we need for this day. In Christ we ask these things. Amen."

✐ ✐ ✐ ✐

"Lillian, I'll visit the farm from time to time with Father," Amy said. "I'll stop to see you."

Reaching into my coat pocket, I pulled out the wad of cash. "I won't need this. Robert, it may come in handy. Take it." He did without protest.

We rode through Alpharetta where we heard Mr. Yancey shout my name. "There's a letter addressed for you two."

Handing it to Amy, she opened it. "Oh, it is from my father. He has the horses bought and paid for at the livery. The swords should arrive today."

"Stephanie," I said. "I hoped Drury and I would string the horses and bring them back so the Guard could ride to Atlanta. If you want, you can take your husband's place."

She looked at Amy. "Do you trust us?"

For a moment, I thought Amy would respond in the negative. She smiled. "I trust George; but for as long as I live, I'll never trust you. Do it. You handle horses better than anyone else in Georgia."

Chapter 50

Amy Yardley

Sarah sat on the porch. In the late afternoon shadows, dismounting, starting up the steps, I saw her stare at Stephanie. "Where's Drury?" No more than a second passed. "You don't have to say. I know that look. He's dead, isn't he?" Without acknowledging me, Sarah passed, making her way to Stephanie, indulging her in an embrace I wished to never feel.

A carriage stopped. The driver assisted Beatrice and Father as they stepped out. Beatrice noticed first. She stared at the embrace and then glanced at me. Handing her purse and parasol to Father, she took three strides wrapping the two women in her arms. There they stood—three war widows. How many? I asked myself. How many women in the eighty or so years this nation had existed experienced that embrace—the embrace of widowhood derived from war? Now, I stared at George and he at me. We need not speak. I knew my husband. We both contemplated the same question. Would I be number four?

Emerging from the chaos of my thoughts, I found myself standing with Father and George. The others had made their way to the porch and then into the house.

"Drury's dead?" Father asked.

George pushed his coat-sides back allowing his hands to find his hips. The action revealed his holster. "Yes sir—died at the cabin in Cherokee."

"Anyone else?"

"Two—Tom and Court."

He shook his head, motioning for George to join him at the carriage. From my vantage point, I saw gleaming silver swords on the floor.

"They just arrived," Father said. "Horatio and I picked them up at the armory." George expressed his gratitude. "Thirty horses along with thirty saddles await you at the livery."

"We don't need that many," George said.

"When it comes to war, you never have too many horses."

"Stephanie and I, with Amy's permission will take the horses to Alpharetta. The Guard will ride into Atlanta horse soldiers."

"Did I hear my name?" Stephanie asked from the porch. She walked down the steps, eyeing the swords on the carriage floor. "George, Amy, may we ride to tell Mother and Father of Drury's demise?"

"Yes," George said. "On the way, I need to inform the stationmaster that we'll need livestock cars for the horses."

"Let's go," she said. "At this hour, we'll spend the night with my parents and return in the morning. Besides, I'd hate to think cattle cars more important than my husband's death."

Chapter 51

George Yardley

Alpharetta
May 25, 1861

"We leave today less three fallen comrades," I spoke in the town square. Before me, twenty-eight Milton Guards stood next to their saddled horses wearing their leather coats. Each saddle-horn held a sword strapped over it. Folk from the county surrounded us, including Robert, Lillian, and the girls. "We go to Virginia. We hope and pray all twenty-eight return; but if not, may God's eternal blessing and peace be upon us. We take with us three riderless horses to honor Tom, Court, and Drury. We honor their service to God and country. Reverend Woolridge, will you please send us off with prayer?"

Men, soldier and civilian alike, removed their hats. Heads bowed. Until our pastor said "Amen," I heard not a word. When I looked up, Mr. Yancey approached, carrying three poled banners: a Confederate flag, a Georgia state flag, and a triangle gray flag with an insignia of a striking copperhead snake. He handed the Confederate flag and the Georgia flag to Tim Egan and Bobby Paul Green. The other, he handed to me.

A brief stirring resulted. Holding the banner high, I gave the order, "Men of the Milton Guards, mount." Stephanie rode to the front guiding Drury's horse. Nathaniel did the same with the two riderless horses. I handed the banner to Kinchen.

We rode away to words of encouragement, but mostly words of God's blessings and protection. Lillian stood next to Robert, arms at her sides, chin up, tears rolling down her cheeks.

At the Chattahoochee, I declined the ferry. Guiding them down river, I opted for our first river crossing as horse soldiers.

Nearing the city, I turned, riding past each man. "Sit tall in your saddles as we enter Atlanta," I repeated. Each stretched. They looked like cavalry, dressed in their jackets, their swords clanking at their sides, rifles sheathed across their saddles. What is the line between courage and appearance? Certain we would find out before the end of summer, I studied every passerby wishing I knew his or her thoughts.

Approaching the armory, a commotion erupted from those who saw us. Atlanta Grays ran in every direction pointing others toward the horse soldiers.

"You are late," Colonel Bingham shouted. "Lieutenant Yardley, what is the meaning of your tardiness?"

Looking around, I saw soldiers by the hundreds waiting my explanation. "May I request, Colonel, we meet in your office?" He granted the audience. Before dismounting, I signaled Nathaniel to join me. For fifteen minutes, I expounded upon the events in Cherokee and the demise of Captain Stith. With each passing minute, Bingham grew more anxious.

"Do you mean to tell me," he said, "that you engaged in battle, and men died?"

"Yes, sir. Some died—some wounded on both sides."

The colonel cowered, taking a seat at his desk. "What was it like? I've never faced gunfire."

"To tell the truth," Nathaniel said, "we pissed ourselves, and some threw up at the sight of death. Fear eradicates bodily control. Now, Colonel, twenty-eight soldiers—horse soldiers await our destiny in Virginia."

Bingham squirmed, fiddling with a quill. "Who addresses me in this manner?"

"My cousin, Nathaniel Thomas."

"He has a quick tongue. How is he as a soldier?"

"Better than anyone you've seen fight—a lot better than me."

Bingham stood. "That being the case, Lieutenant Yardley, I commission you a captain in the Confederate Army. Private Thomas, I bestow upon you your sergeant stripes."

Chapter 52

Amy Yardley

Father and I went to the armory and watched George lead the Guard to the train station. I dared not interfere, knowing a woman had no place in such doings. Stephanie rode at the rear of the column mounted on Drury's horse.

"She gets to see my husband off, and I don't?"

Father placed his arm around my shoulders. "Calm yourself. Stephanie has seen her husband off in a manner I hope you never experience."

The comment froze me. How could I begrudge her? What if George had taken the bullet that killed Drury?

At the station, we stood at a distance observing soldiers load cannons, cannonballs, and boxes of gunpowder. Four Guardsmen, supervised by Nathaniel, boarded the horses in the livestock cars. Stephanie tied Drury's horse to a post and approached us.

"Your husband's efficiency stands second to his appearance."

I wanted to make a snide, jealous comment about trust; but, I held my tongue, opting for a compliment. "The Milton Guards would be well served to have you accompany them. You could teach them horsemanship."

Hugging me, she stepped back. "Your husband's sense of honor exceeds all that is humanly possible. He loves you." She turned to Father. "Good afternoon, Mr. Frey."

He tipped his hat. "I hope it is. I hope that which we stand before and observe is rooted in an honorable cause." He stared at the activity near the train.

Stephanie stood beside him. "Do you question the Confederacy's motives?"

"In my waking hours and in my sleep."

After the Guard entered their car, George said something to Nathaniel, then turned and walked in our direction. I moved toward him, separating myself from Father and Stephanie. We embraced, but not the loving, romantic embrace I'd felt for more than a year. Rather, the embrace filled me with desperation.

"I will write you on the train and upon our arrival in Richmond. There they will assign me a military postal code. When you receive it, write everyday—write every night. Until then, we share the moon and sun."

He kissed me, taking my hand, walking me to Father. Beatrice and Sarah had arrived. As we concluded good-byes, the far end of the station drew our attention. Stephanie rode Drury's horse to the car holding the Guard. She sat tall, erect, determined. George kissed me once more, making his way to the platform. Stephanie slowed to a stop.

"Would you do me the honor," she asked, "of taking my husband's horse with you? Let him serve to remind you of the honor of war. It is better to fight and die for honor than live in bondage to a government that refuses liberty. May Dixie's heritage live through the sacrifices you make." She dismounted to cheers from inside the car, allowing George to take the reins. Nathaniel loaded the horse. On this day, the platform stood empty—no dignitaries, no prayers, and no send off. Twenty-eight men departed to do their duty.

Chapter 53

George Yardley

The accommodations on the train proved different from what I experienced on the trip to Savannah. Hard wooden benches with harder wooden backs made it impossible to rest. According to the conductor, we would travel across Georgia, then northeast through South Carolina and North Carolina until we reached Richmond. If all went well, with the stops we had to make for other militia, we would arrive in three days.

At every station, we got off the train to stretch and relieve ourselves. Even in the middle of the night, we fumbled around in the dark in strange villages and hamlets. Some stations provided outhouses; but, most provided large latrines. If a creek or river presented itself, we washed. After the second day, I decided our car smelled worse than the horse car. Twice a day, we exercised the horses.

"We'll cross the Appomattox River within the hour," the conductor announced. My watch showed four o'clock in the afternoon. Richmond stood less than two hours away.

We pulled into the Richmond Depot before six. Once we unloaded the horses and equipment, Major Ely Remington, who appeared taken aback by the horses, greeted us. "We expected foot soldiers, not cavalry."

"Plans changed," Nathaniel said. "If you want foot soldiers, we'll return to Georgia."

With my right hand, I nudged Nathaniel behind me. "What Sergeant Thomas means is we made arrangements to bring the horses. We've had a tough go of it. Three of our men were killed in a skirmish. We're in no mood to hear about what you expected. Do you want us to stay or return to Georgia?"

"Stay," a voice said from behind us. Colonel Joshua England smiled. "Major Remington, you are in the company of one of the finest soldiers in the entire South. Captain Yardley already proved himself in battle, as have his men. We can't afford to run them off."

"Yes sir," the major said, while I wondered how Colonel England knew about us.

"There's an encampment by the James River. Bivouac there until those assigned to your company arrive. Major Remington will see to your needs. Until then, Captain Yardley, I request the honor of your presence at dinner tomorrow night for the officers of the Army of Northern Virginia. General Lee desires to meet you."

"Colonel England," I said pausing to assure I had his attention. "When will we receive our postal codes?"

"In the morning."

Militia from every southern state filled the encampment, with a significant number from Virginia. As far as Nathaniel and I could tell, we were the only troops present with horses and, for certain, the only ones with uniforms. Major Remington assigned us two tents that slept twelve. Two rows of six cots lined each wall. When Nathaniel pointed out we needed four more cots, Remington scoffed. "We'll see to it in the morning."

"We'll see to it tonight," Nathaniel said. The major glared.

"Major," I said, "which side are you on?"

Remington continued to stare. "This is neither a hotel nor a dock in Savannah."

Nathaniel glared back. "Major, I'm sorry you feel that way—because by the time my cousin gets done with you—you'll think you're in Savannah." In two hours, Nathaniel had mouthed off to an officer and picked a fight.

"Is that right, Captain?" The major asked. "Can you make me wish I was in Savannah?"

"Not tonight—but if those cots aren't here tomorrow, I will apprise Colonel England of your behavior."

"Slaves will deliver the cots tomorrow," Remington said. "Maybe, Captain Yardley, you can wash their feet while they're here." He turned to walk away.

"Major," I said, "we have a problem that needs resolution."

"I don't have a problem—you do."

The Guard gathered round joined by other soldiers who listened to the disagreement. "Throw the first punch," I said, offering my jaw. "After we fight, I'll need verification from witnesses as to who started this."

With fists clenched, Remington stepped toward me. He swung his right arm; his fist glanced my jaw. Soldiers wagered the outcome as I circled my adversary. Others shouted jeers and taunts. I stopped. "You men have your bets placed?"

"Major," a voice said, "he'll wear you out while he circles, and if that fails, he'll talk you to death."

"He's afraid of you," another said.

To achieve credibility and respect, I had to fight fair. It ended with three punches: two jabs to his mouth and a right hook to his left eye. He fell backwards and lay motionless. The winners collected their bets while I ordered four soldiers to take the major to his tent. Each grabbed either a leg or an arm and carried him away.

"Where can we get cots and tents?" I asked.

"The quartermaster's tent yonder," one said, pointing away from the river. "They have what you need."

"Nathaniel, take five men."

They returned with four cots and two two-man tents. I claimed one tent for Nathaniel and me. The rest divided up as they desired.

"How much trouble are we in?" Nathaniel asked as we bedded down.

"What do you mean?"

"If others know about you here the way that Major knows you, you'll have to fight every night. Soldiers who advocate slavery will get you."

"We'll talk in the morning," I said, blowing out the candle on a box between our cots.

Chapter 54

George Yardley

Dawn brought a chill and dense fog. Eerie, faceless shadows meandered through camp sometimes bumping into each other as they did their business.

"Geez," Nathaniel said returning to the tent. "Hope we don't have to fight in this stuff. To be safe, you'd have to shoot everything that moved, friend or foe." He laid down on his cot.

"You think my reputation preceded me, and I'm in for a fight every night?"

"Could be."

"Don't egg it on."

"I'll do a better in the future."

"Did good last night. Don't entice others to fight me."

Silenced, we laid there, falling back to sleep. When we awoke, the fog had lifted granting a hot, humid day.

"Don't move," Jimmy Smith said as I emerged from my tent. "If you take a step, you'll sweat worse than a pig." Jimmy and others sat around shirtless on rocks and wooden benches.

"Did you all forget to dress?" Nathaniel asked as he came out of the tent.

"No," Randolph Loy replied. "We've sweated in every shirt we brought. We're drying them out."

"Wait until your clothes stick to you," Wesley Butler said. "It'll take two of us to unglue them and pull them off you."

"That river looks inviting," I said. "Why aren't you cooling off?"

"Don't have the will to walk that far," Tip Liller said. "Thought about it; but then, thought against it."

Wearing pants, socks, and a long sleeve under shirt, I pulled the shirt over my head, starting for the water. At the river, other men rinsed off and cooled down. Seating myself on a rock, I undressed.

"Give it up," a man in the water said. "By the time you put your clothes back on, you'll be soaked with perspiration."

Noticing others wore their pants, I waded into the water. Memories of Amy and me at the falls with Drury and Stephanie surfaced. Sadness to the point of tears overcame me. I plunged under to hide my emotions. Seeing me swim enticed the others into the water.

"Maybe someone will serve us breakfast here," Randolph Loy said.

"Hey, you men," a voice shouted from the riverbank, "don't go in too far. Currents out there run deep—they'll sweep you away—drown you in a heartbeat." It was Colonel England. We moved closer to the bank.

"Good morning, Colonel," I said reaching shore.

"Morning, Captain Yardley."

Hearing my last name attached to my rank made me feel I had addressed the colonel disrespectfully. "I'm not acquainted with military etiquette. Should I use your last name when I address you with your rank?"

"That is appropriate."

"My men are hungry," I said. "Where do we eat?"

"The mess tent on the other side of the quartermaster's tent. Breakfast is about over—better get moving."

I hollered, pointing up river. "Get to that tent there if you want to eat."

"Have they been issued tins yet?" the colonel asked.

"No, sir."

"Gentlemen," the colonel said as we walked toward our tents, "go to the quartermaster to requisition eating utensils, and then get your food."

"Do we have time?" Bradley Burke asked.

"They won't feed you unless you have tins."

Lining up at the quartermaster's tent, we remembered our horses. In a roped pen about thirty yards away, they appeared listless.

Tim Eagan spoke. "If we take care of ourselves before we take care of our horses, we'll be without horses in short order." He turned toward the sergeant behind the makeshift wooden counter. "Do you have buckets and brushes?"

The sergeant nodded, turning to a private. "Get buckets and brushes for these men." Looking at Tim, he asked. "How many?"

"Five brushes and five buckets." In a moment, Tim's request sat on the counter. "Four of you come with me and the rest of you eat. By the time you're finished, we'll be done with our horses. We'll wash them down, brush and feed them." Tim looked at the sergeant. "Where can we get oats?"

"Right here," he said, turning to the same assistant. He retrieved a forty pound sack. Four of us, including myself, grabbed the buckets and brushes. Tim carried the oats. When Splinter saw me, his ears perked. He pranced through the other horses.

Holding a bucket of oats to Splinter's mouth, watching the others feed and brush horses, I realized the importance of what we did. "This must be the second order of each day. Once up, we tend the horses, and then eat. I'll tell the others when they get here."

We went about our work. Two men made repeated trips to the river filling four buckets. They emptied two buckets over Splinter and two over Tim's horse.

Bradley scooped oats into a bucket. "This is a lot of work for five men."

"It is," I said. "We'll divide the work up—five groups of six men."

Tim peered over his horse. "That's thirty men. We're down to twenty-eight. I'll work the horses every day."

"Sounds good," I said. "Some of the Guard never owned or tended horses. They'll need your direction.

"We saved a little food for you in the mess tent," Nathaniel said as he and a few others approached.

"If we don't get this horsehair off us before we eat, we'll scratch and itch till Christmas," Tim said, looking toward the river.

"Don't wash off in there," Nathaniel said. "You'll contaminate it till Christmas."

"Well, what do you suggest?" I asked.

Nathaniel wedged his thumbs behind his belt buckle, a habit he acquired of late. "Stay out of the river. With the way you stink, head north and enlist in a Yankee regiment. Of course, if they smell you coming, they'll shoot you."

"They might smell us coming. They'd hear your flapping tongue miles away," I said. "It's an honor to do a hard day's work. The Yankees will write on your grave marker, 'We shot Nathaniel Thomas before he talked us to death.'"

"Bring those buckets," Tim said, picking up two. "If we stand around much longer listening to you, we'll miss the war."

I followed Tim and the others to the river. We cleaned up and filled the buckets, returning them to Nathaniel. By noon, all the horses and all the men were washed. Afterwards, we sat around in hot, humid conditions finding relief in the shade of willows along the riverbank. About five o'clock, I cleaned up, dressed, and made my way to England's tent accompanied by Nathaniel.

"Have you written Amy, yet?" he asked.

"Yes. Why?"

"I need to write my parents."

As we approached the colonel's tent, Major Remington emerged with two officers. "Think I'll hang around for a minute," Nathaniel said.

I glared, waiting for someone to speak. "Is there a problem?" England asked, stepping out of the tent. Peering first at me and then at Remington, he measured the situation. "Would you gentlemen join me in my tent?" Inside, Remington and I stood a few feet apart. England folded his arms. "What is the meaning of this, Captain Yardley?"

I collected my thoughts. "We had an altercation last night."

The colonel stared at Remington. "Your face is bruised."

"We fought. That's all."

"Officers in the Confederate Army do not fight each other, Captain Yardley. What justified the fight?"

"The major made allegations regarding my involvement in an incident in Savannah."

"Go on," he said. "What was the nature of this incident?"

"My wife and I assisted slaves working on the docks. Some considered the act grievous. Major Remington took issue with my participation."

"What assistance did you give slaves?"

"We tended to cuts and wounds on their backs and feet."

"You did what?"

"We washed their backs and feet—salved their wounds—that's what we did."

The colonel turned away raising his hand to this forehead. "Were you sent here as a joke? How can I commit you and your militia to battle alongside men who would kill you if they knew you did such a thing? This is preposterous. No wonder Major Remington took you on."

"Colonel," the major interjected, "if I may?" He waited permission.

"Go ahead."

"I heard today of how Captain Yardley led his Guard in battle and how valiantly he fought. I concur with your conclusion that there are Confederate soldiers who would kill him if they knew what he did. However, I am contrite over my senseless behavior and beg the captain's forgiveness."

"That will solve one problem with one officer—you," the colonel said. "Even if Captain Yardley forgives you, I am concerned others will hear about his ordeal in Savannah. How many times are you willing to fight?"

"First, I forgive you, Major Remington, as I am required to do within my faith." Remington bowed, acknowledging the gesture. "Second, I am not ashamed of what my wife and I did, except there is more. After that event, I rescued a runaway slave from slave hunters. They wound up dead."

"This is a joke," the colonel shouted. "What commanding officer sent you here? Did he have any sense, and did he have concern for you safety?"

"Guess I won't be meeting General Lee tonight?" I said.

"Oh, yes you will. Someone else will bear the brunt of this, not me. I will inform General Lee of the matter."

"Well then," Ely Remington said, "let us go to dinner. Enough brandishing of tongues."

We exchanged glances, stiffening as we prepared to exit the tent. "Besides, George," Ely continued, "if we're in battle, I'll be honored to fight next to you."

The colonel gazed at me. "Major, I don't see bruises on Captain Yardley's face. Is there a reason?"

"Yes—he finished the fight before I landed a punch."

Chapter 55

Captain George Yardley

On horseback, we rode up a hill away from the river. From my vantage point, I studied the buildings, some five and six stories tall. Richmond appeared a grander place than Atlanta. Accompanied by a colonel, a major, and two lieutenants, we approached a hotel, tied our horses to hitching posts, and went inside.

Negroes dressed in white waist-coats, black trousers, and string ties opened doors and led us to a registration book, which we signed giving names, ranks and units. Polished wooden floors and marble columns glistened in sunlight that streamed through huge windows. A large sitting room contained eight crystal chandeliers. It also contained, I thought, at least two hundred officers, talking and smoking cigars. Overwhelmed, I turned to Ely. "Do you know these men?"

"All," he replied. "Most graduated from the Academy or Virginia Military Institute."

"What academy?"

"West Point—are you joshing?"

"I know no one except you and the colonel. I feel out of place, like the moon in daylight."

"You outrank half these men. Don't let on you feel intimidated."

"I was a lieutenant four weeks ago—I don't outrank them by much."

"Also," Ely said, "these men have not fought. If they hear tell you've engaged an enemy, you'll become an instant hero."

Looking around at the youthful faces, the realization that politicians committed us to war with so little preparation and experience angered me. The more I studied the surroundings, the more I concurred with Ely. Very few, if any, had seen a man die like I saw Drury.

Negro waiters circulated amongst the crowd serving glasses of champagne. When everyone had received, eyes turned upward. From a balcony on the second floor, six officers, including General Lee, made their way to a curved staircase and proceeded down. With voices stilled and eyes staring at the white-haired and white-bearded southern gentleman, I felt God had entered the room.

In the silence and standing on a small platform, he spoke. "Good evening, my fellow Virginians," he peered around the room, "and, tonight for the first time, my fellow southerners. As you know, officers and militia from the seceded states have joined us. We form the Army of Northern Virginia. Our responsibility is the first line of defense against Yankee invasion. I accepted this honor you bestow upon me for one reason. Union politicians seek to subjugate states and champion causes contrary to those our forefathers instituted. Mr. Jefferson intended that each state govern itself. He intended our nation to consist of a union of freed and liberated states, not a nation of states subjected to a federal government. Tonight, before we dine, I offer this toast." He held his glass up. "To the free and individual rights of states and to the citizens of our confederacy. May the God of history bestow his grace upon us." A chorus of "Here, here" echoed through the marble columns, followed by the clinking of glasses.

"Take just a sip," Ely said as our goblets met. "These toasts go on forever." I sipped and waited.

"Here's to the Confederate States of America and to her general, who will lead us to victory." Again, a chorus sounded. Before anyone else spoke, General Lee introduced Chaplain William Jones who gave the blessing.

As the prayer concluded, I held my glass out to Ely. "May I finish this? I need it."

He smiled, turning his glass up. I followed. A slave, holding a tray accepted our empty glasses. Directions were given to follow the waiters through large wooden doors opening to the main dining hall. Once seated, they served a four-course supper.

"Any chance," I asked Ely as we sat at a large round table with Colonel England and five others, "that my men are eating like this?"

"None," Ely said. "Biscuits and gravy is their meal, and most of that, unless they made it to the front of the line, will be cold."

"I'll have a hard time explaining this."

"Explaining what?"

"What we ate in comparison to what they ate."

Ely feigned a choke. "Don't explain. What they don't know won't hurt them."

"It hurts me. Those men are friends and neighbors; and one, the one who egged us on last night, is my cousin. I may be an officer; but I'm one of them—not one of these. I won't eat like this again unless the Guard partakes of the same meal." Ely knew I meant it, refusing to debate. "I'll excuse myself." Lifting my napkin, I placed it on my plate. As I stood, a Negro tended my chair. "Good evening, gentlemen," I said to the others. "I shall eat with my company." Turning, making certain not to stumble over my chair, I exited through the nearest door. By then, darkness on a moonless night had set in. Loneliness ravaged my heart. Tears came as I thought about Amy. By the time I returned to the camp, the Guard had a fire going that smelled like home.

Nathaniel met me at the tent flap. "You better get out here and tell us what's going on before we mutiny."

"Give me a minute."

He honored my request, returning to the fire. Undressing to my undershirt, keeping my pants on, I removed my boots. With my suspenders hanging to my side, I approached the circle of men. "It's pretty hot. Do we need a fire?"

"Not about warmth," Tip said. "It's about the temperature of our evening repast. Seems like most," he made a semi-circle with his right arm referring to the other camps, "got used to eating cold food."

"At that," Randolph said, "it fails to qualify as food. Cold gravy and biscuit briquettes don't strike us as southern cooking. And then, to think these other men wouldn't take the initiative to warm it up is revolting." Some laughed.

"What did you eat, Cousin?" Nathaniel asked.

Hesitating, I thought to lie. "Whatever it was, I didn't enjoy it." Truth was, I didn't enjoy it. "We're in trouble," I went on deciding to change the subject.

"Trouble?" Tip asked.

"If what I saw and heard is truth, no one here ever fought a battle except us." I paused letting the thought sink in. "Men, we have to train and drill and train and drill, or we'll wind up like Court, Tom, and Drury. It's my job to make certain that doesn't happen; but, I need your cooperation. We must keep our horses and ourselves in the best possible shape. We have to target shoot and practice with these swords. If we don't, they'll bury us in a Virginia pasture—that is if anyone is left to bury us. Worst case—the buzzards will pick us clean."

"Well," Nathaniel said, "that's the kind of bright and bushy news we need to cheer us up. When we practice with those swords, why not stab each other to death to put us out of our misery." No one laughed. An anxiety crept around the circle.

"It's my job to keep you alive. I'll do my best. I'll tan you into leather hides. And you're going to be the best damn militia in this entire army. Get some sleep. We start in the morning."

"Men," Nathaniel said. "George is serious. Our lives are at stake. It's time to become the best horse soldiers on God's green earth."

Nathaniel and I moseyed to our tent. Lost in thought, we didn't speak until we bedded down and extinguished the candle.

"You're serious, aren't you?" Nathaniel said.

"Yep—no one dies because I was irresponsible. We may all die. We're not dying because we didn't know what to do."

"Thanks," Nathaniel said. "I mean it. It's time we take this war to heart. We know we're outnumbered. The only way to even the odds is to out shoot, out ride, and outwit the enemy."

Chapter 56

Alexander Frey

A telegram from the Bank of Boston declared the federal government refused to transfer my accounts to the Bank of London. My next telegram to the bank requested they send the assets to the Atlanta National Bank. To that petition, I never received a response. With inflation and interest rates rising, three million dollars sat helpless.

In Atlanta, the heat stifled activity. A torrid June dawned, leaving the entire South incapacitated. Never had I remembered such heat without an evening rain bringing relief. Horatio and Alexander Stephens greeted me as I arrived at the office.

Standing in the parlor, Stephens spoke first. "We need your money."

"I've made a grievous mistake. The Bank of Boston impounded my funds. The last draft I received was used to complete the forge and boot factory. Ample funds—a million and a half dollars—remain in Atlanta and two million in England. I fear the money in Boston lost."

"Would you consider traveling to Boston to demand the money?" Horatio asked.

I cast a cold, steel glare in his direction. "Would you make that journey? I'll purchase a train ticket if you wish to impersonate me."

"No thank you," he said. "My suggestion was foolish."

"Yes, it was," Stephens said. "We'll make do with the funds in the Bank of Atlanta. How might we acquire the assets in England?"

A silence invaded the moment. "All right—I'll sail to London. Horatio, make the arrangements. I've lost contact with Captain Percival."

"You may have to sail from New Orleans or Jacksonville."

"New Orleans. I could take the train rather than travel by land to Jacksonville in this heat."

"I will not tolerate such foolishness," Amy said emerging from my office, startling us.

"Young lady, what are you doing here?" I asked.

She remained silent, enhancing my indignation. Crossing her arms, stomping her left foot, she glared. "I dare say, what are you doing here?"

"This is my office."

"My question referred not to logistics, but business. How could you consider sailing to England? Are you stupid enough to think the Yankees will allow you to cross the Atlantic and return with funds intended for the Confederate cause? Have you lost your mind? Mr. Stephens—Mr. McClerken—the next time you ask Father to do such a thing, I will shoot each of you between the eyes." She removed a pistol from her purse. Horatio cowered, followed by Stephens.

"Put that away" I said. "You will not hide in my office and then brandish a weapon."

"If these are your friends, God help you." Replacing the weapon, she walked through us, out the door, slamming it.

"Why do you ask me to risk my life when neither of you, I take it, would sail into these political waters?" Neither man responded. "I will discuss the matter with my wife and inform you of my decision."

Chapter 57

Amy Yardley

"He'll go. We know that; but, he's not going without me," Beatrice said as we sat at her kitchen table.

Returning my cup to the saucer, I stared out a window. "I may lose my husband and my father and even you. War has changed my happiness to despair."

"Have you heard from George?"

"No—he told me not to expect mail for two weeks. I feel helpless. There's nothing for a woman to do in war, except wait."

Beatrice stood. "My first husband taught me that lesson, and that is why I will insist on traveling with Alexander. I'd rather die at sea than wait for his return."

"So, I'll wait for my husband and for you," I said. "I pray for a short war."

"There's no such thing except in the hearts of women whose husbands and sons have gone to fight. War is long and drawn out, and so is the agony of waiting."

"Then I shall wait in Richmond," I said rising from the table. "Keep this quiet. After you depart, I will go to Virginia." I started for the front door. It opened. Father stepped in. Unable to control myself, I confronted him. "Well, when do you depart for England?"

He stared down the short hall leading to the kitchen. "When Horatio makes the arrangements."

"He better make arrangements for two, because you're not going unless your wife accompanies you."

"She's right," Beatrice said. "If you go, I go. I refuse the anguish of waiting for another husband's return. If you die, I die with you."

Father attempted a protest, but realized its futility. "I'll inform Horatio." Then he turned to me. "Now, young lady," he said repeating the phrase he used in his office, "what is the meaning of your behavior this morning?"

"The meaning of her behavior," Beatrice said, walking toward us, "stems from that which women have endured since the beginning of time when their husbands and fathers go to war. If wise, you will refrain from self-righteous indignation."

Silenced, he entered the parlor, placing his hands in the pockets of his leather jacket, seemingly in an attempt to constrain his emotions. Not able to constrain my love for him, I went and embraced him.

"This Saturday," he said, "I would appreciate it, if we could take a ride to your farm. Time in the country will do me good."

"That sounds wonderful," I said. "I wish to see Lillian."

Chapter 58

Amy Yardley

As I stepped into the brutal heat, I searched for a carriage, but found none. Walking toward Peach Tree Street under the shade of a parasol, a surrey came along. I gave the driver Stephanie's address. Upon arriving, I found her standing on the front porch. We embraced.

"Why do I feel you're up to something?" she asked.

"Because I am."

In the parlor, she offered me a chair. "Well?"

"How would you like to travel to Richmond by train?"

"What? Your father won't allow such a thing."

"He and Beatrice will be gone."

"Gone?"

"Yes—he plans to sail to England to bring his money back for the Confederacy." Stephanie waited. "While they're gone, I am traveling to Virginia to see George."

"Does George know?"

"No—but Beatrice does." Pulling my purse to breast, I sought her eyes. "Please go."

Stephanie gasped. "I can't afford it, and I wouldn't do such a thing to my parents.

"Would you go if Drury were there?"

"Why," she paused, "I would."

"Then, why don't you go now? You know money is not an issue."

"When?"

"When Father and Beatrice set sail, I will inform you ahead of time." We stood and embraced. "There's a lot to be said for friendship."

∾➳∾➳∾

"Well, where have you been all day?" Sarah asked as I walked up the front steps.

"To Father's office, to his home, and to see Stephanie."

"Maybe you should have gone to the post office." She held up an envelope. "Here's a letter from your husband; but, don't get excited. The postmark is Raleigh, North Carolina."

I rushed inside and upstairs, removed my dress and undergarments, and put on a robe. Sitting in the chair next to the window, I opened the letter and read.

My Dearest Amy,

We arrived outside Raleigh, N. C. It has been a long, hot trip, though no one complains much. The Guard enjoyed the railroad. However, the accommodations are not what we experienced on our way to Savannah. The wooden benches are hard, and the food tolerable. When we stop, we walk the horses and water them. We should be in Richmond in a couple days.

How are you? I miss you very much and love you more than I miss you. As soon as I arrive at our destination, I will get the postal code for my address. I cannot wait to hear from you. Have to stop so I can mail this. Please love me forever.

George

It wasn't much, but something. My excitement about the letter and dreams of Richmond produced giddiness. Never would I spend another day in Atlanta without going to the post office.

Downstairs, I informed Sarah that George was well. Noticing an apple halved on a saucer, I picked it up and took a seat at the table. "I have news. Your brother and his wife will sail for England. He must retrieve his money deposited in the Bank of London."

Sarah stood, turning away, peering out the window. "His money means more than his life—not to mention Beatrice's."

Swallowing a bite of apple, I taunted. "Maybe the meaning of life increases when one believes he is involved in a cause greater than himself."

"Causes mask the meaning of life. Love produces meaning. You will do anything for someone you love, even die for him. A cause manipulates and coerces—that's happening to your father. It's a strange line he crossed. He loves you and George. He loves Beatrice. He loves me. Those in power blind him to that love; so, he does what they need. What a sad state of affairs."

I sat amazed at Sarah's wisdom, refusing the remainder of the apple. Sarah described what I felt as I eavesdropped on Father and his friends. I could not imagine how he allowed himself guided into such folly.

"This may sound odd," I said, "but I need a glass of wine." I went to the cabinet in the dining room and retrieved a bottle.

"I'll take some, too," Sarah said. "Maybe we should store fifteen or twenty bottles to help us wait for George's return from war and Alexander's return from England. I'll spend every day wishing them here."

Chapter 59

George Yardley

Each morning the Milton Guards awoke and commenced training. At times, the routine felt inhuman. We ran two miles carrying our rifles. After breakfast, we practiced cavalry charges in nearby pastures—up hills, down hills, and most difficult of all, through ravines and gullies that narrowed our feigned attack. With drawn swords and rebel yells, we rode at full gallop. Every horse seemed to grasp the energy of the attack. Convinced I had the most well trained militia in Richmond, I took pride in our accomplishments. Though ignorant of what made a cavalry outstanding, I held my horse soldiers in highest esteem. Someone else noticed. I received an invitation to serve under General Beauregard.

Moving through the River Camp one morning, Colonel England stopped me. It was the second day of July. Debates and arguments flourished over whether we should celebrate Independence Day. The consensus reached was the Confederacy fought for the same rights for which our forefathers fought— freedom from tyranny.

"George," the colonel said above the arguments in our vicinity, "General Beauregard wants the Guard to join with the Black Horse Cavalry. They train north of Fredericksburg at Stafford Courthouse. Report within the week."

"Is that near Washington?" I asked.

"Yes, and nearer to war. Word has it that the first land battle will take place by the end of July in northern Virginia. Lee has taken a defensive posture awaiting the Yankee attack."

"Why don't we attack?"

"The rule in military school is that your best offense is a good defense. Though our army consists of novice soldiers, we have devised a line of defense west of Manassas. General Johnston controls the Valley of Virginia. A railroad runs between Front Royal and Manassas. If war starts in Manassas, Johnston will support Beauregard."

"You make it sound easy."

"Are you willing to report to Stafford Courthouse?"

"If that is where the general wants us, we will go. How long will it take to move a troop of horse soldiers that far? Now that I think about it, how far is it?"

"About sixty miles—you can make it in three days." He turned toward soldiers participating in a heated argument. "If you leave tomorrow, you could rid yourselves of this senseless talk about Independence Day."

"We will leave in the morning."

"Thank you, George," the colonel said. "It is an honor to know you."

We parted company. I made my way to camp noticing Nathaniel and six Guardsmen standing outside a tent. "Well, what was that about?" he asked.

"Pack up—we're headed to Stafford Courthouse to join the Black Horse Cavalry under the command of General Beauregard."

"Beauregard commanded troops at Fort Sumter?"

"Yes."

"He started the war in South Carolina. Do they expect him to start the next battle?"

"Don't know," I said, "but when it starts, we'll be in the thick of it." The entire Guard gathered, listening. After repeating the details, I ordered the men awake by six o'clock and ready to ride by eight. Breaking camp filled me with anxiety and excitement.

❧❧❧❧

There was more to do than I realized. From the quartermaster, I had to requisition the tents and equipment assigned us upon our arrival. We couldn't leave the River Camp with that equipment without orders from Colonel England. At the colonel's tent, his sergeant informed me England had begun a staff meeting and was unavailable. Rather than wait, I returned to the quartermaster to see what else we needed. Owning our horses and saddles proved beneficial. We had used our ammunition during training. Requisitioning powder and shot also necessitated a written order. Last, the quartermaster assigned us one cannon.

"How do you make a cavalry charge pulling cannons?" I asked.

He scratched his head. "You don't. Before you charge, you blast a few balls to decrease the enemy's potential. Then, you charge hell-bent for leather."

Feeling embarrassed, I sought mercy. "What else?"

"If in your shoes, I'd requisition a buckboard and team of horses. Take all the food, ammunition, cannon shot, tents, and blankets you can manage."

"Do we have to keep ourselves in provisions?"

"Exactly—if you don't, you'll be dependent on someone else, and someone else always has something more important to do."

"Thanks."

"One more thing," he said. "The fight with Major Remington didn't go unnoticed. Soldiers don't want to fight beside you. Take care—don't rely on anyone. And," he hesitated, "your reputation scares most."

"What do you mean?"

"If your commanding officer's politics agree with Major Remington, your commander might send you into battle as a sacrifice. Do you understand?" I nodded. "If he believes your presence a detriment to other troops, he could hold you in reserve. It's not a bad thing to be held in reserve. You'll know where you stand."

"Thanks again," I said.

"See if the colonel finished the staff meeting. I'll have what you need when you return."

"Why are you doing this for me?"

"Well, I don't cotton to slavery. Your militia drilled harder than any. Our side needs fighting men like you."

I made my way through camp. Deciding to take an aggressive approach, I went right to the colonel who stood outside his tent talking with Ely Remington.

"Good morning, gentlemen," I said. Surprised at the interruption, England turned, flashing a disgusted frown. Before he could reprimand, I continued. "The Milton Guards need supplies and equipment before we head to Stafford." I eyed Remington. "Colonel, may I obtain my written orders to make requisitions?"

"See the quartermaster. He'll give you what you need."

"He won't without written orders."

The colonel looked at Remington and then directed an aide to write the Guard's orders to serve under General Beauregard.

"May I requisition what the quartermaster believes we need?"

"You may. What is the meaning of your demanding behavior?"

"The meaning is, begging the colonel's pardon, if my men go to battle, I want them supplied." The aide returned holding a piece of paper which he offered to the colonel. England signed it, handing it to me. "Should I report to you before we depart?"

"Yes, Captain. When ready, send a messenger. I would like a word with your company."

"Yes, sir," I said.

A buckboard with two horses waited at the quartermaster's tent. At the rear, one cannon stood facing backwards secured by ropes.

"Glad you made it," Nathaniel said. "We hoped to leave without you."

"Here are the orders," I said to the quartermaster, handing the paper to him.

After reading, he returned it. "We'll have you ready in fifteen minutes."

"Nathaniel, rather than run your mouth, run over to Colonel England's tent and report we depart in fifteen minutes."

"Yes, sir, Captain," Nathaniel said. "Anything else?"

Chapter 60

George Yardley

In the commotion, I realized something stopped my cousin in his tracks. Two women approached on foot, escorted by Ely. With each step, they gained the attention of hundreds, if not thousands of soldiers. Amy smiled as she picked me out. Stephanie, her jaw set, head bowed, appeared solemn. Breaking away from Remington, Amy ran to embrace me. I returned the gesture, realizing silence fell upon the Guard.

"What is the meaning of this?" I asked. "Do you bear bad news?"

Amy glanced at Stephanie. "Nothing is wrong."

"You got it in your head to take a train ride to Richmond?"

"No—I got it in my head to visit my husband."

"There's something more to this than a visit," I said.

"What news do you bring from home?" Paul Gilbert asked.

"None," Stephanie said. "Everyone is fine except it is hotter in Atlanta than here."

"You men get back to work," I said. "We have orders to embark within the hour. Get back to work before you wear yourselves out gawking."

Nathaniel's arms extended, gaining Amy's attention. "Gawking is work." She granted him an embrace and a kiss on the cheek.

Taking each woman by the elbow, I walked them toward the willows near the river.

"Where are you going?" Amy asked.

"Stafford Courthouse—assigned to General Beauregard's brigade."

"You're leaving today?"

"Yes."

"Let me catch you up on a few things. Father and Beatrice are on their way to England from New Orleans. He went to retrieve his money for the cause. He does not know we are here; but, Beatrice does."

"Sarah?"

"She knows, but refused to give her blessing to this trip."

"Imagine that," I said. "Anything else?"

"Not at the moment."

"Where are you staying?"

"At the Marshall Hotel. Before you ask, we plan to remain in Richmond to help in whatever manner possible. War exacts a toll enumerated by wounds that need tending. We offered our services as nurses."

"Word has it we will fight the first battle in northern Virginia by the end of the month."

"Is that why you're being sent there?"

"That is correct." I waited a moment, assessing whether I should tell her about Remington. "There's something else. Men here know about Savannah. Some will hold you in disdain if they discover your identity. Do you have your revolver?"

"In my purse."

Stephanie snickered. "The last time she removed it, she pointed it at Horatio and Vice President Stephens."

"I'll talk to you about that another time," Amy said. "No harm done."

"George, I mean, Captain Yardley," Nathaniel hollered. "Are you going with us?"

I turned. Each Guardsman stood next to his horse waiting my order. "I have to go. Any man comes near you with evil in his eye, shoot him." Kissing her, embracing her, I returned to my men. "Soldiers of the Milton Guards, mount up." As if in unison, they did so. Slowly, we rode through camp toward Broad Street. The buckboard, full of supplies and pulling one cannon, followed. In the commotion, I forgot Colonel England's request to address the men. A last look at Ely Remington standing with Amy and Stephanie made me hate him.

Chapter 61

Amy Yardley

"He didn't seem upset with you," Stephanie said. "His reaction surprised me."

"He appeared detached and yet, he wasn't." We walked to the hotel taking in the sights of Richmond. "Maybe I did wrong. He has twenty-eight soldiers to worry about and now, he'll worry about his wife and her friend."

"Should we return home?"

"Not yet. Let's see what the next few days bring—especially since the full fury of civil war may be unleashed."

At our hotel, a slave ushered me to the desk clerk. A telegram had arrived from Sarah expressing indignation we had not notified her of our arrival. Scanning the lobby, I saw a small room with a glass window on which the words, Telegraph Office, were painted in gold. Entering, the operator informed me it would cost seventy-five cents to send a telegram, and so I did.

"Is there a telegraph office in Stafford Courthouse?" I asked, completing the first transaction.

"Yes, there is," the operator said.

"My husband's military unit departed this afternoon. He plans to arrive there in three days. If I send a telegram, might he receive it?"

"As long as you know his company."

"The Black Horse Cavalry under General Beauregard." I said, hoping for an affirmation, but received none. Turning to Stephanie, I smiled. "George is worth seventy-five cents."

"Write your message. I'll send it," the operator said.

"Will you see what I write?" Before the words sped from my mouth, I realized their foolishness.

"The operator on the other end will see it also," he replied. "Don't be embarrassed. If you want to tell him you love him, tell him. We send that message a lot." I wrote one brief line: 'Thanks for understanding. I love you.'

For the remainder of the afternoon, we addressed two concerns. We found a Baptist Church to attend, and we sought avenues by which to offer our assistance when war came.

An elderly couple entered the hotel lobby as we approached the dining room for supper. We waited to be seated. They stood next to us.

"Good evening," I said.

"Good evening," the woman replied while the man paid no attention. "You are not from Richmond, I take it?"

"No ma'am—Atlanta, Georgia."

That drew the man's attention. He looked at his wife and then at us. "I was born there. Please do not think me discourteous. Are you unescorted?"

"Why, yes," I said. "My husband is a Captain in the Georgia Militia, and Mrs. Stith," I hesitated realizing what I was about to say. "Mrs. Stith's husband was killed in a battle north of Atlanta."

"A battle north of Atlanta? Whatever do you mean?" he asked.

Stephanie refused to speak, so I did. "The Milton Guards, to which both husbands were assigned, fought against The Association that had kidnapped Mrs. Stith. The Association had ties to the Kansas statehood dilemma. My husband and I and others in north Georgia oppose slavery, but also oppose the federal government denying our states' rights. My husband, Captain George Yardley, led the Milton Guards into Cherokee to free Mrs. Stith. A battle commenced in which Major Stith and two others were killed along with members of The Association." The man grimaced, expressing sympathy to Stephanie. A Negro waiter made his presence known and asked if he could seat Stephanie and me.

"Just a minute," the woman said. "We are James and Mary Alice Branner. My husband is a physician and teaches at our medical college. If not an imposition, we would be honored if you joined us for supper."

"Doctor Branner, would that be acceptable?" I asked.

"More than acceptable." He turned to the Negro. "May we have a table for four?"

"Yes, sir, Doctor Branner," the Negro said. Mrs. Branner went first followed by Stephanie and me. At the table, two additional Negroes assisted the ladies with our chairs.

"Mrs. Yardley," Mrs. Branner said, "I don't think we heard your first name."

"Oh, I apologize—Amy."

"Amy and Stephanie," Dr. Branner repeated.

One Negro filled our water glasses, starting with Mrs. Branner. Another handed each person a menu. The prices seemed high. At that point, I didn't care. Meeting the Branners seemed what I refer to as a 'God appointment'.

"What is your favorite meal here?" Stephanie asked.

"By the limited size of the crowd, you might surmise nothing on this menu finds favor with anyone in Richmond," Doctor Branner said. "Let me assure you the first casualty of war is a restaurant's menu. Inflated prices deprive many friends the opportunity to dine. You will enjoy your meal."

With our orders taken, the waiter retrieved our menus. "Would anyone care for a beverage?" he asked. Relaxed in the

Branners' company, I requested a mint julep. Stephanie did the same. Though appearing conflicted, Mrs. Branner ordered one.

"A unique evening," Dr. Branner said with a smile. "In the presence of three beautiful women, I will drink in public for the first time in my life—Scotch and water."

"If that's the case, you departed Atlanta too soon," Stephanie said. "No one dines there without enjoying a drink."

He laughed. "Maybe I did. Tonight, I make up for lost time." As the waiter placed the drinks on the table, Doctor Branner raised his. "Here's to the joy of youth and the wisdom of old age. May this war destroy neither." We touched our glasses and proceeded to sip. For a moment, I recounted our train trip, the encounter with George and the Guard, and our hope of staying in Richmond to help with the war.

"You are serious about offering your services?" Dr. Branner asked. We nodded. "If you like, I can introduce you to the doctor who oversees our program in which young ladies train to care for wounded and dying soldiers. The program takes a month to complete."

"Wonderful," Stephanie said. "What do we have to do?"

"First—enjoy our meal. Second—meet me Monday morning that I may make appropriate introductions."

"And third," Mrs. Branner said, "tomorrow we will take you to our home where you can room and board while in Richmond."

"We couldn't impose," Stephanie replied.

"Nonsense," Mrs. Branner said. "I've made up my mind."

Sipping my drink, I spoke. "Do you ever think God sees to His divine ends and that He destined us to meet tonight?"

"Part of the wisdom we toasted," Dr. Branner said, "is refusing to understand God's divine ends." He held up his glass again, tipping it toward me. Something in the exchange made me aware of Savannah and what George said. I decided to inform the Branners of the incident. If offended, best to settle the matter now.

Upon hearing the account, Doctor Branner spoke. "I would like to meet this young man of yours. The fact you cared for the wounds of slaves lends more credence to my conclusion that you are excellent candidates for the nursing program. What's more, Mrs. Branner and I would be honored to have you as guests in our home."

"Thank you," I said.

"We have a great deal to do tonight," Stephanie said. "Maybe we should retire."

Folding my napkin and placing it on the table, I turned to Mrs. Branner. "We plan to attend the Baptist Church on Broad Street in the morning. If it is convenient and you would give us your address, we will hire a carriage to transport our baggage to your home."

"Nonsense," Mrs. Branner said. "We will return tomorrow at two o'clock with our carriage to provide transportation."

"Baptist?" Dr. Branner repeated. "Finally, an unsavory quality, but I'll get over it. We are Presbyterian."

"I was Baptist once," Mrs. Branner said, "until I married. Now, I worship God according to what He predestined rather than according to free will."

"And you should thank God and me that He chose you to see the light of truth," Dr. Branner said. "What more could a woman ask?"

"Please," Mrs. Branner said, "with that sentiment, it is time to rescue you ladies from Doctor Branner's humor."

Chapter 62

George Yardley

The Richmond Highway led the Milton Guards on a winding path north to Ashland. We covered fourteen miles. Asking permission of a farmer, we camped in his pasture. Laziness set in. The men desired to sleep under the stars, not wanting to put the effort into pitching their tents. I refused their whining, believing routine disciplined soldiers. Besides, to the southwest dark clouds formed.

The blackness of night and the blackness of the storm hit at the same time. After the rains, I heard a buckboard. Peering out my tent flap, I saw the farmer. He brought dry kindling and firewood. Two flaming torches attached to the wagon illuminated his cargo.

"You boys need heat," he said. "A soaking like that takes a fire to dry things out."

The pasture grass proved slippery, and splotches of mud made it difficult to off-load the wood. Three men built a blazing fire while I acquired local information from the farmer. In his estimation, we might make it across the South Anna and the North Anna Rivers if lucky. He was certain the swollen rivers washed out at least one bridge.

"Who repairs the bridges?" Nathaniel asked.

"First one to come along. Of course, that depends on how badly they want to cross." He looked around. "Don't you have buckets?" I shrugged. Pointing to buckets in the buckboard, the farmer continued, "Damn shame to waste a rain like that without collecting water."

"Got busy making camp—hobbling horses—didn't give it a thought."

He climbed up on the buckboard. "A lot we don't think about when we don't know what we're doing. A few more nights—preparation will come natural—if you live that long." He whipped the reins.

"Thanks. Thank you very much," I said as he drove off.

He waved. "Hope to see you again."

About half the Guard gathered around the fire while the other half sought the refuge of sleep. "Mac Bruce," I shouted over the crackling flames, "anytime it rains—you're responsible for setting buckets out to catch rain water. That's an order."

Settled in my tent, I spent time thinking about Amy and about the Anna Rivers. Thoughts swirled. How many more mistakes would I make because of ignorance. Scared, I realized I had never built a bridge.

Chapter 63

Amy Yardley

"Pardon ma'am, but are you ladies unescorted?" Two men in blue military uniforms asked as we approached the hotel steps.

"We are married to Confederate officers," Stephanie said. She stepped upward.

"Oh," one said. "We heard you were widowed."

"I choose to remain so. You may excuse yourselves."

"You are Major Remington from this morning," I said.

"I am, and this is Captain Jordan Banks." He bowed.

"Amy, come now," Stephanie said.

Turning, I smiled, excusing myself. We ascended the steps without speaking.

"What was that about?" I asked, closing the door to our room.

"That was about two men ascertaining if we were available. Lock the door before you allow half the soldiers in this city to enter."

"What? They were gentlemen."

"If given an opening, they'd be here undressing us rather than us undressing ourselves," she said, unbuttoning her blouse. "Lock, and chain that door."

I did. "You scare me."

"After tonight, we'll room in the safety of the Branners' home."

Reaching into my purse, feeling for the pistol, I wrapped my fingers around the handle. "Doubt I'll sleep a wink." Rain pelted our window.

Chapter 64

George Yardley

The storm brought cool air and decreased humidity, but a thick morning fog. One after another, we walked into the pasture to relieve ourselves. An eerie sense came over me as I watched their figures move through the mist. What if under attack right now, I thought, as I re-buttoned my pants? What would I do? How would I lead? The thought of an early morning surprise attack alarmed me. I called the Guard together.

"Before we eat, here are your orders. We number twenty eight. Seven are to stand guard in rotating two-hour shifts around the clock with loaded rifles and pistols. A surprise attack would have devastated us this morning. I'm dividing you right now. The Fourth Platoon consists of Sergeant Richard Grogan, Bobby Paul Green, Jeremy Glass, Corporal Richard Lindamood, Tim Eagan, Jimmy Smith and Randolph Loy." Looking around, I sized up the men. "Third Platoon: Kinchen Cross, Sergeant Harvey Gibbs, Bob Gibbs, Noah Tucker, Reuben Reece, Levi Cross and Asa Donald. Second Platoon: Nathaniel, Francis Pugh, Calvin Pruitt, Jesse Martin, Josiah Langford, Tillman Holcombe and Elijah Herring. First Platoon: Corporal Paul Gilbert, Wesley

Rachford, Tip Liller, Bradley Burke, Mac and Green Bruce and myself."

Feeling as if I forgot something, I searched my memory. "Oh, from this day forward, when you bed down, do so with your weapons loaded. Rack your muskets and rifles against each other. Don't accidentally shoot someone. For that matter, don't shoot yourself. It's been done." Again, it surprised me as to how much attention they paid.

"First Platoon, prepare breakfast. Second, break camp. Whoever breaks camp tends to the buckboard that day. Third, water and feed the horses, and Fourth Platoon stand guard. When you stand guard, stay in groups of two with the platoon leader walking between you." They went to work. By the time the fog lifted, they loaded the buckboard, saddled the horses, and ate breakfast.

"Mount up," I ordered, feeling confident. "Let's see if we have to build a bridge." The platoons rode together, with the second managing the buckboard and cannon. The Richmond Highway, soaked and muddy, burdened our travel.

The farmer's prognostication proved correct. The bridge over the South Anna remained intact; but, the rain washed out the North Anna's. Broken sections lay wedged and scattered about thirty yards down river.

"Our next challenge?" Nathaniel asked. "Can that buckboard and cannon float?"

"Why don't we tie you to the cannon and see?" I said. "Did anyone requisition a saw?" No one answered. A couple shook their heads.

Nathaniel stared behind us. "Something's strange. This is a busy road. Why aren't others here? Calvin Pruitt, come with me. We're riding upriver to see if there's a place to cross. Tillman and Elijah, go down river. See what you can find."

"You're comfortable giving orders," I said.

"The rest of you," Nathaniel shouted, "have a party." He tipped his hat at me. "How's that for an order?"

The four disappeared, going in separate directions. Having never built a bridge, I rode back to the one at the South Anna to take a look. Tip and Green accompanied me.

Twenty minutes later at the South Anna, I examined the bridge. One look convinced me it was hopeless to rebuild the broken one. We would have to return to Richmond to get what we needed. "Let's go," I said. We mounted and started back. As we rode toward the spot where I left the others, a void confronted me. The Guard had vanished. From across the river, I heard a noise. Nathaniel sat on Winsome looking as winsome as his horse's name.

"How'd you get across?" I hollered.

"Found an old geezer half mile upriver. For a dollar, he sells wings grown on a great bird they raise here. He attaches them to your horse with magical paste. As soon as he does, the wings start flapping. Next thing you know, they've flown you across. When you land, they fall off." The men snickered.

"Tell me how to get across; or, I'll shoot your flapping tongue."

"Boys," Nathaniel said, "ever seen a soldier who picks more fights with his own men? First, he fought Ely Remington and now me." He paused, turning toward the men and then back to me. "Hurry upriver before he sells out for the day. With the bridge gone, he's doing a sizable business. We'll mosey along until you catch up." Everyone busted up laughing.

Disgusted, I looked back at Tip and Green, who also laughed. "You boys have any money?"

"What for?" Green asked.

"The wings." Tip laughed so hard he almost off his horse.

"What's wrong over there?" Nathaniel shouted.

Tip stretched upward in his saddle. "George wants to know if we have money to buy wings."

Nathaniel laughed. "Hope so. If not, you'll have to spend the war on that side of the river. Hurry up. We'll take Washington by the time you catch us."

We rode along the river a couple hundred yards and found a shallow. As we crossed, I gave Tip and Green fair warning. "If you make fun over this in front of anyone other than the Guard, I'll whip your hides." Kicking Splinter, I galloped off. In fifteen minutes, we caught up.

"How'd those wings work?" Nathaniel asked.

"Fine, but I'd like to find one of those birds."

"Why's that?"

"To stuff it down your throat."

Chapter 65

Amy Yardley

Stephanie and I bathed and dressed for church. As we waited for breakfast, a knock sounded. Stephanie responded. Ely Remington and Captain Banks presented themselves in full military regalia.

"We wondered if we might escort you to church," Ely said.

Stephanie attempted to close the door. "No, you may not."

Ely blocked the door with his foot. "We apologize for our behavior last evening."

"Apologize all you want," Stephanie said, "but we are not interested. Remove your foot." He refused, pushing his way into the room, shoving her aside. The captain followed.

Turning to me, Ely looked me up and down. "So you are Mrs. George Yardley?" Captain Banks closed the door. "You desire slaves, we're told." His words froze me. I inserted my right hand into my handbag without speaking. "Since your husband departed, we thought you might desire us."

Holding my purse out, I did speak. "Major Remington, I have a gun. If you do not remove yourselves, I will use it."

Smiling, he turned toward Banks. "We heard you make mention of that gun through the door last night, but concluded you pose a hoax." He started toward me.

Letting the purse drop to the floor, I pointed the firearm. It went off. The bullet penetrated his chest.

"Oh, my God," Banks shouted. "What have you done?" He stepped toward Remington.

"Captain Banks, stay there unless you want the same fate." As he knelt, he stared upward at me.

"I didn't mean to shoot him," I said. "The gun went off."

Stephanie stood trembling against the door, her right hand spread across her mouth. Calling her name, I tried to gain her attention. "Go downstairs. Tell the clerk to send the police."

The hotel clerk and two others came through the door before she moved. Seeing Major Remington bleeding and Captain Banks kneeling, the clerk pushed my right hand downward. "What happened?"

"These men pushed their way into our room. I carry a revolver. As he," I nodded toward Remington, "came toward me, I pointed it, and it went off. I didn't mean to shoot."

"Get the police," the clerk said to one of the men. He turned and ran down the hall.

"You may get up," I said to Captain Banks.

He did. Blood reddened his left hand. When he saw it, he grabbed a towel hanging next to the washbasin. Never removing his eyes from me, he wiped his hand. "Your husband beat Ely in a fair fight, and now you killed him."

"When my husband hears you pushed your way in here, you'll be as good as dead."

"It wasn't my idea."

"You didn't choose to leave."

"Meant no harm."

Three policemen with guns drawn came through the door. When they saw me, one asked for the gun.

"You may not have it. I will put it away." Stooping, picking up my handbag, I replaced the weapon. Clutching the bag to my abdomen, I approached Stephanie and embraced her. Though not crying, she trembled. "It'll be all right as soon as we get to the Branners."

"Branners?" One policeman questioned. "Doctor Branner?"

"Yes, sir," I said. "They invited us to room and board with them. If acceptable, my friend and I would like to attend church. Afterwards, we will return here for our noon meal." I turned to the clerk. "Please have our room straightened."

"Officers," the clerk said, "these men sniffed around last night and this morning. I overheard them speak about these women. I have no reason to doubt Mrs. Yardley."

"You may have a porter take our baggage to the lobby," I said. "We will return after worship." Taking Stephanie's arm, I guided her down the hall.

❧❧❧❧

Seated in the hotel dining room, a policeman approached. "Ladies, the circumstances under which Major Remington died necessitate a few questions. If permissible, may I join you?"

"Yes," I said. "Please be seated."

"Why do you carry a gun?" he asked.

I explained the circumstances in Georgia, indicating my husband taught me to shoot. Next, he wanted to know if I gave a warning.

"Officer, the shooting was accidental. The circumstances were not. If you do not report that the two men pushed their way into our room, it will appear we invited them. That was not the case. I pointed the pistol at Major Remington in self-defense." Pausing, I opted to repeat myself. "If you don't report the forceful entry, I will require the services of an attorney. Our reputations shall not be impugned."

He wrote notes. "That will be included in the report. I leave you to your meal. If necessary, I will contact you at the Branners." He stood, bowed, and departed.

At two o'clock, Doctor and Mrs. Branner entered the lobby, greeting Stephanie and me. Slaves gathered our luggage, placing it in the rear of the carriage. We rode five blocks on Broad Street, making a left turn at Grace. On that corner stood a beautiful three-story house that appeared much like my home in Atlanta.

The Negro driver belonged to the Branners. He helped us from the carriage and went about the business of unloading the baggage. Doctor Branner escorted us up a few stairs to the front porch. A middle-aged female slave opened the door, greeting us. Standing in the entranceway, Mrs. Branner introduced Dinah. She had slaved for thirty years.

Along with Dinah, Mrs. Branner escorted us to our rooms. "If not summer, I would put you on the third floor, for privacy," Mrs. Branner said. "It is too hot at this time of year up there." Stephanie chose one room, leaving me the other. We returned to the first floor where Dinah served lemonade.

"Tell me more about you," Doctor Branner said as we sat in the parlor.

"My parents live on a farm south of Atlanta," Stephanie began. "It is not a plantation, though we do own slaves. For the most part, we raise horses and crops. Amy and I met because she came to our equestrian school to learn to ride. My family has owned that land since the mid 1700's. I am their only daughter. We told you last night that my husband, Captain Drury Stith, was killed in battle." Dr. Branner turned his attention to me.

"My mother died after I was born. My father and his sister, Sarah Frey, raised me in comfortable conditions. He is a cotton broker—and also brokers other crops—along with trading merchandise from Europe."

"Frey? Your father isn't Alexander Frey?"

"He is. Do you know him?"

"Do I know him? Your grandfather Frey and my father, Horace Branner, were best of friends. I never knew your father because I was sent to Richmond to study medicine. Do you still live on Wheat Street?"

"Yes."

"If this doesn't beat all. I became a poor doctor, and your father, from what I understand, became the wealthiest businessman in the South. Where is Alexander?"

"He and his wife, Beatrice, sailed to England." I went on to explain the purpose of the voyage.

Doctor Branner grew concerned. "With war coming, the Union rules the seas." It is hard to imagine Alexander putting his life in jeopardy."

"My fears coincide with yours," I said.

"However, it is difficult to imagine Alexander putting his life in jeopardy. It was foolish to speculate about your father's safety when I know so little about war and sailing ships." His head bowed as if lost in thought.

Trying to reassure our benefactor, I expressed my prayerful concern for Father and Beatrice. For a few moments, conversation felt awkward until Mrs. Branner changed the subject to our training as nurses. Doctor Branner had discussed the matter with individuals at church and had received affirmation we could begin our classes Monday. Wanting to take a walk to become familiar with the neighborhood, Stephanie and I did so.

Chapter 66

George Yardley

By mid-afternoon, the Milton Guards approached Matta Creek. It, too, ran strong. Deciding to cross in case it rained that night, I ordered the Fourth Platoon to move the spare horses and buckboard. We crossed without incident.

Nathaniel and Second Platoon tied ropes to the cannon and started across. Out of nowhere, a large limb carried by the current crashed into Winsome's left front leg. Nathaniel jumped into the swollen creek, bracing himself against his horse. Seeing the trouble, I raced Splinter toward the creek throwing a rope to Nathaniel. Others pulled the cannon to dry land. Josiah and Tillman lassoed Winsome, rescuing the horse from the waters. Winsome's front leg dangled. As soon as the gelding found footing, he collapsed.

"Don't waste time," Tim said. "Put him down."

"He is down," Nathaniel said, wide-eyed.

Tim pulled his revolver from its holster. "If I'm ever in that condition, shoot me." Holding the gun inches from Winsome's head, he pulled the trigger.

"What do you do with a dead horse?" Tillman asked.

Tim replaced his carbine. "Drag it to the side of the road and let nature take its course."

Tillman and Josiah tied their ropes around the horse's legs, remounted, and dragged the carcass about a hundred yards.

Nathaniel stood and watched. "Two weeks," he said, "three dead militia, one bruised major, and one dead horse."

Making camp, we accomplished our duties. By supper, we hobbled the horses and dug a latrine, while Fourth Platoon stood guard. From the other side of the creek, I heard galloping hoofs. A uniformed soldier approached at full speed until he saw our posted sentry. Slowing, he waited. Neither Noah nor Reuben knew what to do. Finally, the rider asked if we were the Milton Guards. When confirmed, he asked for me.

"If I'm the one you want," I shouted, "there's no sense getting wet."

"Captain Yardley?"

"Yes."

"I'll cross—not returning to Richmond tonight."

"Be careful. We lost a horse in that current."

He urged his gelding into the stream, one step at a time. Dismounting, he looked at me. "If you don't remember, I'm Colonel England's aide."

"I remember."

"You married a helluva woman."

Panic poured down my spine. "She all right?"

"Fine. Major Remington is dead."

"What?"

"Mrs. Yardley shot him through the heart. He and a friend came gallivanting to their hotel and made advances. When he wouldn't back off, she shot him." I felt relief and anger. "Captain Yardley, your wife and Mrs. Stith have boarded with Doctor and Mrs. Branner. They met at the hotel. Both women feel safe and will train to nurse the wounded."

"She is a helluva woman," I said.
"Why do your men stand guard?" he asked.
"Discipline."

Chapter 67

Alexander Frey

The Merchant of Orleans embarked a day late, but sailed through the Keys in good fashion. With three masts, it captured a stiff breeze eastward. Never having seen such a vessel, Beatrice expressed fascination, spending hours walking the deck, gazing over the rail.

The ship, laden with cotton and tobacco, cut through the gulf waters into the Caribbean. Captain Emmett Foster hoped to accomplish the crossing in three weeks. Due to the bombing of Fort Sumter, he planned to sail southeast between Puerto Rico and Cuba, eastward to the Canaries, and north to England. From what he knew, Yankee warships remained stationed off the east coast waiting for cargo vessels. As yet, the Yankees had not prevented shipping from leaving New Orleans.

Striking into the Atlantic, Beatrice felt challenged. Twice a day she became ill. Though no storms appeared, the seas rolled, upsetting her stomach.

"Maybe you're pregnant," I said in jest.

Holding the rail, her eyes widened. "I hope so."

After a sleepless night, she sat in our cabin. "A pregnancy would give this sickness meaning."

The thought of a child enamored me. Considering her age, I realized parenthood a possibility. "Might your breasts be tender?" I asked.

She wept. "They hurt constantly. I feel bloated." In the jar next to the bed, she wretched.

"Forgive me," I said, embracing her, caressing her back.

"Time will tell," she said.

"Maybe it's both. Maybe you're pregnant and seasick."

"At times, I want to eat, and at times I have no appetite. Right now, I need fresh air."

Dressed in nightclothes and wrapped in a blanket, I led her to the deck near the bow. The sun peeked over the horizon, a godlike fiery ball demanding attention.

"God," I prayed as I held her, "please keep us safe, and please relieve Beatrice, and if you mean to bless us with a child, please see her through this time. Amen."

"I've never before heard a prayer from one's heart," she said. "Along with the breeze, I feel God's love and my husband's."

"Enjoying the morning?" a voice asked. It was Captain Foster. We both jumped. "Didn't mean to intrude. The bow is my favorite place in the morning when I sail eastward."

"We enjoy the beauty," Beatrice said. "However, I have felt sick the past four days."

"Your eyes are set deep. I'll have a porter serve you juices." He walked away. Before we regained eye contact, a galley slave came toward us carrying two pitchers and two glasses. Without a word, he placed them on a table and backed away. I poured water and orange juice, presenting them to my wife. She opted for water. Sipping, she turned her attention to the ocean and the myriad of glistening whitecaps stretching to the horizon.

"I'll try some juice," she said, seated at the table. Handing it to her, I saw in the morning light how dreadful she looked.

Taking a seat, I peered first at the Sun and then at her. "Something burdens me."

"Well, your son-in-law is on his way to war; your daughter is pining over his absence; and your wife is helplessly sick, not to mention, you stand at the axis of this war. No one else sails to England to collect funds for the cause." I shook my head. "You have reason to feel burdened." She stood, pulling the blanket around her. "Thank you for being my husband." She kissed me until I returned the kiss.

Chapter 68

Amy Yardley

Richmond's hospital stood four stories high surrounded by spreading oak and maple trees. During our first hour, Doctor Branner introduced us to every doctor and nurse we encountered. At nine thirty, he ushered us into a classroom where we met Doctor Perry Littlejohn.

"Doctor Branner told me your plans yesterday at church," he said. "Three ladies will join us. Until they do, please share your backgrounds." We went through the same routine we gave the Branners Sunday afternoon. Stephanie's widowhood drew his attention.

As the other three students arrived, Doctor Branner excused himself. Settling into a desk, I felt happiness for Stephanie. The more I studied Doctor Littlejohn, the more handsome he grew. His actions declared attraction for Stephanie.

His presentation about wounds and tending them captivated me. "You will see bullet holes, amputations, burns, and broken bones attended on the battlefield. To prevent infection, we must keep wounds cleansed, which is easier said than done. Soldiers fall in fields and woods where dirt and mud cake open abrasions. If you have nerve and stomach, I will show you a tended wound to give you a mental image. When war comes, you will have opportunity to view infected wounds. What do you say? Are you up to it?"

One woman spoke. "How might we tend wounds if we can't look at them?"

"Well then, let's go."

Exiting the classroom, he led us through one hallway after another until we reached a door with a sign that read, Morgue Staff. Seeing the inscription, I felt queasy, but mustered courage. In the room, two men tended a body lying on a wooden table. As we approached, Stephanie saw first that it was Major Remington, naked from the waist up. A dark, blood-stained hole presented itself to the left of his breastbone. I gasped. Doctor Littlejohn turned to me.

Stephanie took charge. "Gentlemen," she said, "are you familiar with the circumstances under which this man died?"

"Yes," Doctor Littlejohn replied, "He made an unwanted advance toward a young lady who carried a pistol. She shot him."

"Correct—that young lady is Amy Yardley."

Doctor Littlejohn gasped. "Oh, dear—are you all right?"

"Yes, though, I would like fresh air." Stephanie and one man led me to an outside door where I stood collecting my thoughts and emotions. "I want to go back."

"Are you certain?" Stephanie asked.

With a nod, I turned and opened the door. Approaching the table, I took a place in full view of my dead assailant. "May I clean the wound?"

"Why yes," Doctor Littlejohn replied. "There's nothing like getting back on a horse after one falls off." He handed me a cloth and water basin. Dampening the rag, I wiped the outside and inside of the wound.

"Be careful," the doctor said. "If you poked a cloth that deeply into the wound of someone living, the pain would kill him."

Stephanie watched, appearing as if she wanted nothing to do with either Major Remington or his wound. However, Doctor Littlejohn wanted something to do with her.

After class, the doctor dismissed the five of us and departed for his noon meal asking us to return by two o'clock.

Mary Ruth Sessions knew of a café a short distance away. We walked in the noon heat. Entering the front door, we saw Doctor Branner and Doctor Littlejohn seated in a corner.

"It will be good for the five of us to get to know each other," I said, as a waiter seated us.

"How long have you been a widow?" Mary Ruth asked Stephanie.

"A month," I replied. "To use your analogy, Mrs. Stith, the doctor admires your face."

"Funny," Stephanie said. "Doctor Branner looks us up and down from head to toe."

"Maybe," I said, "but he can only look." The others laughed.

"Do they know we're talking about them?" Patricia Ann Cummings asked.

"No," Stephanie said. "Men believe women incapable of dialogue and original thought. Most women do all in their power to create that image. The day will come when that will change." She turned and stared at Doctor Littlejohn who stared at her. His smile faded. "See what I mean? Stare them down. They crumple like a piece of paper." A nervous laughter circled our table.

"How will you face him in the classroom?" Celeste asked.

"The question is how will he face me?"

Chapter 69

George Yardley

"Have you named that horse?" I asked Nathaniel. We rode up a rise south of Fredericksburg.

"Winsome the Second."

"Original," I said, looking back as we topped the hill. "This would be a helluva place to surround an enemy. You could control everything from this hilltop."

Nathaniel turned to look. "Maybe so—if battle takes place here, let's remember to claim the high ground."

Riding on, I asked Nathaniel how he thought his first night on guard duty went. His response was positive; but, he was certain it would get old. "Besides," he said, "battles don't take place at night—they take place during the day. The men will question the necessity."

"Nothing to prevent a Yankee from slipping into camp and slitting a few throats."

"Maybe not, but we're fighting Yankees, not Indians. Don't confuse your enemies." Nathaniel hesitated. "An Indian could slip into a camp. A Yankee couldn't slip into his pants without everyone knowing it."

"Maybe we could."

"What? None of us could slip into our pants without the whole world knowing."

"Tonight," I said, "when everyone's asleep and Third Platoon is on guard, let's see if we can sneak up on them."

"Let's sleep," Nathaniel said. "Besides, what if one of our own men shoots us?"

I hadn't thought about that, which alarmed me. "If you're scared, I'll go myself."

"If you make it into camp unscathed, don't practice throat slitting."

"If I make it, I'll slit your tongue. Then, I won't have to listen to you for the rest of this war."

"Glad we're fighting Yankees and not Indians," Nathaniel said. "They're prone to slit throats, tongues, and something else."

Viewing my maps, the Rappahannock loomed. A railroad bridge spanned the river. It seemed strange that we hadn't encountered Confederate troops.

Crossing the river proved easy. Maneuvering our way around rocks and a few obstacles such as tree limbs, we made it to the other side. Ascending the riverbank, we entered Falmouth, stopping at a general store. The owner offered information I needed. General Beauregard's army had marched south from Stafford Courthouse and west to Warrenton. From there, they planned to camp near Manassas Junction. Word had it the Yankees had inundated that town.

An advance troop of Yankee cavalry had followed Beauregard to Falmouth and turned back having gained the reconnaissance they sought and having spotted us crossing the river. If we had continued north, we might have confronted them. Thankful for the information, I pushed westward toward Warrenton, hoping to make another mile before dark.

Before eating, I gathered the men. "There are Yankees in these parts. We almost bumped into them. They might creep around tonight. Don't go lax. We need you alert. If anything moves, ask for identification. If none is forthcoming, take cover and shoot or," I hesitated, "shoot and take cover. Nathaniel, you and Second Platoon eat first—guard the perimeter. First Platoon take the next watch."

❧❧❧❧

After eating, Nathaniel placed Francis and Calvin on the road behind the camp in the direction from which we traveled and then stationed Jesse and Josiah about fifty yards into the woods to the north. When he returned, he expressed a strange feeling someone should guard the road toward Warrenton. He ordered Tillman and Elijah there. If anyone on guard heard two sharp whistles, it denoted Nathaniel's presence.

"If Yankees come at us from Warrenton, I'll slit the throat of the man who owns the general store," I said.

Taking his musket, Nathaniel made his first round. Heading toward Francis and Calvin, he whistled, hearing like replies. They hadn't seen or heard anything, though they expressed jumpiness. "Good," Nathaniel told them, "stay alert. I'll see you in forty-five minutes unless you scare each other to death." He left walking at a forty-five degree angle into the woods. Again, he whistled twice and heard the response. Jesse and Josiah believed they had something to be anxious about. Smoke filled the air as the breeze blew from the west.

"Someone's nearby," Josiah said.

"We suppose it's General Beauregard's brigade," Jesse said.

"Hope so," Nathaniel said. "I'll check with Tillman and Elijah. They're guarding the road toward Warrenton." He walked another forty-five degree angle toward the road, but came to it before he thought he should. For safety's sake, he whistled twice, but received no response. Cresting a small incline, the smell of smoke strengthened. Three campfires came into view. He whistled again but to no avail.

"Something's wrong," he said upon his return. "What should we do?"

Looking into the darkness, I thought. "If I find Tillman and Elijah asleep, I'll cut an ear off each. Let's go."

We put the Guard on alert and exited the camp walking at a cautious pace. Every so often, Nathaniel whistled but received no response. Then, we saw the campfires.

"What next, Captain?" Nathaniel asked. Before I replied, we heard two whistles. Nathaniel responded. Tillman and Elijah hurried toward us, out of breath.

"What's happening?" I asked. We knelt in the darkness.

"Forty or fifty Yankees camped down there," Tillman said.

"How do you know they're Yankees?"

"They're wearing blue uniforms," Elijah said.

"That doesn't mean anything. Both sides have blue uniforms, and both sides have gray uniforms."

"Well, how do we know who's who?" Elijah asked. "We'll shoot our own side."

We stared over the crest of the hill again trying to pick out anything that would identify the soldiers in the camp.

"How close did you get?" Nathaniel asked Tillman.

"Close—fifteen yards."

"Why didn't you ask where they're from?"

"Let's go," I said. "We'll crawl."

Knowing the blackness hid us, we moved until within earshot of the first fire. About twenty uniformed soldiers sat around on logs and rocks talking and swapping stories. Restless and tired, a few bedded down.

"Don't move," I shouted. "You're dead if you do."

We stood about fifteen feet apart with muskets trained. No one moved. "Where are you from?" I said.

After a hesitation, one responded. "North Carolina."

"How do I know you tell the truth?"

Another stood, pulling a paper from his shirt. "Orders signed by General Lee."

"Walk toward my voice." I turned to Nathaniel. "Read what they say."

"I'm not going in there."

"Cover me," I said. "If anyone twitches, shoot him." I stepped from behind a tree, entering the camp. "Don't you men move or you will be shot." Taking the paper, I held it to the firelight. When finished reading, I stretched out my hand. "I'm Captain George Yardley, Georgia Volunteers, Milton Guards."

"Captain Allen Stewart. You scared us to death."

"Didn't mean to. Why you here with no guard posted?"

"Why would we need one?"

"If we hadn't scared off a Yankee cavalry troop in Falmouth, they'd have found you." The captain grimaced. "We're camped about a quarter mile away. My men smelled your smoke—so we came looking. You're lucky we're friends. You'd best post a guard. Maybe we'll see you in the morning." I turned and walked away.

"Something's wrong," Nathaniel said as I rejoined them.

Wary of my cousin's premonitions, I waited. "What?"

"Don't know." We continued through the darkness. Near camp, Nathaniel whistled twice, drawing two shrill responses.

I decided two platoons should stand guard—one on the road at the crest of the hill and the other surrounding our camp. "Second Platoon—get some sleep," I said. "First and Fourth stand the next watch. I'll take my platoon to the hill." I paused. "Men, this is serious. Do your best."

The night proved long. One by one, the campfires over the hill went out until my platoon stared into blackness. Again, no moon appeared. When the first light of dawn broke, neither did any North Carolina soldiers. They were gone.

Running into camp, I ordered Tim to saddle Splinter and Winsome II. Yelling for Nathaniel, I grabbed venison and biscuits. "Kinchen, keep the Guard here until we return."

"Guess you were right," I said to Nathaniel as we rode through the deserted camp looking for signs and direction.

"Here," Nathaniel said. "Over here—they went into the woods—tracks head north."

"How did they dismantle that camp without us hearing them?"

"We're either deaf, or their horses make less noise than ours."

We followed through the trees. Broken branches and loosened rocks told the story. Suddenly, Nathaniel turned Winsome II, signaling me with his right hand. Having learned not to argue with his instincts, I followed a few yards, waiting for him to speak.

"Counted eight rifles pointed at us at about thirty yards."

Not having seen one, I kept riding. "Trap?"

"Sure enough—few more yards—we'd be dead."

"Before we get back to camp, we have to figure this out. If these are Yankees spies, I believe the store owner misled us. Second, where is General Beauregard—Warrenton or Stafford Courthouse? And third..." Rifle shots reverberated from our camp. We pushed through the woods entering the road where it crested finding the Milton Guards surrounded and taking fire. Six blue uniformed soldiers in front of us fired and reloaded. "Let's take them first," I said. We rode to within fifteen yards, halted and fired our rifles, each downing a soldier. With my revolver, I dropped two more while Nathaniel wounded one. Drawing my sword, I ran and thrust it through the remaining soldier's heart. Seeing movement to my left, I raced, wielding my sword, plunging it into a soldier's neck. The Guard, having formed a perimeter, continued firing, taking turns loading, firing, and reloading. Nathaniel ran toward me, handing me my rifle. Before I drew a bead, a bugle called. The blues ran into the woods, dropping weapons.

"Go after them," I shouted. "Take one alive." Nathaniel and I remounted. "Load your pistols." The guardsmen fanned out through the woods. Tim saddled his horse.

"Let's go," Nathaniel said.

Tim joined us. "Two ran in that direction," he said, pointing to the southeast. We kicked our horses, picking up the trail.

"They can't get far on foot," Nathaniel said.

In front of us stood two boys clad in blue uniforms, with their hands up. "Please don't shoot us," one said.

"We won't as long as you talk," I said. "Tim, get down—tie their hands behind their backs." He did.

From the direction of our camp, two shots reported. "Get them back to camp," I said. "Let's see what the shooting is about." Nathaniel and I rode off leaving Tim alone with the prisoners. Then, from behind us, we heard another shot.

"Oh, God," Nathaniel said. "What have we done?"

Turning, we rode toward where we left Tim. There, we saw Tim's rider-less horse and Tim lying in the leaves.

Nathaniel jumped down. "He's still alive. Looks like a scalp wound."

"Get him to camp. I'll go after the others."

Tim moaned. "There are four."

"Did you hear that?" Nathaniel said. "There are four."

Hesitating, I decided against the chase. "I'll help with Tim."

Laying him across his horse, we walked back. As we came into view, guardsmen ran to help and see what happened.

"Did you capture any?" Nathaniel asked.

"Killed two," Tillman said.

"Wish we'd taken one alive," I said. "Search the woods. Make certain they didn't leave anyone behind."

Men fanned out. Nathaniel tended to Tim, laying him on a cot inside a tent. Tim went in and out of consciousness. Blood clotted and caked the wound on the back of his head.

"I'll get water and heat it," I said. "Mother use to say hot water cleaned better than cold."

At the fire, I watched men saunter into camp. Once the water boiled, I lifted the bucket with a branch, carrying it to the tent. Taking my kerchief, I drenched it, cleaning the wound. Tim lurched and settled. About an inch long slash presented itself across the back of his scalp. Parting his hair, I placed a clean cloth over the wound and tied another strip around his head to hold the first cloth in place. Finished, I heard a commotion. Mac and Green Bruce carried a man in a blue uniform toward the fire. I ran through camp, looking as they dropped their captive to the ground.

"You didn't beat him to death, did you?" I asked.

"No sir. He's alive. Kick him in the ribs—he'll quit playing possum," Green said.

"Do you want a kick?" I said to the man on the ground.

He stirred, rising to all fours. "I'll talk."

"Where you from?"

"Pennsylvania."

"What are you doing here?"

"We're spies—sent to gather information."

"How long you been in Virginia?"

"Last night is all. We rode from Alexandria yesterday."

"Nathaniel, take Second Platoon—ride west. Kinchen, take Third Platoon, head to Falmouth and then to Stafford Courthouse. I want to know where General Beauregard is. If he's in Stafford, we'll hang that general store owner in Falmouth."

"Beauregard is west of here," the prisoner said. "That's who we trailed."

"Makes sense," Nathaniel said.

"Let's find out for ourselves. Get going. Keep your eyes opened. We busted up this pack of spies. They'll move about trying to regroup. Fourth Platoon—take the watch."

"Kinchen," Nathaniel shouted, "if you find Beauregard, return with a doctor. We'll do the same." Kinchen nodded.

"We'll camp here tonight," I said. "Try to return before dark. Now, get going."

Tim floated in and out of consciousness, talking out of his head at times. Never having been in this situation, I did not know what to do. Until a doctor arrived, I chose rest as the remedy. What happens in battle, I questioned, doubting the enemy would care for the wounded or bury them. The prospect of leaving a man on the field dead or wounded nauseated me.

Chapter 70

Amy Yardley

"Pressure," Doctor Littlejohn repeated. "Apply pressure with a cloth to an open, bleeding wound. Count to sixty. Get the feel for this." He folded a cotton cloth four times. When finished, he walked toward me holding out his hand, instructing me to pretend he had been stabbed through his palm. Giving me the cloth, he encouraged the pressure. I took his hand in my left and pressed with my right counting to sixty. Moving from woman to woman, he directed each to press firmer until he came to Stephanie. She, too, took his hand, applying pressure to the point he grimaced. "Ah," he said, pulling his hand away. "For such a slightly-built woman, you exhibit remarkable strength." Again, she eyed him until her gaze turned him away.

Doctor Littlejohn retreated to his lectern. "There is an appropriate amount of pressure," he continued. "Press firmly—check the wound every sixty seconds. The wound will tell you if you have met its needs. If not, it must be cauterized or sewn. Advise the surgeon, and turn the treatment over to him. Are there questions?"

Celeste stood. "Doctor Littlejohn, we are women. What if we encounter a wound near a man's private parts?"

An agony of embarrassment and suppressed laughter emanated. Before he spoke, Stephanie did. "Let him bleed to death," she said, giggling. "Most men would rather die than have us see their 'private parts.'"

"That will be all, Mrs. Stith," Littlejohn said, eyeing her until she turned away. "Miss Browder raises a sensitive issue. Contrary to what Mrs. Stith espoused, the main objective, if presented with such a situation is to do all in your power to save a life. If you develop an attitude wherein you look upon the wounded man as Christ would look upon him and if you care for him as our Lord would so do, you will please God and your patient."

The moment froze. No one responded. No one breathed. The depth of Doctor Littlejohn's teaching and the seriousness of his analogy caused me to contemplate my place in life and my place in serving a wounded soldier.

After class, we walked home. A breeze provided relief from heat and humidity. Extending my left arm, I placed it around Stephanie. "You miss Drury, don't you?"

A tear streamed down her cheek. "More than I can say."

"Dr. Littlejohn is lucky I didn't shoot him through the heart after he accosted you."

"Not his fault—I had that coming. Don't be hard on him."

"Do you having feelings toward him?"

"No—I have no heart to give except a heart of grieving."

"If George had died in my arms as Drury died in yours, I wouldn't have strength to do what you do. I wouldn't have strength to go on."

"You are my strength. May I never have to be yours."

We completed our walk, arriving as Doctor Branner stepped from his carriage. We stood on the porch discussing the lessons. Mrs. Branner appeared with a telegram from Sarah. All was well, but she missed me and hoped my return imminent. Knowing that impossible, I excused myself, proceeding to the bedroom. For the next hour, I wrote describing everything that happened, including the incident with Major Remington. I finished by expressing my hope to remain in Richmond throughout the war, serving as a nurse.

Chapter 71

Alexander Frey

By Wednesday, Beatrice knew she was pregnant. Her breasts enlarged and ached. Even though the sickness ceased during the night allowing her to sleep, illness overcame her each afternoon. No matter what she ate, it came up.

"Captain," I said, "please forgive me for the intrusion."

Sitting at his desk, searching maps with a magnifying glass, he looked up. "No forgiveness necessary. How is Mrs. Frey?"

"Pregnant—she needs privacy."

"Do you wish for a boy or girl?"

"I have a grown daughter—a son might be nice, but more than anything—I desire comfort for my wife."

"If all goes well, she will step onto land in two weeks—if not sooner."

"Thank you—that information will provide peace of mind."

Chapter 72

George Yardley

Nathaniel and his Second Platoon returned, having made it to Warrenton and back without finding General Beauregard. The journey took five hours.

"Why aren't we seeing more troops?" Nathaniel asked, sitting on his cot.

"Don't know—we may fight this war by ourselves if no one else shows up."

"Maybe Kinchen found something."

"I hope—be better than something finding us."

Nathaniel faded off to sleep. He awoke to a commotion as did I. Kinchen returned with a blue-uniformed soldier, Doctor William McAllister, who carried a black bag. Nathaniel and I followed him into Tim's tent.

McAllister bent down, separated Tim's hair, and studied the wound. "Concussion—ball cracked his skull. He'll live. Keep him awake the best you can. Every hour walk him around camp whether he wants to or not."

"Let's start now," I said. "He hasn't stood since the shooting."

Looking outside, I yelled for Jimmy Smith and Randolph Loy. For the next fifteen minutes, much to Tim's dismay, they goaded him to walk. As I looked on, I decided the doctor meant to either kill him or cure him. By the looks of Tim, I considered digging a grave.

Fourth Platoon prepared the evening meal, which the doctor and six additional soldiers, who accompanied him, also ate. A husky sergeant from Petersburg, Alton Peerce, sat near me.

"Have you had conversations with the owner of the general store in Falmouth?" I asked.

"You mean Mr. Speakes?" Peerce said.

"Don't know his name. I'm suspicious."

"What? He wouldn't hurt a flea."

"He sent us in this direction after telling us General Beauregard headed to Warrenton. If we hadn't stopped to make camp, we'd have ridden into a covey of Yankees in broad daylight. He's either a spy or a Yankee sympathizer."

"Damn—that makes sense. He makes two trips to Alexandria each week for supplies and goods—gone overnight. When he returns, he never has enough in his wagon to have made the trip worthwhile. He's the one telling the Yankees what's happening here, and where we are."

"What should we do?" the doctor asked.

"Nathaniel and I might follow him the next time he makes a trip. No sense giving the Yankees free information."

Nathaniel sat, staring at me. "If anyone would like to go in my place, I'd be honored."

"I'll go," the doctor said.

Nathaniel stood. "Deal."

"No deal. I didn't ask you to consider the matter."

"That's how I want to end my life—following a spy into enemy territory. Doc, why don't you cut my heart out? That way, I could have a proper burial. If I go, they'll either kill me, or I'll die in a dank prison."

A silence ensued until Sergeant Peerce turned to me. "Take him with you. We won't have to listen to his babbling."

Mild laughter circled the campfire, silenced by the sight of Tim walking from his tent.

"Going to be a helluva war," the doctor said. "Right now, soldiers on each side wear both colors, blue and gray. If we don't decide who wears what color, we'll shoot our own."

Nathaniel kicked a rock. "We won't know who to shoot."

"Do us a favor," Peerce said. "Start with yourself."

∽❧❦❧∼

We arrived in Stafford Courthouse at noon having retraced our way to Falmouth and then to our destination. Doctor William McAllister had taken to Nathaniel and me. As the Guard made camp on the brigade's western periphery, Captain McAllister sought me out. We sat on two benches in front of my tent. "I'm heading to Richmond," he said. "Word has it the brigade will march toward Warrenton and Manassas Junction. If all goes well, you should arrive by the fifteenth of July."

"You've been ordered to Richmond?" I asked, paying attention to the spectrum of soldiers before me.

"We've trained field nurses at the medical college. I am to oversee them—set up a field hospital at Haymarket, west of Manassas. I'll collect the nurses—bring them north."

"Could I accompany you?"

"Doubtful," he said. "Word spread here about your arrival. Seems some make you out a hero already. There's talk you took a ball at Sumter and led a fight in Cherokee. Sergeant Peerce tells everyone about you taking on those Yankees the other night. You have more war experience than this entire brigade."

"We're in sad shape if that's the case."

"We're in sad shape, regardless. Soldiers harden in battle. You hope to not lose the war while recruits learn. The Yankees are in the same stead. Their soldiers have never fought."

Nathaniel strolled across camp holding a paper. "What's the matter?" I asked.

"Two things. Speakes rode by in a buckboard, and here's a telegram from Amy."

"Did you read this?"

"Only the part where she says she loves me more than you." I read and looked up.

"Is she all right?" McAllister asked.

"Yes. She's in Richmond, and she's the reason I want to go with you. Be nice to see her before we fight. I'm heading to Alexandria."

Nathaniel kicked the ground. "Be glad to stay here."

"We're going—get saddled."

"Did you tell anybody—like your commanding officer— what you're doing?" Doctor McAllister asked.

"Don't have a commanding officer yet. If we get out of here, I won't have to explain. Something about Speakes I don't like."

Nathaniel hurried to the corral. With Josiah's help, he saddled the horses.

"What's your rush? You seem willing to go all of a sudden." I asked him.

"We have to talk. Let's go." He mounted Winsome II. Josiah held Splinter's reins waiting for me to mount. "Didn't change your mind, did you?" Nathaniel asked.

"No." I watched Nathaniel gallop toward the Richmond Road. "What's wrong with him?" I asked Josiah.

"Don't know—something's got him. If you don't hurry, he'll get to Alexandria before you depart camp."

Kicking Splinter, I rode off. Heads turned as we passed through camp. Nathaniel slowed, allowing me to catch him. "What's wrong?" I asked.

"What's wrong? We're the only troops ready to fight in the entire brigade. Overheard the officer corps plans to hold us out of battle because of Savannah. Nobody wants to fight with us."

"What?"

"It's all over camp. Word spread before we arrived."

"What else?"

Nathaniel hesitated. "Amy killing Major Remington hasn't helped."

"What?"

"I'm telling you, it's all over camp. Two companies followed us north. They're the ones with the information. They arrived yesterday while we tried to find Beauregard. No one likes you or your wife."

"Should have beaten the bastard to death."

"Something else—Amy and Stephanie board with a Doctor Branner. He arranged for them to take classes to become field nurses."

"Huh. Doctor McAllister heads to Richmond tomorrow to bring field nurses north to set up a field hospital."

"You think it's important to follow Speakes?"

"Yep—spies in our midst make it hard to win a war. If we find he's trading secrets rather than trading goods, I'll kill him." Nathaniel didn't respond. "Pick up our pace." We shook the reins. In less than an hour, we saw the buckboard crossing Aquia Creek.

"There's something wrong," I said. "At the rate he's going, he can't make Alexandria and return in two days." Nathaniel nodded.

Riding over what my map called Dumfries Hill, we saw the houses of a peaceful hamlet. In front of a sign that read Livery, Mr. Speakes stopped and uncovered his buckboard. Two men joined him. We waited in the woods about a hundred yards away. The men unloaded the buckboard, carrying the contents inside. They returned with two items they placed in the buckboard. After they covered them, they entered a house across the road.

"We're in for a long night," Nathaniel said.

"Maybe not. Look—isn't that an inn?" Nathaniel nodded. "Let's see if we can get a room and a meal."

The innkeeper, a jolly old man whose family owned the hotel since the Revolutionary War, greeted us. A large sitting room to the left of the entrance, accompanied by an even larger dining room to the right, appeared more than comfortable.

"What kind of money you got?" he asked from the sitting room.

"Both kinds—U.S. and Confederate," Nathaniel said. "Which would you like?"

"U.S., but I take Confederate."

"How much for the room?" I said.

"Room? Do you mean rooms? Only one bed per room."

"How much for each room?"

"One dollar a night U.S. Two dollars, Confederate."

"That seems steep," Nathaniel said. "Does that include supper and breakfast?"

"No sir—each meal is fifty cents."

"U. S. or Confederate?"

"Either, but the price includes the livery tending your horses."

"Here," I said, retrieving a wad of U. S. money from my belt. Peeling off four dollars, I handed it over. "What time can we eat?"

"Mrs. Cato will prepare your meal in an hour."

Mr. Cato directed us to our rooms. "George Washington stayed here many times."

"Well, I'm George Washington Yardley—named after President Washington. That won't get us a better rate, will it?"

"No sir. Your name doesn't matter or who you're named after—rate's the same for everybody." At the top of the stairs, Mr. Cato opened two doors, lit candles, and let us in. "See you in an hour."

"Wake me when it's time," Nathaniel said as he closed his door.

"Why don't you wake me?" I went inside, noticed paper, ink, and pen on a desk, and wrote.

My Dearest Amy,

I received your telegram, thankful you wrote. Nathaniel and I are in Dumfries, Virginia, chasing down a Union spy. We received word you accidentally shot and killed Major Remington. It

*grieves me I left the job to you, but am glad you took
care of yourself. I hope the incident has not caused
you distress.*

*Nathaniel also learned that you and Stephanie are
taking nursing classes. We met a doctor, William
McAllister. He has been assigned to bring field nurses
from Richmond to Haymarket to set up a hospital.
Hope you are one of those nurses.*

*Talk has it that the first battle will be near Manassas
Junction. If that is the case, Haymarket is near there
and will serve as the place where the wounded are
taken. You may have your hands full.*

*Nathaniel and I will return to Stafford tomorrow
and receive our orders. I imagine we will head
to Warrenton and then to Manassas. I will do
everything in my power to find you.*
I am,

Very Truly Yours,
George

I had no more than finished the letter, when I realized
Nathaniel and I had failed to discuss a matter. Folding the paper, I
addressed an envelope to Amy in care of the Branners. A moment
later, I tapped on Nathaniel's door.

"An hour hasn't passed," he said, opening the door.

"We have to talk. You think the higher-ups won't let the
Guard fight?"

He let me in and closed the door. "That's what I heard."

"If that's the case, then so be it. A time will come when they'll
need us."

Nathaniel reopened the door. "Let's go to supper."

The staircase creaked with each step.

"Come in, and have a seat," Mr. Cato said. "Would you like
a drink?"

Nathaniel nodded. "I'll have a beer, as will my cousin."

About to protest, I thought better, surmising if Nathaniel wanted a beer I ought to permit it. Mr. Cato returned from the kitchen with two steins, explaining they were gifts from a German duke who stayed at the hotel. "Please take care not to break them."

As Nathaniel took his first sip, the front door opened. Three men entered. One was Speakes. Each carried holstered carbines. Mr. Cato rushed to the foyer, greeting them. Making eye contact with Nathaniel, Speakes turned as Mr. Cato ushered the men into the dining room.

"Mr. Yardley and Mr. Thomas," Mr. Cato said, "Please meet Mr. Hezekiah Wills and Mr. Noel Drinkard, residents of our fine town." We exchanged courtesies. "And, Mr. Samuel Speakes of Falmouth." Speakes didn't seem to remember us. He walked around the table taking a place next to me while the others seated themselves next to Nathaniel. Mr. Cato appeared with three more steins, taking a seat at the head of the table.

"Where you men from?" Hezekiah asked.

"Nowhere in particular," I said. "We drift around waiting for war to break out."

"Well, war broke out," Wills said. "Have you not heard about Fort Sumter?"

Lifting my stein, I eyed him. "I mean a land battle. That was a bombardment. No lives lost, and none wounded."

"True," he answered, "but it was a battle waged by southern insurrectionists against the Union."

"By that remark, I surmise you have Union leanings," Nathaniel said.

"True," Drinkard said. "We oppose secession and oppose the dissolution of the Union."

"How do you stand on the issue of slavery?" I asked.

"We're opposed to that barbaric institution," Hezekiah said, sipping his beer.

"Do you see a peaceful solution?"

"Certainly," Drinkard said. "Set the slaves free. It's that simple."

"So the southern plantation owner exacts the financial loss?"

"He bought the slaves—made his fortune on slave labor—he should bear the cost," Hezekiah said, raising his stein and his voice.

"And all the Yankee traders who stole the slaves in Africa, and shipped them here to sell—their fortunes remain intact?"

"They did what they did because of economic demand," Drinkard explained.

Mrs. Cato entered from the kitchen carrying a tray holding a bowl of carrots, a bowl of green beans, and a serving platter of beef. Returning again from the kitchen, she placed a basket of biscuits on the table, then vanished. For the next few moments, we passed food, including butter and strawberry jam.

"Hope I have the opportunity to compliment Mrs. Cato," Nathaniel said to Mr. Cato.

"She'll return when we complete the meal."

Nathaniel ate faster than normal. After consuming his biscuit and jam, he excused himself. "Had a tough day in the saddle. If it's all the same, I'll lean against the wall and stretch a bit." He rose before Mr. Cato gave permission, standing against the doorjamb at the entrance to the dining room. Whatever sixth sense Nathaniel had, I realized he felt trouble.

"We must maintain the Union," Hezekiah said. "Though too old to fight, we serve through other methods."

"What methods?"

"Information," Mr. Speakes said.

"Information? Spying?"

"That's an unfortunate term; but, it describes our position," Drinkard said. "And that is why we're here tonight."

Before his words settled, I sensed they served as a signal. Two men burst through the kitchen door with guns drawn. The other four men at the table stood and except for Mr. Cato, drew guns. Nathaniel darted to the other side of the entrance gaining cover.

Suddenly, the front door opened. Two armed men stepped in. Not expecting Nathaniel to be in the parlor, they turned toward the dining room. Nathaniel shot both, causing one to fall across the table. In the commotion, I drew my gun and fell to the floor, aiming and shooting the two men from the kitchen. Hezekiah fired toward Nathaniel. From under the table, I shouted for everyone to stop.

"Put your guns on the table," Nathaniel said, "or I'll shoot."

An acknowledgement exchanged between the four remaining men resulted in the surrender of their weapons, which they placed on the table. Two downed men groaned, one pleaded for help.

"George, you can come out now," Nathaniel said.

Standing, I eyed Speakes with an anger surpassing how I felt about Andrew Shelton and Ely Remington. "Collect their guns," I said.

Nathaniel gathered each weapon, including those on the floor. When he finished, he turned to Speakes. "This is fair warning. I've never shot a man in cold blood; but, I'll do so if you return to Falmouth." He hesitated. "If you return to Falmouth, I'll hang you."

Pointing my gun at Cato, I cocked it. "We're heading to the livery for our horses. We better not see any movement here or I'll burn the livery. Do you understand?" They neither spoke nor nodded, but glared. We backed out the door, running down the street, carrying a basket of guns. Crossing a creek, I threw the guns in the water.

"Why'd you do that?" Nathaniel asked. "We could use them."

"Don't know—just did."

At the livery, we found the door locked. Nathaniel aimed and shot the lock. Sliding the door open, I lit a lantern, revealing Splinter and Winsome II in stalls. We saddled and mounted. Nathaniel exited, leaving me inside. I opened two stalls chasing the other horses outside. From the lantern, I dripped kerosene on the straw, igniting it. In the darkness, I did the same to Speakes' buckboard after which I threw the lantern inside the livery. Flames erupted, streaking across the floor. We raced south as the livery and wagon burned. A new moon rose. I hoped Amy saw it.

Chapter 73

Amy Yardley

Stephanie and I walked into class, taking our seats, realizing a second person stood before us. Once settled, Doctor Littlejohn introduced Doctor William McAllister.

Upon hearing my name, he smiled. "Mrs. Yardley, are you married to Captain George Yardley?"

"Yes, sir," I said, returning a smile. "Why do you ask?"

"I had the pleasure of spending time with the Milton Guards two nights ago. Your husband impressed his superior officers. His company broke up a Yankee spy unit."

"Where is he now?"

"Hard to say. He and his cousin followed a civilian shopkeeper whom they considered a spy." He hesitated. "That's not accurate. His cousin opposed the venture. George refuted the protest. They can take care of themselves."

"Agreed—as long as they're together, I'm happy."

"Very astute," Doctor McAllister said.

Doctor Littlejohn cleared his throat. "We have a matter to discuss." He waited, gaining our attention. "General Beauregard ordered Doctor McAllister to establish a field hospital in

Haymarket, Virginia. Ladies, who amongst you would consider serving there? If you agree, you must depart in the morning."

"I'll go," I said. Stephanie and the others gave positive responses.

"Fine," Doctor McAllister said. "Be here at seven o'clock. If possible, bring two changes of clothing along with comfortable shoes. Nurses practice on their feet."

"Realizing you must make preparations," Doctor Littlejohn said, "you are dismissed for the day." We stood encouraging each other while the two doctors talked. I gravitated toward Doctor McAllister.

"If I had my choice," he said, "I'd give up medicine and fight with your husband." He stared behind me. "This must be Mrs. Stith. Would you allow me to treat you both to coffee?"

"Certainly," I replied, realizing he admired Stephanie. "Shall we go to the shop where we eat lunch?"

"Yes," Stephanie said. I led the way from the classroom down the hall out to Broad Street. Once seated in the cafe, the talk turned serious.

"What occurred with regard to you and your husband in Savannah?" Doctor McAllister asked. "It causes consternation among our soldiers."

"Evidently, you know what happened. However, let it suffice to say that some find caring for Negro slaves in a Christian manner objectionable. In case you have not heard, my husband and a Major Remington fought over the matter. Major Remington and a friend made unwanted overtures toward Mrs. Stith and me, which resulted in me accidentally shooting him."

"You killed Major Remington?"

"Yes," Stephanie said.

"Where are you from?" I asked Doctor McAllister.

"Woodstock, Virginia—a town in the Shenandoah Valley. I grew up on a farm my father and I tended while Mother taught school. When sixteen, I was sent to Richmond to study science."

"Where are your parents now?" I asked. "Are they living?"

"Yes—they bought a grain mill in Edinburg where they work with my two sisters. My father farms; but, the mill takes most of his time." He paused. "Mrs. Yardley, how did your husband become such a fine soldier?"

"It seems it's in his blood. He grew up farming and doing leatherwork."

"Well, in the soldiering I've seen, no one commands the respect of his men more than he. They listen and obey. They would ride into the jaws of death if he gave the order."

"I know," I said, feeling my voice weaken. "I pray those jaws never open, because he would do his duty and lead the charge."

"Is that why you love him?"

"I love him because I can't have him. He belongs to someone else or somewhere else. It is as if God loaned him to me. Whatever must be done, he will do, and God help the person who stands in his way." Pausing, I allowed my words to take root. "I do love him. I love him with all my heart; but, I don't own him." Turning toward a window, I wondered why these thoughts flowed forth to a stranger. Stephanie took my hand.

"Have I upset you," Doctor McAllister said.

"It upsets me to think this war might take him before..."

"Before what?" Stephanie asked. I shook my head unable to speak.

"Maybe we should go," Doctor McAllister said. "You have a lot to do before tomorrow morning." Standing, we moved outside while William McAllister paid the bill.

We walked a city block, parting at a cross street. Stephanie and I strolled home. Upon arriving, we found Mrs. Branner watering potted flowers on the front porch. Stephanie explained the morning's events and the urgency of our departure. Sadness overcame our hostess.

"I heard," Doctor Branner said, walking up the steps behind us. "I tried to get here to forewarn my wife. Let's have a drink. Then I'll take us to the hotel for a parting dinner."

Chapter 74

George Yardley

As we crested the Dumfries hill, the glow from the burning stable ceased, leaving us in darkness. For the first time, I felt what it meant to be in a strange land.

"We gonna ride all night?" Nathaniel asked. I didn't answer. "Maybe you didn't hear," he shouted. "Will we ride all night?"

"Don't know—can't believe I wasted six dollars."

"We're lucky we're alive, and you're worried about six dollars? Why don't you ride back to that inn? Maybe happy-go-lucky Mr. Cato will give you a refund."

"That's not what I mean. I should have paid in the morning."

"Remember that the next time eight men jump us in a hotel. I saved your life. You haven't offered one word of gratitude."

Chapter 75

George Yardley

"What is your business?" The lieutenant asked.

"I need to see General Beauregard."

"Doesn't everybody? Half his brigade wants to see him."

My head bowed, not wanting to hear foolishness. "I want to report about Yankee spying. My sergeant and I killed and wounded four spies last night in Dumfries and broke up an entire military company the night before."

"I heard it was the Milton Guards," a voice said. Still on Splinter, I turned seeing a large bellicose man. "I am General Beauregard. What is this business about spies?"

"Captain George Yardley, Milton Guards," I said, dismounting. I explained what transpired. Consternation swept over the general's face. Turning to the lieutenant, he ordered him to take a platoon and burn the general store in Falmouth. Then, turning to me, he congratulated me except for one thing—the four men I let live in Dumfries.

"A spy is a spy, and a traitor is a traitor," General Beauregard said. "If one crosses your path, take his life."

"Yes, sir," I said, remounting Splinter.

"Fine looking horse," the general said. "You are assigned to the Black Horse Cavalry?"

"Yes, we arrived yesterday. I must find my commanding officer."

"See Captain Rabun or Captain Mosby."

৵৵৵৵৵৵

Captain Rabun found me and attached the Guard to his company. Third Platoon packed the buckboard and cannon. Every member of the Guard, including Nathaniel, stood next to his saddled horse prepared to depart. To the contrary, not one of the thousands of men surrounding us appeared ready. A lack of discipline and direction presented itself. Fires burned; tents stood partially collapsed; frustrations exuded from every corner of camp.

"Mount up," I ordered. In unison, twenty-five horse soldiers did so, along with Tim and Josiah, who climbed onto the buckboard. "Milton Guards, forward." With me leading First Platoon, we rode through camp drawing the attention of those we passed.

"Not sure why we're doing this," Nathaniel said, having approached me. "How do we know what to do when we reach Warrenton?"

"We'll do what every soldier does when day turns to dusk. We'll make camp."

"That's good to know. I hope to remember that wisdom for as long as we fight this war. If you keep riding off ahead of everyone, we'll fight alone. Doubt we'll last long."

I paid him no mind, but took in every word, marveling at how Nathaniel grew in wisdom and knowledge, not to mention in his ability to sense a situation and respond to it.

About four o'clock, we reached the outskirts of Warrenton. Coming to a large, white plantation house, I directed Nathaniel to request permission to camp in their pasture.

"What if I receive a denial?"

"Shoot them and burn the house down."

In a few moments, he returned accompanied by a middle-aged man and four boys ranging in age from about ten to eighteen. "I prefer you not use our pasture," the man said. "Won't prevent you. We believe Christianity decries war. We're opposed to slavery and don't own any."

"I feel the same, but don't cotton to the federal government telling me what to do."

"According to Paul's letter to the Romans, our leaders are God ordained and we are to obey them," he said.

"The problem stems from whether you believe federal office holders or state office holders are in charge. I take it you subscribe to federalist control?"

"Correct," the man said. I noticed disgruntled feelings in the two older boys regarding their father's position, but left the matter alone.

"Anyone up the road who might open their pasture to us?"

"Yes, the Gregorys hold your sentiments. They own the next plantation."

"We'll respect your wishes; but, thousands of troops march behind us."

"Thanks for the information."

"Virginia isn't much different from Georgia," Nathaniel said as he remounted. "People disagree no matter what state they're from." We made camp. The rains came.

Chapter 76

Amy Yardley

Amidst the lightning flashes and thunderclaps, a Confederate Army division with five women and a doctor made camp southeast of Warrenton. One lantern illuminated the canvas under which we huddled. The storm proved so loud we couldn't hear each other.

The tent flap opened. Doctor McAllister entered drenched to the skin. "Two of you come with me. A soldier shot his hand. The bullet lodged in the shoulder of another."

Startled, paralyzed, we peered at each other. The realization we had to go out in the weather set in. I stood along with Celeste. Taking blankets, we covered our heads and followed Doctor McAllister. Slipping and sliding in mud, he walked in between us holding our arms. A lighted tent appeared. The rain subsided as we went to work. "Miss Browder, tend to the man lying to the left." A soldier curled up on a cot clamped his hands between his legs. "Wash the wound and bandage it."

Waiting, I noticed another man lying on his back with blood emanating around his left collarbone. "What do you want me to do?"

Four soldiers entered the tent. Doctor McAllister pointed at two, ordering them to help me remove his shirt. As we moved him, he screamed.

"Cut the shirt off," the doctor ordered. Taking shears from his bag, I cut the cloth. Nearing his neck with the points, I prayed he wouldn't jump. The wound revealed itself. One soldier became ill and ran outside. "Clean it," the doctor said as he took the lantern and sterilized his knives and tweezers. When I removed the dried blood, I saw where the bullet entered and the red fleshy hole it made. Applying pressure, I hoped to stop the bleeding. Having counted to sixty, I removed the cloth. The soldier coughed, splattering blood on my face and neck.

"God," McAllister said, "the bullet penetrated his esophagus." He had no more than spoken, when a stream of blood poured from the soldier's mouth followed by gurgling—a sound I never forgot—the sound of death. He lurched, convulsed, and expired. McAllister stepped forward covering the soldier's face with a blanket. Taking a cotton cloth from his medical bag, he dipped it in a basin of water beside the bed and washed the blood from my face. All the while, Celeste cared for the other man.

The rain storm passed. In the distance, a faint thunder clap rumbled. Doctor McAllister ordered the soldiers to find a suitable place for the wounded man to sleep and to leave the dead man until morning when we would bury him. The doctor escorted Celeste and me to our tents.

Outside, Stephanie, Patricia Ann and Mary Ruth begged for information. "One lived and one died," I said.

Chapter 77

George Yardley

The Guard broke camp by mid-morning. As we rode north toward Manassas, two horsemen appeared behind us.

"Let's see who they are," I said to Nathaniel and Tim. When the intruders spotted us, they stilled their horses. Two brothers from the previous day introduced themselves.

"We want to fight," the eldest said. "Would you allow us to enlist with you? If you don't, we'll find another cavalry unit."

In disbelief, I noticed each carried a single shot rifle, pistol, and a couple pouches of lead and powder. "Either of you ever shot one of those things?"

The younger removed his pistol from the holster, aimed at a pinecone hanging on a tree to the side of the road, and blew it away.

"Phew," Nathaniel said. "Guess so."

"We can shoot straight," he said, holstering his gun. "What's your decision?"

"You boys made up your mind, right?" I asked.

"You either want us, or you don't," the older said. "We're wasting time. When our father realizes we're not tending to chores, he'll come after us."

"What'll he do if he finds you?" Nathaniel asked.

"If this interrogation lasts much longer, we'll find out."

"I like them" Nathaniel said. "Come along—we'll see what happens." We rode to where the Guard waited. Before we approached, Nathaniel asked their names.

"Rex and Bartholomew Snyder," Rex said.

"These boys are new recruits," Nathaniel said. "This is Rex, and this is Bart. They've joined Second Platoon."

"Why do you get them?" I asked.

"I invited them. Besides, they like me better than you." He snickered. "Don't you boys?"

"Well," Rex said, "I do like you better." Most of the Guard chuckled.

"You two will fit in fine," Nathaniel said. "Everyone likes me better."

When the laughter subsided, we rode a while until Bartholomew spoke. "The Yankees have surrounded Manassas?"

"How do you know?"

"Pa and me scouted around a week ago. Those bluecoats came to town like bees to a new hive. If you ride about ten miles, you'll stir them up and not have enough help."

"We'll wait for Beauregard," I said. "No sense letting them take us prisoner before the battle starts." We made camp in a pasture along a creek and waited for two days.

Chapter 78

Amy Yardley

By July twelfth, Beauregard's Regiment, including the Black Horse Cavalry, had encamped at Manassas Junction. Thousands of Confederate soldiers lined an eight-mile stretch along Bull Run Creek, while Federal troops held positions around Manassas. The waiting began.

Near Haymarket, Doctor McAllister and his five field nurses established their hospital. Five tents, each holding eight cots, stood in a neat row. In due time, one nurse was assigned to each tent. Mary's tent would treat head wounds; Stephanie's abdominal wounds; Celeste's leg wounds and amputations; Patricia's arm wounds and amputations; and my tent cared for chest wounds. The futility of it all hit Stephanie first when she asked how many field hospitals the Confederacy established.

"Three including this one," Doctor McAllister said.

"Three?" Thousands of soldiers will fight. Do we expect a total of forty wounded?" We sat in a tent eating a noon meal.

He put his fork down and wiped his hands on a cloth. "I expect hundreds if not thousands—not many surgeons beating paths to practice medicine in a battle arena."

"Why did you?" she asked.

"I'm naive enough to think someone may need me—that I may save some boy's life."

"Are you growing a moustache?" she asked, noticing the black shadow on his lip. He squirmed. "Well, are you?"

"Yes—is that all right? Do I need your permission?"

"It would become you to ask." She smiled as the words slipped out. Maybe, I thought, something turned in my friend—maybe she felt ready for a man. Leaning forward, folding her arms, she revealed cleavage. Catching him looking, she smiled again. I wondered if she teased or discovered an attraction. "Please don't shave it until it is fully grown."

"Fine," he replied. "You may judge if I am to keep it."

She leaned back. "I want to straighten my hospital tent and make certain all is in order."

"I would be honored to accompany you if you wish."

"I keep my wishes to myself." She stood. "You may join me if you desire."

Chapter 79

George Yardley

During the morning of July eighteenth, General Beauregard addressed the officers of the Black Horse Cavalry. Gathered under a sprawling oak at Sudley Church, he stood atop a rise.

First, he divided the six hundred cavalrymen into twenty units. Second, he spaced each unit half mile apart along the eight miles of Bull Run with two units at each flank. And third, he ordered each unit to remain at the rear while ground fighting occurred. If, and only if, enemy soldiers broke through the Confederate lines, would the cavalry charge.

Completing the orders, he singled me out. "Captain Yardley, when the attack comes, I plan to send a division against the enemy's left flank to the east. The Milton Guards shall reinforce that flank. The Yankee generals may attempt the same maneuver, which would leave us vulnerable to the west. Your men have seen battle. Prepare to fight to the death."

"Yes, sir," I replied feeling self-conscious. Beauregard mounted his horse. He and his executive officers rode toward headquarters at the Henry house.

As he disappeared over a hill, shots rang out from the direction of Blackburn's Ford. A Yankee division, whose purpose seemed that of making mischief, engaged Confederate troops, but did so without proper support. Routed, they retreated carrying with them dead and wounded. Though still untested, that skirmish gave others a taste of battle.

Three days passed without hostility. As General Beauregard sat eating breakfast on the twenty-first of July, the Union fired a cannon ball toward the Henry House that somehow went down the chimney. Beauregard escaped with his officers, making their way to a temporary command tent from which he launched the attack at the enemy's left flank.

At almost the same moment, General McDowell launched his attack against Beauregard's left flank. During the morning, Union troops sought penetration points at bridges and shallow fords along the stream. Then, McDowell sent a force at the southern center. The Confederate flanking maneuver failed, while the Union maneuver found success.

Between the two major Union thrusts, a division of Union soldiers crossed Bull Run near Sudley Church. Hidden in the woods, I saw the enemy make its way toward the Stone Bridge; but, I heard no bugle call and did not respond. After those soldiers cleared the hill toward the bridge, I ordered my men to ride eastward, remaining in the woods. A Confederate division made limited inroads, delaying the Union advance. Without the bugle call necessitating a charge, I ordered my men to dismount on a hilltop, where we commenced firing into the enemy's right flank. We shot six volleys before the enemy realized from whence the attack came. Union soldiers lay dead and wounded while those standing scattered toward Bull Run where Confederate troops met them with a fresh volley, taking prisoners. Remounting, I ordered the Guard's return to our assigned place near the church.

Further down the Run, the two Union divisions continued to make strides forward, causing Southern troops to flee. One brigade held its ground: General T. J. Jackson's. For a while, Confederates rallied around him, giving General Johnston's brigade time to arrive from the Shenandoah Valley by train.

Those fresh troops, along with timely cannon fire, turned the tide. Wounded and scared Yankees fled eastward toward Washington, dropping their arms as they ran. Private citizens, who had ridden from Washington with their picnics to witness the battle fled, complicating the Yankee retreat.

"If we wait here much longer," I said to Nathaniel, "we might find the battle and the war ended. Let's see who won."

Hearing no bugle call, I ordered the Guard to ride across Bull Run northeast toward Centreville. Cresting a hill, overlooking the main road to Washington, I witnessed the mayhem of retreating soldiers. The sight of my thirty mounted cavalrymen ready to attack, struck fear into the hearts of those running for their lives. Pandemonium broke loose, causing more disruption and bedlam.

"What should we do?" Nathaniel asked.

"Run them all the way back to the White House." Splinter jerked, as if in agreement. Looking to the west and hearing no battle sounds, I gave the order.

"Men, we have the opportunity to cut the enemy asunder. They came to defeat us," I shouted. "Let us finalize their defeat. Take no prisoners; but, spare the civilians. Charge!"

Thirty horses thundered down the hill into the fleeing soldiers. The Guard had no more than drawn our swords, when in the distance, I heard the bugler sound retreat. Not wanting to obey, I allowed the charge to continue, which cast the scene into more mayhem. Yankees screamed, crying for mercy. Seeing the futility of attacking unarmed soldiers, I raised my hand, slowing to a halt. A mysterious pride came over me as I watched the horror before us. Suddenly, from the west a shot rang out. Frances Pugh fell.

"There they are," Rex Snyder hollered. Seven Yankees rose from a shallow gully about thirty yards away, running for their lives.

"Nathaniel, stay here—take care of Frances. The rest, come with me."

The charge progressed. Drawing my sword, I used it for the first time, slicing the nape of a Yankee's neck. Halting Splinter, I turned and watched life leave my victim's eyes. In rapid order, seven bluecoats lay dead, shot and slain. Those from both sides, Union and Confederate, saw the swiftness by which death took its toll. I galloped Splinter to Frances. "How bad is he?" I asked, dismounting, holding Splinter's reins.

"Bleeding from his stomach."

Looking toward the road, I saw an overturned surrey with a horse harnessed to it. "Let's get him to a field hospital." The other men returned. I ordered Third Platoon to bring the surrey. Nathaniel, Josiah, and Frances' friend, Calvin Pruitt placed their fallen comrade in the backseat. "You men follow me, and look like Confederate soldiers. I don't want to be mistaken for Yankees." Getting to the road, we raced toward the Henry House and the Stone Bridge. Nathaniel ministered to Frances as the Guard followed on horseback.

Approaching the house, we saw Confederate soldiers walking and running from one fallen body to another. The horrors of war covered field and pasture. No one paid us any mind. Some tended to fallen comrades, and some scavenged for weapons, powder, and ammunition. At least two details dug mass graves. Not knowing the nearest hospital's location, I stopped to ask. Two sentries on the north side of the Stone Bridge gave two choices: Haymarket or a plantation house at the foot of Bull Run Mountain. One sentry encouraged me to head to the plantation in that most of the wounded, to that point, had been taken to Haymarket.

"How far?" Nathaniel asked.

"About eight miles," the sentry answered. "Follow the road past Sudley Church. Keep going until it dead ends. The plantation house sets a mile away down a long, winding road."

"Hurry," Nathaniel yelled from the backseat. "He's bleeding worse." Whipping the surrey horse, bitterness overshadowed me that I had ridden the Guard into the ambush.

Suddenly, I felt Nathaniel tug at my shoulders. "Stop—stop." He wrestled the reins from me, pulling the horse to a stop. "All the doctors on earth can't help Frances now." The Guard gathered round. "He's dead."

"George," Calvin said. "I'd like to bury Frances here in the woods—not in one of those big graves they're digging."

Looking at the body, I turned to see a small clearing. "What about there?" Calvin looked and nodded, keeping his head bowed. "Nathaniel, ride to the Stone Bridge—find shovels."

"Would it be all right," Calvin asked, "to camp here for the night after we bury him? I'd like to write his mother."

"We don't have our tents; but, we can send for the buckboard."

"I'll go," Reuben said.

"I'll go with him," Levi offered.

"Fine, but be careful. Yankee stragglers may lurk. Get back here fast." I wished I had reminded Nathaniel of this warning.

The remainder of the Guard unsaddled their horses and hobbled them. Three cavalrymen rode up. "Are you the Milton Guards?" a lieutenant asked.

"Yes, sir," I said.

"General Beauregard wants to see Captain Yardley. Is he here?"

"I am."

"Would you come with us?" Before I made a gesture, Tim went to saddle Splinter.

"What's this about? We have a burial to perform."

"Burials are being performed for miles around," the lieutenant replied. "We're at war. Your commanding officer requires your presence."

Tim led Splinter to me. Before mounting, I gave Kinchen instructions about digging the grave. "Hold off on the funeral until I return."

We rode away in a fast gallop reaching the Henry House in about fifteen minutes. The lieutenant escorted me through the front door. At a table in the dining room, I was introduced to

General Johnston and eight other officers. When Beauregard saw me, he paused, turning everyone's attention toward me.

"Captain Yardley," he said. "Would you please give a full report of your activity today?"

"Yes, sir." I described how we hid in the woods until a Yankee division crossed Bull Run at Sudley Church, moving toward the Stone Bridge. "I maneuvered my men eastward through the woods, up a hill, remaining out of sight. We came to a clearing overlooking the road. There, I ordered my men to dismount and fire at my command. The Guard did so, six times inflicting heavy casualties. The Yankees ran in disarray toward the stream where other Confederates cut them asunder."

"Then what happened?" Johnston asked.

"I returned to where General Beauregard assigned us to protect against additional flanking moves the enemy might make."

"So," Johnston said, "you spent the day hiding in the woods while the battle raged?"

I liked neither his tone nor the expression on his face. "I followed orders."

"If a few more officers followed orders today, we would not have suffered the heavy losses we did," another voice said. Turning toward the archway, not recognizing the person speaking, I felt better for the comment.

"Did you engage any enemy troops?" Johnston asked.

"No sir. When the battle died down, I led my men northeast toward the main road to assess our situation. Cresting a hill, we saw the mayhem of the Yankee retreat. A small enemy contingent fired upon us wounding one soldier, who later died. We attacked, killing all seven. The Guard awaits two men to return with shovels and two to return with our buckboard. We plan to bury Frances Pugh, spend the night, and report tomorrow." Hesitating while all eyes measured me, I had to speak. "Did I do something wrong?"

"Captain," the officer who supported me said, "I am General T. J. Jackson. You served your state and your honor well this day. You provided time and support to allow General Johnston's arrival. Some around this table expressed concern over your lack of presence for the remainder of the battle. You explained yourself. We stand appreciative regarding your abilities."

"Thank you," General Beauregard said to me. "Return to your men to perform the burial. Please join the officers here for a meeting tomorrow at ten o'clock."

Chapter 80

Amy Yardley

Covered in blood, I cared for eight wounded soldiers all shot or stabbed in the chest. Two died. Their corpses lay on cots. Doctor McAllister had removed lead balls from five boys, instructing me to stop the bleeding. The July sun made the tent unbearable with heat. I stepped outside. The fresh air seemed a gift from God until I reckoned the scene before me. Hundreds of bodies—many more continuing to arrive—spread across the grounds. Hopelessness stirred within me. Reentering the tent, I noticed one patient moving. I went to him.

"Are you an angel?" he said, taking my hand.

"I'm your nurse."

"You look like an angel. My mother looms beside you." Turning, I saw no one. "Thank you for coming," he said squeezing my hand. The squeeze ended. Lifelessness... I felt cold lifelessness, and wondered if George lay lifeless on some battlefield.

Doctor McAllister joined me, opening the front and rear flaps. "How goes it?"

"Three dead—don't know about the others."

He moved to the front flap, shouting for help. Six boys appeared. "Take these corpses to their graves," he ordered, pointing to the bodies. "Bring four soldiers with chest wounds."

"Did I kill them?"

"No, you tried to save them. Don't confuse the issues. You'll have more work in a few moments. If you find bullet wounds close to the surface, use tongs to pull the lead out. After you do, clean the wound and stop the bleeding." He left.

Fear returned. What if George or Nathaniel were outside? What if they lay alone without anyone tending them? I rushed to the door wanting to dash around the grounds. Two boys, carrying a litter with a wounded soldier, stopped me, and placed him on an empty cot.

After cutting his shirt, I examined the bloody hole. Sticking my index finger in, I felt the ball below the breastbone on the left side. One soldier I cared for, I decided, will live. Retrieving the tongs, I inserted them, extracting the bullet. My patient never moved. Blood gushed. Grabbing a basin of water, I poured it over the wound. He groaned.

"You stay awake," I hollered. "You're not dying. Do you hear me?"

He awoke, remaining conscious. While treating others, my attention returned to him. Whenever he dozed, I roused him, even if it meant slapping his face. Talking to the wounded seemed to have a positive effect. At every opportunity, I spoke, sang, or recited scripture. By nightfall, flies, gnats, and mosquitoes swarmed. If I closed the tent flaps, the stench overcame me. Beside myself with exhaustion, I took a blanket and coiled up on the ground between the two rows of cots. When I awoke, Stephanie lay beside me. The light of dawn shone.

Chapter 81

George Yardley

After the burial, I gathered the Guard around the campfire. A silence ensued. Every eye turned toward their captain.

"Men, war consists of two sides: one personal and the other military. Personally, we lost a friend for which I am responsible. Rather than watch for the enemy, I saw the Yankees retreat. I need your help at such times. Be alert. Look out for one another. Militarily, we routed the enemy. Victory took its toll. The South suffered many casualties. From the look on the faces of those general at the Henry House, we lack cause to celebrate. To the contrary, I believe the North will use this battle as a rally cry. Tomorrow, I return to the Henry House to receive orders. We'll see where God wants us."

Concluding, my attention turned to Calvin. "You want time to write. Get what you need and use my tent. Tomorrow we'll find a post office. Fourth Platoon stands the watch, then Third Platoon, and so on."

Chapter 82

Amy Yardley

Mercifully, a morning breeze blew as I exited the tent. Hundreds and hundreds of dead, dying, and wounded lay before me. Walking through their midst, I sought anyone with a chest wound. I found none and found no one I recognized.

"How many dead?" a male voice asked. Doctor McAllister stood scanning the site.

"Don't know, but I'd guess half. Some breathe and groan."

"I meant in your tent."

"All were alive when I left."

"When I looked in minutes ago, I saw Stephanie sleeping— didn't disturb her."

"She joined me during the night. Didn't know she was there until I awoke."

I looked around causing Doctor McAllister to do the same. "My husband could lay here. It would kill me to think he died while I slept."

"He didn't die. His men made a flanking attack on a Yankee division that crossed the Run. In doing so, he spared enough time for General Johnston's brigade to arrive. George may have saved the day. That's what some soldiers say. George and General

Jackson seem to be the heroes of the day." I breathed a sigh of relief and again wanted to weep, but steeled myself.

"Casualties?"

"Don't know. They're encamped near Sudley Church."

"How far?"

"Far enough you can't make the trip unescorted, and besides, we have work to do," he said gesturing toward the wounded.

"How could George and I be so near to each other, yet so far away? I wish I could see him. He doesn't know I'm here."

"Let's eat and get back to work."

Stephanie stood in the door of my tent appearing dreadful. At least four insect bites covered her face. Deep bags sagged under her eyes. Staring at the scene, she appeared listless.

"Would you like something to eat?" Doctor McAllister asked.

"Sure."

Stephanie walked toward a mess tent with us. Her expression changed to one of determination. "Are you hungry?" I asked.

"Yes, I want to eat and get back to work. I want to stop feeling sorry for myself."

Chapter 83

George Yardley

I requested Nathaniel's presence for the ride to the Henry House. Not in a hurry, it took a half an hour. Upon our arrival, we saw a red flag with crossbars hanging from two upstairs windows. Each bar contained stars I didn't bother to count. Two women handed smaller replicas of the flag to sergeants and lieutenants.

"It's a grand day," General Johnston said from the front door. "Come in. We must talk."

Whispering, I addressed Nathaniel. "Let's see if I can get you inside. Walk fast with a sense of urgency."

A sergeant allowed Nathaniel entrance. Around the table, Generals Beauregard, Jackson and Johnston sat.

"Captain Yardley," Johnston said, "have a seat. Join us for breakfast."

Turning to Nathaniel, I introduced him. "I'd like to extend you the courtesy of meeting my cousin, Nathaniel Thomas."

Beauregard and Jackson stood. Johnston followed. "You may join us," Johnston said.

With hat in hand, I sat. "Thank you—we'll have coffee; but we ate."

Johnston motioned to a slave who returned with two filled cups.

"Captain Yardley," Beauregard began. "We want your cavalry to return to Fredericksburg. General Jackson and General Johnston will move to the Shenandoah. We're concerned the Federalists will present a two-sided attack—one south using the Richmond Highway and one through the Valley of Virginia. Reinforcements from Fredericksburg will join General Beauregard using the Rappahannock as a line of defense."

"We intend to give up northern Virginia?" I asked.

"That is where you come in," Johnston said. "We want your Guard to make intrusions into Yankee lines. You are to wreak havoc on the enemy by picking your battles and by using the element of surprise."

"General Beauregard, are you my commanding officer?"

"I am. You are to leave today. Set up camp near Falmouth on the north side of the Rappahannock. Be vigilant in your watch. My brigade will follow in a couple days, after we tend to the dead and wounded. General Lee's brigades should arrive within the week. After the beating the enemy took yesterday, we don't expect incursions for at least a month. They must regroup and inaugurate a new battle plan. We have spies in place."

Before I could speak, General Jackson spoke. "Captain Yardley, please return here with your cavalry on your way to Falmouth. A promotion is in order. We will conduct a ceremony to raise you to the office of major." I eyed Nathaniel. "Select two men for promotion to lieutenant, preferably men who hold the rank of sergeant."

"That would mean promoting Nathaniel and Kinchen Cross."

"Whomever," Jackson said.

"Will that be all?"

"Yes," Johnston answered. "Please return in two hours."

"Amazing," I said as we headed for camp. "They expect us to hold off a Yankee invasion."

"They don't expect us to hold it off. They expect us to disrupt it."

"Regardless, I'd rather take a position on the south side of the Rappahannock."

"So would I. That's not where they ordered us."

❧❧❧❧

We left the cannon stored in the camp north of Warrenton, finding it slowed us down. "Please hear me out regarding the following promotions." I recounted Kinchen's and Nathaniel's. "Richard Grogan, you are the sergeant for the entire Guard. Corporal Lindamood, I promote you to sergeant for Fourth Platoon. Paul Gilbert, sergeant for First Platoon. Tillman and Levi, you are sergeants for your platoons."

At the Henry House, Johnston and Jackson stood on the steps at the front door. Every Guardsman wore his leather jacket except Bartholomew Snyder. Calvin gave Frances' to Rex leaving Bartholomew without one.

"That's a smart looking company of soldiers," Johnston said to Jackson, loud enough for me to hear. "I wonder where they got those jackets."

"Let's ask," Jackson replied.

I explained Amy and I made them, and why Bartholomew didn't have one.

"Well, I hope none of the rest of you has to die in order for this young man to receive his," Johnston said.

"I can make one in due time," I said, not liking the insinuation.

"You might want another hat," Johnston said to me. "That one looks like it belongs to a backwoods country boy."

"I'll die in this hat. My father made it—gave it to me the day I killed my first deer and, that's who I am, a backwoods country boy."

Johnston withdrew from the conversation turning the promotion ceremony over to Jackson. Once carried out, the

Guard received orders to go south toward Warrenton and east to Falmouth.

Mounted, General Jackson approached, accompanied by a lieutenant. "Captain Yardley, we need you to deliver five buckboards of medical supplies to the field hospital in Haymarket."

"Certainly," I said. "To whom shall we deliver them?" Jackson searched his memory, but couldn't remember. "Find someone assigned to the hospital. They'll tell you."

"Leave the wagons there?"

"Yes," he said.

Ordering five men to drive the buckboards, I headed the Guard south. At Haymarket, a large pasture presented itself about three hundred yards from the road. Nine immense tents stood in a line. What I saw next turned my stomach. From one side of the pasture to the other, wounded and dead soldiers lay: some on stretchers; some on the ground.

We proceeded, not wanting to look at the carnage. Approaching the tents, a corporal greeted us. We emptied the buckboards, storing the contents in the first tent. By then, it was noon. The corporal offered a meal in the mess tent, which we accepted. Not having anything else to do and not able to assist, I ordered he Guard mounted. We rode away.

Chapter 84

Amy Yardley

"You afraid George lays out there?" Stephanie asked, gesturing toward the bodies as we walked to the mess tent.

"No—I looked. I fear he lays wounded without help."

"If that's the case, the entire Guard is decimated. Forgive me," she pleaded. "I meant to compliment the Guard. I meant it to reassure you. It didn't come out right."

"Don't worry—I thought the same thoughts."

"What thoughts?" Doctor McAllister asked.

"Oh, nothing," Stephanie said. "I misspoke." As we went through the line dishing food, Doctor McAllister told us a new shipment of medical supplies arrived.

"When did that happen?" I asked.

"About an hour ago. Corporal Weed informed me."

"That's good news," Stephanie said as we sat down.

We ate, soothing our hunger. "Mrs. Stith, you appear much better compared to this morning," Doctor McAllister said. Her bug bites had diminished in size.

"Your patients do well," he said to me. "Each of you has a special way about you when you care for these men. I know it is a small percentage, but some will live because of you."

"I wish I could see my husband."

"I'd like to see him," Doctor McAllister said. "You are married to a remarkable man."

"He is remarkable," Stephanie said. "Every eligible woman in Atlanta eyed him until he bumped into Amy. He couldn't take his eyes from her." She paused. "Now that I think about it, every woman in Atlanta had her eyes on him. It mattered not whether she was eligible." I smiled, admiring my friend's honesty. "I'm most fortunate, though," she went on. "The four of us, including my husband, went skinny dipping one day. I happened to steal a peak at his..."

"Stephanie, you shouldn't say such things."

"You're jealous because you're not the only woman who ever saw him naked."

"How could you?"

"I could because I wanted to, and I'll look again if I get the chance." She laughed.

McAllister eyed me. "I was not aware women enjoyed the kind of friendship you share."

Corporal Weed entered the tent, spooned some food, and joined us. "Just met the most famous soldier in the Confederate Army," he said. I stared, waiting. "Captain George Yardley and the Milton Guards delivered and unloaded the supplies."

"What?" I screamed. "Where are they?"

"Gone—headed to Warrenton and then Falmouth. Do you know him?"

"George Yardley is my husband." I wanted to run through the mess tent door, but knew it useless. Placing my elbows on the table, I bowed, clasping my hands behind my neck, exasperated. If I could take a horse and ride after him, I would; but, I knew my duty.

Stephanie touched my forearm. "If nothing else, you know he's all right."

"He is all right," Corporal Weed said, "but I heard his men say one of their company died—don't reckon I heard the name."

"Please remember," I asked.

"Frances," he said. "His name was Frances."

"Frances Pugh," Stephanie said in a whisper. "They've lost another."

Chapter 85

Alexander Frey

The ship docked, leaving Beatrice and me to make our way to the guest lodgings I enjoyed during stays in England. A horse-drawn carriage wound its way through London, causing a racket as hoofs pounded the cobblestones. Pointing out the Tower and Parliament, I suggested we tour a few castles before returning to America. Mesmerized by the architecture and the well-dressed manner in which English gentlemen sauntered from place to place, Beatrice beamed and expressed gratitude her sickness had passed for the most part.

The lodge, a stone two-story building encircled by a brick wall, was located at the city's outskirts. I remarked as to the beauty of the countryside, but elicited no response. When the carriage stopped, two older men appeared at the front gate. Their presence did elicit a response.

"Are they slaves?" she asked, touching my arm.

"No, my dear—employees."

Seeing me, their eyes sparkled through smiles. Shaking hands, I introduced Beatrice. "Brian Troop—Charles Bondiforce, please meet my wife, Beatrice Frey." They bowed, their eyes filling with questions.

"Who causes this commotion?" Sylvia Grace asked as she walked through the front gate. "Alexander," she shouted. "How wonderful to see you." We embraced, kissing each other on the cheek. As we did, Sylvia took notice of Beatrice. "And who might this charming woman be?"

"Mr. Frey's wife," Charles said. "The Georgian got himself married."

Sylvia smiled. "Married? How wonderful."

"Mrs. Grace, please meet Mrs. Beatrice Frey. Beatrice, this is Sylvia Grace." Sylvia extended her hand encouraging Beatrice to do the same, which she did.

"Where might that scalawag of a husband be who overcharges when I stay here?"

Sylvia pointed across a pasture. "In the fields tending to the harvest. Brian, inform Peter we have company. Do not say who—surprise him." Turning, Brian walked down the road, disappearing behind the wall. "Come in," Sylvia said, directing Charles to bring the baggage.

Through the gate, Beatrice gasped. "What a beautiful garden. There must be hundreds of red roses in bloom. The aroma takes my breath." Holding my hand, she kissed my cheek. "I've entered a fairy tale."

"You have. This is my favorite place on earth. I've tried to buy it from Peter. He refuses my offers. And what's worse, the prices I pay to stay here are such that I've probably paid him four or five times what it's worth."

Sylvia's eyes narrowed. "Beatrice," she said, taking a small knife from her apron pocket, cutting a rose, presenting it to my wife, "wait till you have to endure a meal with Peter and Alexander. If one didn't know better, you might think they hated each other."

"I do hate Peter. He's a scalawag, a cheat, a thief, and besides, he's British."

"Alexander," Beatrice said, "how could you?"

"Wait until you meet him—you'll find yourself in agreement. Not to mention, he will do all in his power to dishonor you and our marriage vows."

"Alexander," Sylvia said, stepping onto the wooden porch, "you stop at nothing to demean my husband's good fortune and reputation. Beatrice, don't believe a word. For supper, I'll put the men—notice I did not say gentlemen—in one room, and we shall eat in another. They can have their fun, and we can get to know one another."

We had no more than entered the house when a voice bellowed from behind. "Oh my God," Peter shouted, "I hoped that with the start of your civil war, the Yankees had captured and imprisoned you."

Beatrice Frey

When I turned, I saw the handsomest and most striking man I had ever beheld. Somehow, I thought my eyes deceived me. How could I have encountered the rose garden and now this human specimen in a matter of seconds? He wore woolen tweed pants, knee high boots, and a pure white shirt opened at the top. His black hair glistened as if all the stars of heaven shone upon him. Strutting through the door, pretending to clock Alexander, he froze, eyeing me. "O my God, is right. Who is this perfectly beautiful creature?"

"My wife," Alexander said, "and if you so much as look at her cross-eyed, Sylvia will enter widowhood."

"My wish is for your wife's widowhood, so she will no longer have to endure the rigors and boredom of marriage to a scoundrel. You have my heartfelt sympathy, Mrs. Frey, and how, may I ask, did he persuade the most beautiful woman on earth to marry him?"

"I had to persuade the man of my dreams to marry me."

"There," Alexander said, "is the perfect answer from the perfect wife. The next time you insult me, she'll slit your neck with a knife rather than slit your pride with her tongue."

Peter threw his arms toward heaven. "'Tis not fair that God bestowed upon you—the wealthiest and vilest man on earth—such an exquisite creature. Where is justice?"

"Obviously, in the eyes of God," I said.

"Enough," Sylvia said. "Shake hands, and stop feigning hatred." They did more than that. Approaching each other, they embraced as if long lost brothers.

Alexander Frey

"Peter," I said, "I am pleased to introduce Mrs. Beatrice Frey. Beatrice, this is Peter Grace."

"May I have the honor?" Peter held Beatrice's shoulders in his hands, bowed, and then kissed each cheek. "Never has a kiss brought me such pleasure, save the kisses of my wife."

My head shook and bowed. "Sylvia, pay him no mind. When he says he is harvesting, he is eating that with which we in the south fertilize."

"Is my husband full of manure?" Sylvia asked.

Charles returned from taking our baggage to my favorite room. I escorted Beatrice upstairs, settling her in bed for a nap. Making it clear I would return within the hour, I went downstairs to Peter's study where I found a glass of scotch on a coffee table.

Peter joined me. "You certainly won yourself an elegant bride." Holding up his glass, I clanked mine to his. We sipped the golden liquid.

"She's a marvel."

"Did you stop in London before coming here? The reason I ask—every banker in the city awaits you. Confusion abounds about money sent here from Boston."

"They sent it? I received notice they refused my request."

"From what they say, yes, it is here."

"I wonder how much?"

"Haven't revealed the sum. They sent couriers here to see if you arrived."

We reclined in two leather chairs. "Wonder if my son-in-law could make a chair like this."

"Son-in-law? Your daughter married?"

"Forgive me. So much occurred since my last trip. I find it difficult to recall what you know and don't know. Amy married a young man—quite capable in many fields. He is a hunter, a farmer, and a leatherworker, not to mention, well-spoken and capable of caring for Amy. At this time, he is in Virginia fighting for the Confederates."

"And your daughter?"

"I hope she is with my sister in Atlanta."

"And what have you been up to?"

"Built two factories during the past six months—one produces weapons and the other produces boots. I've also tried to get my money out of New England to support the Confederacy."

Peter sipped his scotch. "All of it?"

"Most of it. That is why I am intrigued by its presence here." Hesitating, I too, sipped my drink. "Beatrice and I have another problem."

"Can I help?"

"She may be pregnant."

"Oh, jolly good. Why is that a problem?"

The crossing—she didn't sail well—didn't know if she was seasick or nauseated from the pregnancy. In either case, I did not expect to stay long. Now, we may be here for some time."

"That suits me."

"I knew it would, you old bastard. If we stay, you'll swindle me out of my gold that concerns your banker friends."

"Hadn't thought that, but a longer stay appeals."

"I'd live on the streets before paying you for nine months of lodging."

"Nine months?" Sylvia said from the kitchen door. "What about nine months?"

"Beatrice may be pregnant. She didn't sail well, and Alexander questions whether they can return to Georgia before the baby's birth."

"It's more complex," I said. "I must return to Georgia. Beatrice may have to remain here until the baby is born."

Peter's eyes gleamed. "If just Beatrice, she can stay at no charge."

"That's sporting," I said.

"Pregnant women appeal to me, but Beatrice—pregnant—and in my own home—that may be more than I can fathom."

"Pay him no mind," Sylvia said. "He's all talk and no action."

During the afternoon and evening, we ate together allowing, Sylvia and Beatrice to become better acquainted and discussing the pregnancy, along with my travel concerns. Beatrice expressed interest in how well Grace Lodge and farm prospered without slaves. It gave her hope that if America freed her slaves, our southern culture and economy might endure.

∾☙✄☙∽

After breakfast, Peter and I mounted horses and made our way to The Bank of London. Entering the building, Mr. Lawrence Cooke welcomed us.

The Bank of Boston had sent a draft for three million dollars to my account in London seeking instructions as to what they should do with the gold. Mr. Cooke had already responded with a request to Boston that they ship the gold to London. As far as he knew, the gold should arrive within the month.

Chapter 86

George Yardley

We made camp west of Falmouth near where the Guard had routed the Yankee spies. My mind turned to another spy. Rex Snyder knew Mr. Speakes. While Nathaniel and I waited, Rex entered the general store. Minutes passed. Growing edgy, I feared Rex had slipped and revealed his mission. Maybe they held him hostage—bait for a trap.

"What do we do?" Nathaniel asked as we stood with our horses in a wooded area about a hundred yards from the store.

"Return to camp—get a couple men Speakes doesn't know, and send them in, or take care of it ourselves." I pointed toward the store. "Did you see that?"

Nathaniel strained to look. "What?"

"The back door opened." It opened wider. Rex walked out with his hands tied behind his back, his mouth covered with a kerchief. From the look on his face, I surmised they pointed guns at his back. "Wait here." I said.

Nathaniel grabbed my shoulder. "Let's get help."

I mounted Splinter and started for the store. "It will be too late. If they shoot either Rex or me, hang the son of a bitch. Hang him from that oak tree on the other side of the street from his store—after he watches you burn the store down." As I cleared the woods, Rex shook his head side to side trying to prevent me from riding in. It was too late. Three to four shots rang out. At least one downed the boy while a couple whistled past me.

Jumping off Splinter, shooing him away, taking cover in a ditch, and drawing my revolver, I saw the terror of war. The Guard, mounted, riding in a full charge with pistols drawn, unloaded their lead at the general store. Where did they come from? I asked myself. The crack of black powder filled the air. Every man fired as he rode past except Bartholomew, who pulled his horse up, jumped down, and ran toward his brother. By then, the Guard reversed itself for the second charge, protecting the Snyders. I raced toward the two boys, shooting at the door twice before the next flurry of lead from the Guard perforated and shattered the wooden planks. Placing myself in front of the Snyders, I waited for the cavalry charge to pass. Eight guardsmen stopped, jumped down, and surrounded the building. I neither heard sound nor saw motion inside. From behind I heard what I wanted to hear.

"Are you all right?" Bartholomew asked his brother, loosening the kerchief.

"Yes—cut the rope." Bartholomew did.

"Are you shot?" I hollered transferring my gaze back and forth from the door to the boys. "You men—inside—come out with your hands up."

Nathaniel heeded my former order, appearing with a torch. Crouched at the corner of the building, he shouted, "Come out, or we'll burn you out."

"Throw it," I ordered. Nathaniel crept along the back wall, tossing the torch inside the door. It extinguished as it rolled across the floor. "How many in there?" I asked Rex, kneeling next to him.

"Four."

Bartholomew ran to the door disappearing inside. Seconds later he reappeared. "They're not here."

Nathaniel raced to the back door. "Anyone see them go out the front?"

"There must be a trapdoor to a cellar or a loft," I said. "You men inside—we know you're in there. Come out, or we will burn you out." No response was forthcoming. "Torch it."

"I saw two women and a child in there," Rex said. "Don't want any part of killing them."

"They'll come out when it burns," Nathaniel said.

"We'll come out now," a woman's voice cried. Standing near the door, I saw a large shelf move, revealing the two women and child.

For a moment, I sensed silence, stillness. "Where are the others?"

"An escape tunnel runs underground across the road," one said. "They went there."

"Where does it come out?"

"In that field," she said, pointing around the building. Everyone followed as I ran around front leaving the women and child alone. At the field, I heard horses' hooves. From a shed about a hundred feet north of the store, four men rode for their lives north toward Dumfries.

"Let them go," I said. "We can't ride our horses into the ground over the likes of them." As I finished speaking, something came over me I'd never felt. I wanted to harm the women, but knew I couldn't because of the child. "Tim, take some men— find a wagon, hitch some horses to it, and send the women north before I hang them."

Riding to our camp, I asked Rex what had happened. "One man inside the store saw the Guard make camp. They hoped Nathaniel and you would show up. When I entered, they used me as bait."

Settling down for the night, I realized three days had passed without giving Amy a thought. The center of my life seemed a vision. War had taken her place. Reaching under my cot, I fetched a leather satchel containing writing paraphernalia. For the next hour, I wrote everything I remembered about Bull Run and about the field hospital at Haymarket. Folding and sealing the letter, I addressed it in care of the Branners and fell asleep.

Chapter 87

Amy Yardley

No nurse had a full night's sleep for four nights. The wounded decreased in number, but not due to medical care. Mostly they died, carted off to mass graves. From the initial wave of injured for whom I cared, only one man passed away. The rest thrived on my sensitivity to their needs. Stephanie's patients did the same. She also found herself caring for Doctor McAllister's needs.

General Jackson requested and ordered Doctor McAllister's field hospital moved to Front Royal. In the middle of August, we boarded a westbound train. Sitting next to a window, Captain McAllister approached me, smiling, and handing me a stack of envelopes. "These are for you." I counted nine letters—seven from George and two from Sarah. "Enjoy the ride," he said, taking his seat two in front of mine. Stephanie walked down the aisle seemingly intent on sitting next to me until Captain McAllister persuaded her otherwise.

Curling up, facing the window, I ordered the letters by postmark. Saving George's for last, I opened Sarah's. All was well, except she felt loneliness. No word had arrived from Father.

One by one I started through the letters from George until I read the second to last wherein he described the scene at

Haymarket. As odd as it seemed, his appraisal depicted a more gruesome portrayal than what I had experienced. I concluded I had steeled myself against the horror to better serve. Finishing that letter, I peered across the Virginia countryside as the train clacked along. Awaking later, not knowing how long I napped, I opened the last letter.

My Dearest and Most Beautiful Amy,

Tonight, I lay in a camp west of Falmouth from where the Guard will carry out raids against Federal troops. Today, we scattered a band of civilian spies whose intent was to kill Nathaniel and me because of what we did in Dumfries. They escaped their building running for their lives. We helped ourselves to what we needed in their general store and left the rest for whoever wants it.

A strange sensation came over me tonight as we rode into camp. I have been so busy leading these men and fighting battles, that I failed to realize the void in my life, which is you. A couple months ago I couldn't breathe or take a step without thinking about you. Now, hours go by, especially those in the heat of battle, in which you never cross my mind. War takes a terrible toll! Who would have thought I could become so intent on soldiering that I could put you out of my mind for even a minute? I live in fear I will make a decision that will cost someone his life. Please forgive me for this. If we were together, I would think of you every moment. For as I lie here, even now, I wish you beside me, for I know I love you very much.

I hope all is well with you and Stephanie and the Branners. We have moved around often. I have not received a letter from you, but hope to do so soon. I wish I could be with you, and I look to the time when we will be together.

All of my love and best wishes,
George

Pulling the letter to my breast, I knew what I had always known, that I could never completely have him. War produced new loyalties and commitments within him. As hard as I tried to believe his words, I concluded that even if I encamped with him, his attention would be elsewhere. I did not doubt his love; but rather, I doubted myself. Now at twenty-one, I had been shot, had killed two men, and had married the man of my dreams. In a matter of days, I had tended wounds of injured men and watched hundreds die. What else in life could be worth doing, except having a baby?

Lost in thought, I jerked around realizing the train had stopped. A wooden sign hanging over the railway station door read, Front Royal. As soon as I could, I knew I had to write to George telling him how much I loved and respected him for his honesty and to inform him I was one of the nurses caring for the wounded and dying at Haymarket.

A lieutenant escorted Stephanie and me, along with the other three nurses, to a hotel for the night. General Jackson's staff had arranged for us to room and board in different homes around town; but, that would commence the next day.

At dinner that evening, Doctor McAllister described our duties. He expressed hope that the war would be brief. If Confederate forces in the west could rebuff a Federal invasion along the Mississippi while General Johnston and General Jackson prevented a northern assault through the Shenandoah Valley, we might demoralize the enemy. General Lee's army positioned itself to deter an attack through Fredericksburg.

"That's where George is," I said, waiting for a response but receiving none until Stephanie spoke.

"That's where the Guard is?"

"Anyway," Doctor McAllister said, "we remain stationed here to receive the wounded. Pray God blesses our military plans— abbreviating this war."

We ate a meal of chicken and dumplings followed by coffee, which we took on the front porch. Doctor McAllister invited Stephanie for a walk, which she accepted, giving me cause to rejoice. Lighting a cigar to keep gnats away, he offered Stephanie his arm.

"Do you think they're in love?" Celeste asked.

"No thinking about it," Mary Ruth replied. "It's only a matter of time until one dishonors the other."

Celeste chuckled. "They could mutually dishonor each other."

"Well," Patricia Ann said, "he could dishonor me if he wants." I gasped, but the gasp did not prevent her from continuing. "Being around these men—wounded or not—hasn't quelled my emotions. I wonder how many boys died without experiencing the pleasures of sex."

"And how would you know of such pleasures?" Celeste asked.

She shrugged. "I don't know of such pleasures."

"We should be concerned about more than this," I said. "Seeing Stephanie and Doctor McAllister together arouses passions we need to put behind us. If God plans for them to marry, He will get them married. That's His concern, not ours."

Stephanie Stith

We walked toward the Shenandoah River through encroaching darkness. The physical contact afforded me joy. When certain the darkness hid us, we turned and kissed. Only my restraint and my fear of snakes prevented us from reclining in the lush grass along the river.

✤✦✤

"Well," Amy said as I entered our room, "you don't look worse for the wear; but, you do look as if in love."

Lying on my bed, I teased with silence for a moment. "I'm in something. Whatever it is, it feels different from what I felt for Drury and still feel for him." Pausing, I stared at the ceiling. "He seems innocent. Could a doctor see all he sees and not understand the passions of the flesh?"

"I had this conversation with the others tonight," Amy said. "You're the expert on these matters. Have you met someone you can't figure out?"

"He would have lain with me by the river; but, I prevented it. I'm not ready, and I'm not certain what he wants. Does he want me? Does he want sex?"

"Sounds to me that your young doctor isn't as innocent as you make him out to be."

"No, he's innocent. I'm the one who isn't."

"And, as far as I'm concerned, you've never been." We laughed, making eye contact. "What do you want from him?"

"Companionship and security. I don't want to be alone. And, I don't want to have another husband die in my arms. I fear that most. Every morning I awake to that memory of holding Drury's head in my lap. Seeing those wounded men has not helped me forget. Whatever you do, don't feel sorry for me. That is the most cherished gift you give. You never feel sorry for me."

"But I do feel sorry for you. I can't imagine what you feel—what you went through the day Drury died. I think about you all the time—what I would feel if I lost George."

"I need a man to take away that fear," I confessed. "However, until certain Doctor McAllister won't die in my arms, I cannot give myself to him—sexually or in marriage."

"There are risks in life. You and Drury took one. Concentrate on what your love meant to him. You gave him pleasure and joy. You can do that for someone else and for yourself."

Chapter 88

Alexander Frey

As the weeks passed, so did Beatrice's nausea. The first news reached England regarding the Battle of Bull Run and how the Confederates routed the enemy. When I read in The London Times one paragraph about a young cavalry captain protecting the southern flank, I wondered about George.

The Liverpool made the crossing, holding in her safe the gold representing my three million dollars from the Bank of Boston. In the captain's quarters, I watched as he and three bank representatives inspected the bags of gold. Satisfied with the weight and worth, the bankers loaded the gold onto a wagon, transporting it to the bank, where they locked it in a vault. Peter and I accompanied the bullion the entire way; though, before we left the ship, I asked the captain if he knew the whereabouts of The Sea Lion and Captain William Percival. He informed me The Sea Lion should arrive in London in less than a week.

Leaving the bank, we dined at The Long Street Tavern. Exquisite oak tables and fine appointed leather benches greeted us. Mirrors provided the backdrop for the bar. While eating, I offered my thoughts to Peter.

"If Captain Percival will sail for Savannah with the gold and return me immediately, I could be here for the baby's birth."

"That is if Captain Percival will make the crossing twice in such a short period," Peter said. "Where do you think Beatrice stands?"

"She desires to remain here, safe from the horrors of war." I paused giving consideration to what I said. Looking my friend in the eye, I couldn't resist. "Maybe Beatrice would be better off in Georgia than dealing with your treachery and deceit."

"Now, now," Peter said, "my relationship with your wife has grown to a fond friendship."

"Which you would seek to grow into something more if I left her to your lust. But, she will refuse you no matter what."

"Maybe," Peter said. "Maybe not."

༂༚༂༚

The ride to London from Grace Lodge took an hour. Beatrice and I made the trip each day to visit the harbor. Worry over missing The Sea Lion enveloped me.

The London docks proved no place for a lady. I found an inn overlooking the Thames. For five consecutive days, we rode past the docks, did not see the ship, and then went to the inn for our noon meal. Beatrice found this time enchanting, giving us privacy to discuss what it meant for her to become a mother and for me to become a father again. Those talks also gave her the insights she needed to accept my mission regarding the gold and the Confederacy. Knowing she would pine for me, if not fear the worst while I made the journey, I truly expressed my great joy about our marriage.

"I'll trust God in this, and pray every day for your safety," she said as we sat eating fruit at the window overlooking the river.

"I won't give you a smug answer like, 'Everything will be fine,' because I love and respect you. I realize full well the predicament in which I leave you."

"I couldn't hold you here if I wanted to," she whispered.

"I'm not certain of that."

೪ು೩ೕ

"I think this our lucky day," I said at the breakfast table, directing the comment to Peter. "Would Sylvia and you accompany us to the docks?"

Peter looked toward his wife awaiting her response. "That sounds pleasant. How long until I must be ready?"

"Half an hour," I replied, "but we'll wait if you need more time."

She finished the dishes, strolled through the house, and up the stairs. Beatrice followed.

"Is there something wrong?" I asked.

Peter turned sideways in his chair. "Yes and no. Beatrice's pregnancy affects Sylvia, in that we never had children. Furthermore, your return to Georgia after the baby is born causes her sadness. She had grown fond of Beatrice. A baby in the house appeals to her. Before long, she'll offer you free room and board to keep you here." We laughed. "What happens if we find Percival today?"

"Well, he's a good friend. If he has leeway, I'm certain he'll get me to Savannah, though I'm wary about Yankee warships sailing in Confederate waters. I'd hate to be sunk by either the enemy or my own country."

"We're ready," Sylvia announced, descending the stairs. "Are you? Are the horses harnessed to the carriage?"

"No," Peter replied. "We talked, and the time passed. I'll see to it." He darted out the back door shouting for Brian and Charles.

೪ು೩ೕ

Though sunny and cool, storm clouds appeared to the southwest. "The Sea Lion is in dock," I said.

"How can you tell?" Sylvia asked. "Every ship appears the same."

Pointing, I smiled. "I would know that mast anywhere."

Crews unloading ships occupied the docks. Wagons filled with lumber and sacks of grain. Two accountants, one representing the shipping company and one representing a federation of merchants, counted every item.

"William Percival," I shouted from the carriage. The captain squinted, making his way down the gangplank. By then, I exited the carriage, greeting him with a handshake.

"What are you doing here?" he asked. "And how did you get here without me?"

"I'm here to transfer money to the Confederacy. It arrived from Boston. The Bank of London holds it. We sailed from New Orleans because of the war."

"The war is on," William said. "The crossing took two more days than planned. I sailed south toward Bermuda and then west. Not sure why, but my owners told me to." He turned toward Peter and the ladies. "We have company." He squinted again. "Oh, Peter and Sylvia, 'tis grand to see you." He greeted them leaving Beatrice alone. Finally, he turned his attention. "And who might this lass be?"

"William, she would be my wife, Beatrice. Beatrice, this is my dear friend, Captain William Percival."

"Your wife? You went and married?" He peered at me waiting for a confirmation.

"Yes, we're married and expecting a child."

"Congratulations," William said.

"How long before you could join us for a meal?"

"Within the hour. Where shall we meet?"

"The Long Street Tavern," Peter said. "Do you know it?"

"Certainly," William replied. "I'll see you there."

William Percival

We parted company giving me time to finish business and clean up. It also gave me time to return to my cabin and read instructions I had from my employer in the event I came across Alexander Frey. Opening a letter, I sat at my desk and read.

Captain Percival:

In the event you encounter Alexander Frey, please be cordial even though he represents the enemy. If he asks you to transport his money to the Confederacy, please agree to do so. However, we ask you to sail to Bermuda. At that time, your ship will be boarded by Federal troops. They will search the ship, find the money, and confiscate it. We know Mr. Frey is your good friend. We will protect that friendship in such a way that he will not know you have betrayed him. It is important his money not reach the South. Thank you for your cooperation.

Sincerely,
Robert Tankard
President, New England Shipping

Folding the letter, I inserted it in the envelope. Sullenly, I walked across the cabin and opened the lock box in my wooden cabinet. Placing the letter there, I turned to the washbasin feeling dirty with sin. Never had I been asked to perform such a task, and never would I have thought it possible. As I dried off, one question ricocheted through the crevices of my spirit. Where were my loyalties? Were they to country, friendship, or employers? At that moment, my friend awaited me, my friend who had made me rich. I couldn't imagine betraying Alexander Frey.

A knock sounded. The mate informed me he completed the work of offloading the cargo, and that the crew stood ready for recreation.

"So do I. Choose three seamen to stand guard. The rest may have leave. Have the purser pay the men. I will hire a new crew in three days in case they wish to sail to America." The mate affirmed he understood. I began a slow walk to the Long Street Tavern.

Chapter 89

George Yardley

Boredom set in the likes of which I had never known. Our camp, Camp Autumn, was surrounded by changing leaf colors of golden red tints and felt as if it, too, moaned with tedium. Rain refused to fall, creating dry, dusty roads. Day by day, the Rappahannock water level dropped, exposing mammoth rocks. We trained, and we wished for home, for parents, for spouses.

"Have you thought about what we're up against?" Nathaniel asked as we prepared to sleep. "With the river low, our backs are to a wall."

I lay naked from the waist up. "What do you mean?"

"If Yankees come at us, where might we go? We're out here by ourselves. They would chase us across that trickle of a river without any trouble."

"Should we move to the other side?"

"We need a natural defense."

"Our orders state we stay on this side to disrupt enemy incursions."

"Well, we haven't seen a Yankee in months. What if they plan to march through Fredericksburg? The thirty of us can't stop them. I don't mind being a disruption; but, I don't want to be a sacrifice."

"What should we do?"

"Place an advanced guard maybe five miles north and while we're sitting around doing nothing pick out a spot on the other side where we can build a natural defense. Maintain this camp as ordered, but if attacked, we'll have somewhere to go."

Yawning, I turned on my side. "I'll take care of it in the morning—glad someone's here to think up plans."

"Don't doze off. Put Fourth Platoon north of Stafford Courthouse. Order Third Platoon to maintain Camp Autumn while the remaining platoons prepare a defense across the river."

𝔖ℯ𝔰ℯ

Next morning, as we finished breakfast, Nathaniel reminded me of his plans. "Everyone gather round—listen up," I shouted. For the next ten minutes, Nathaniel described his goals.

Richard Grogan and Richard Lindamood took responsibility for the camp near Stafford Courthouse. Within the hour, Fourth Platoon packed and rode away with orders to keep a two-man guard posted throughout the night, and once a day to send someone with a report.

Kinchen and his brother, Levi, took charge of Camp Autumn. Third Platoon received orders to refresh the camp and dig new latrines. At first, they felt they had the easiest job. Then, the tedium surfaced.

First and Second Platoons saddled their horses and rode across the river to scout appropriate defensive positions. Calvin Pruitt found a place near the Richmond Highway from which we could catch the enemy in crossfire. I established it as our second camp, naming it Camp Crossfire. We started back to Camp Autumn when Nathaniel found it necessary to speak.

"You boys glad I'm here to take care of you?"

"We couldn't get along without you," Tillman said.

"Matter of fact," Rex offered, "we'd all be dead if it weren't for you."

"What do you mean by that?" Nathaniel asked.

"Those Yankees at Bull Run saw you and thought you looked like Goliath. When they did, they took off running—fortunately, they ran in the other direction. One Yankee we took prisoner told me they'd never seen anyone as ugly as you, so they ran—scared to death." Laughter rang out, leaving Nathaniel's pride wounded. "If you had kept undercover and out of sight, they would have killed us."

"That'll teach you to brag on yourself," I said, riding next to my cousin.

Chapter 90

Alexander Frey

Our afternoon meal completed, William and I joined each other at the bar for brandy. "We must talk," I said. "Can you sail me to Savannah, and if so, when?"

"You know I can," he said, sipping his drink. "However, 'tis something that goes against my grain."

"What do you mean?"

"Alexander, think. I am a New Englander with Union sympathies. You ask me to deliver money that will cause my side to suffer."

"Forgive me."

"It's all right. Our friendship means more than our politics. Why take the chance of running a naval blockade? You might die at sea."

"Right now, with this child coming, I hate to think about dying."

"Stay here until the war ends. Your money won't make the difference between victory and defeat."

"Probably not, but I keep my word."

"Allow me this compromise. What if I sail you and your money to Bermuda? You might gain passage to Savannah or Charleston from there."

"When do we sail?"

"Two days hence on the afternoon tide."

"I'll have the gold transferred that morning. Thank you." Holding up my glass, I proposed a toast. "You truly are a friend."

❧❧❧❧

On Friday, I had the money previously deposited in the Bank of London converted to gold. The two sums totaled over five million dollars in U. S. currency. Giving the details to Peter, I took Beatrice for a walk. The air, thick with fog and moisture, caused the newly cut hay to reek. Taking her hand, we strolled down the road into the countryside. During the last two days, Beatrice had become noticeably pregnant. Her abdomen filled with child.

"Beatrice, half a million dollars remain in the Bank of London. It is your money." Pausing, I expressed my fears and hers. "If the worst happens, and I do not return, stay here until the war ends, and then decide if you should sail to America. That amount should see you through the rest of your life and the child's." We walked for a moment in silence. "I have given Amy her inheritance. I had a will written that states if anything happens to you and our child, your remaining assets transfer to Amy. When I arrive in Atlanta, I will take the same legal precautions there. If George and Amy fail to survive this war, their assets will transfer to you and our child."

"I wish you wouldn't go," she whispered, turning to embrace me. "Why don't you give Captain Percival the gold? Let him deliver it."

"As he pointed out, he is a Yankee."

"Can you trust him?"

"After you and my family, I trust William more than anyone else on earth."

ᥫᥬᥫᥬ

On the way to the bank, we stopped at a solicitor's office to sign the wills, after which we proceeded to transfer the gold to The Sea Lion. Captain Percival waited on deck. His crew finished stowing a cargo of carpets and furniture intended for Boston and New York. In less than half an hour, the crew delivered the three locked strong boxes to William's cabin. William and I removed six floor planks, placing the wealth inside a vault, and replaced the planks.

"Say good-bye to your bride," William said. "It is time."

"I'd rather say, 'I will see you later.'"

"It's your choice."

Striding down the gangplank, I walked toward Beatrice, Peter, and Sylvia feeling a tide of emotion rise within as I again noticed my wife's pregnant lines. I embraced and kissed Sylvia and shook Peter's hand.

"Please take care of her," I said, knowing Peter would die before he allowed anything to happen to Beatrice and the child.

"I will. Safe journey, and God be with you."

Turning, looking into my wife's eyes, I cowered. "I'll need to remember this embrace for months." She stepped into my outstretched arms. Tears streamed down her cheeks, resulting in pitiable sobs. "I love you very much."

"I love you, too," she said. "Please be careful, and God bless you."

I walked up the plank and boarded the ship. The crew brought the plank onboard while shore men untied the vessel. Slowly, The Sea Lion maneuvered into the river.

Chapter 91

Amy Yardley

News spread that the Confederate States of America inaugurated Jefferson Davis and Alexander Stephens as president and vice-president. Frigid temperatures froze Stephanie and me to the bone. Winds blew snow south across the open expanse between Winchester and Front Royal. From the locals, we heard more talk about the weather than about the war. Days passed in which warmth failed me, no matter how long I stood by the fire in the field house we converted to a hospital. Tedium set in, except when Stephanie contemplated Doctor McAllister's advances.

She and I developed a morning routine. Upon awakening on alternating mornings, one jumped up, ran into the kitchen, stoked the coals in the fireplace, and lit the fire in the iron stove. Temptation abounded to return to bed and enjoy the last vestiges of warmth under the quilts; but, if the fires were extinguished, we'd rise to bitter cold.

By the end of November, fighting in the northern Shenandoah ceased, allowing soldiers to return to their farms and homes. The exodus gave Doctor McAllister an idea. Having joined the nurses for breakfast, he offered an alternative: either winter in Richmond or at his home in Edinburg.

"Where is it warmer?" I asked.

"The cold penetrates both towns. It takes two days to get to Edinburg and a week to make Richmond."

"In our travel, would we sleep outside in tents?" Celeste asked.

"Yes, though friends in Strasburg and Woodstock would provide us rooms for a night."

"I won't go anywhere until this cold breaks," Mary Ruth said. "I'd prefer Richmond."

"Me too," I said. "There, the opportunity may present itself to see my husband."

"Outnumbered," Doctor McAllister said.

"Where is General Jackson wintering?" Stephanie asked.

"Winchester," he said. "Until the weather breaks, we remain here. Let us see what December brings." We agreed. "Oh, by the way, I received an invitation to a dance and social at the hotel this Saturday night. The ladies auxiliary giving the party invited you all."

George Yardley

I sent word to General Beauregard requesting orders, wishing he would grant permission for The Guard to return to Georgia. Those orders never came. Fourth Platoon kept vigilant watch at Stafford Courthouse, never once seeing a Yankee soldier. The others maintained Camp Autumn, which they renamed Camp Winter.

Not able to stand the isolation, I sought Beauregard, finding him in Fredericksburg living in the comfort and warmth of a house. After a lengthy discussion, he gave permission for The Guard to return to Georgia for the winter. We stowed our tents and supplies in a barn west of Fredericksburg, waiting word as to when we might depart. I, on the other hand, became introspective and aloof.

"What's wrong?" Nathaniel asked.

"I won't go without Amy. Last I heard, the nurses resided in Front Royal. I must find her."

"You're not going without me. And, if that's the case, let's saddle up and move out. We'll go by Rex's and Bart's home, and take them with us."

"All right," I said. "Give Kinchen the written orders and directions to the train station in Fredericksburg. I'll tell Rex and Bart."

The trip went as planned. After spending the night with the Snyders calming Mr. Snyder over his sons' disobedience, we headed north to Marshall and west to Front Royal.

Dusk settled as we entered town. Finding the hotel, we rented a room and received information about the nurses.

"If you wait about an hour," the hotel owner said, "the ladies will arrive to attend a social. That will give you time to clean up— and, believe me," he sniffed the air, "you need to clean up."

"Make it two rooms," I said.

Nathaniel scoffed. "You don't want to spend the night with me?"

The hotel owner laughed. "That will be four dollars Confederate or two dollars, U. S."

"Pay him," I said.

"Why should I spend my money?"

"Well, I'd like to see you spend money once before I die."

"I'm amazed," Nathaniel said, standing in the hallway on the second floor, "that you're willing to remain here and wait for Amy."

"Surprise is a wonderful thing in love and war. It's worth the wait."

We entered our rooms, waiting for warm water, which arrived in short order. I spent time shaving and washing, hating to wear the same clothes I wore the past five months. Not knowing what else to do, I re-dressed, deciding to wait on the second-floor landing to see if I could catch a glimpse of Amy as she entered.

Stephanie came through the door accompanied by Captain McAllister. Three women followed. Amy entered wearing a gray wool dress. She appeared thinner, if not gaunt, but still beautiful. McAllister escorted them to a large side room for the social.

As others arrived, emotions I had forgotten welled. Not able to stand it, I knocked on Nathaniel's door, but received no answer. Turning the knob, I entered, finding him asleep.

"Wake up," I said. "They're here." Nathaniel refused consciousness.

Giving up, I left and started downstairs. Captain McAllister spotted me. Putting my hand and finger to my lips, he nodded affirmation he would keep the secret. An orchestra played a waltz.

Approaching from the back, I grasped her shoulders with both hands, preventing her from turning. "Mrs. Yardley, may I have the pleasure of this dance?"

She did turn, and attempted a scream, but to no avail. Throwing her arms around me, we held each other. The music stopped. Realizing everyone's attention targeted us, we separated, keeping our arms entwined behind us. The hotel owner gestured for the music to start. Taking her hand, we danced around the room. People gave us the entire floor. Tears descended upon her smile.

Chapter 92

Alexander Frey

The Sea Lion made excellent time. Assured we would make Bermuda within the week, Captain Percival isolated himself in his cabin. Though William's behavior appeared strange, I accepted the aloneness.

As we sailed around the horn of Bermuda toward the Great Sound into Somerset, Captain Percival made his presence known. Looking strained and out of sorts, I concluded my friend ill. We exchanged words as we entered the harbor. Nearing the dock, a contingent of armed soldiers and naval personnel appeared, carrying rifles and revolvers. Not knowing what to do, I headed for William's cabin, bursting through the door.

Stunned, he rose from his chair. "How dare you enter like that?" On his desk, I spied an opened Bible along with four pieces of paper.

"Excuse me. What is the meaning of your behavior?" I collected my thoughts. "Never have you holed up in your cabin ignoring me. Explain yourself."

Before he could, the military personnel streamed past the portal, entering the cabin. "Alexander," Captain Percival said, "please forgive me." With those words, he raised a pistol to his head and shot himself. I rushed to his side, not understanding what happened. Blood oozed from his right temple. His eyes refused light.

"Are you Mr. Alexander Frey?" a voice demanded. Hesitating, I confirmed the identification. "You are under arrest for aiding and abetting the enemy of the United States of America." He ordered me taken into custody.

"What is the meaning of this? Who are you?"

"We are United States naval personnel. You and your gold are remanded to our custody to prevent entrance into the Confederacy."

"You have no right..."

"We are at war, sir. Your right to habeas corpus is suspended by the President of the United States."

"We are in Bermuda—not the United States."

The officer looked as his men shackled my wrists in front of me. "Where is the gold?"

"What gold?"

"You know what gold. The gold you transferred from Boston to London and now from London to here."

"I know not of what you speak. My friend lies dead while you demand information I do not have."

"Your friend is dead, and you will join him if you do not identify where the gold is hidden." He studied the cabin trying to ascertain the treasure's hiding place.

Certain the whereabouts of my money had died with William, I realized the officer had no idea about the false floor. Rather than tell, I decided the secret would die with me.

"Will you tell me or not?" he said. I remained silent. "Take him to the stern; slit his throat; and throw him overboard. When you return, we'll tear the cabin apart."

Two soldiers horsed me around, moving me to the back of the ship. As they did, one drew his knife. Resolving to die on my own terms, I broke loose, ran a couple steps, and thrust myself overboard. Hitting the water, a chill crashed through my clothing. Kicking, I surfaced, met by a hail of bullets. Having no recourse, I submerged, continuing to kick and swim until out of breath. I surfaced; another round of shots echoed. Sliding under the water, I found I could swim better by moving my shackled hands in a downward motion from head to stomach. Keeping up the repetitive motions, I found shallow water where I gained my footing. Rushing to shore, hearing shouts of my pursuing assailants, I ran across the sand into vegetation, gasping for air. Taking a few seconds to catch my breath, I ran deeper into the reeds and undergrowth. Within a few hundred feet, two black skinned boys met me.

"Do you speak English?" I asked.

"Yes, sir," they said in tandem.

"Can you help me?" Pointing toward the docks, I bent over. "I was on that ship. It was taken over by armed men. They are trying to kill me."

"Come," one said. They led me into another area of vegetation down a path worn by use. In a moment, we entered a clearing where a small ramshackle hut stood. "Wait here," the boy said. He entered the hut.

Two men came out, one holding a machete. "Who are you?" he asked.

"Alexander Frey—from Georgia."

"What are you doing here?"

"I sailed to Bermuda on The Sea Lion. When we docked, military personnel boarded the ship, seeking to steal my money. They cuffed me," I said, holding my hands up, "and threatened to kill me. I jumped overboard and swam ashore. These boys found me. Can you help me?"

The men looked at each other. The one with the machete spoke. "If we help you and are caught, they will kill us."

"Please, if you won't help, will you try to break these chains?"

They looked at each other and nodded, sending a boy into the hut. He returned carrying a hammer and chisel. Setting the chain on a rock, they took turns beating upon the chisel until at last a link broke.

"That's better," I said. The cuffs remained around my wrists. The boys returned the tools to the hut. "Something is amiss. We sailed from England. Are these military personnel English?"

"We don't know," one said. "They arrived five days ago on a ship without any markings. They room and board in Somerset."

"Where can I go for help?" The men didn't respond. "Please, help me."

"Remain here for the night until we find out what is happening."

"I would appreciate that." They ushered me into the hut. One woman and two teenage girls waited inside, appearing scared.

"My name is Bernard," the older man said. "This is my friend, Homer. And these are my sons, James and Thaddeus." We shook hands, turning our attention to the females. "This is my wife, Anna, and our daughters, Corey and Amelia." Anna gave a polite nod. In the fading light, I saw the whites of their eyes. Anna lit a candle and prepared food and a straw mattress. Never could I remember such humble accommodations, and never could I remember feeling more thankful.

I slept, but off and on. Every sound alarmed me, as I feared my pursuers might discover my whereabouts. Every time I awoke, I felt gratitude I had slept, even if I had slept only minutes.

When light dawned, it came through the windows and the crevices of the hut. I jumped up, awaking everyone in the home.

"Is something wrong?" Bernard asked, joining me.

"No—thought I heard something."

He smiled. "There's a lot to hear in the wilds of Bermuda. Relax, those men don't know you're here and wouldn't know how to find you if informed."

"Thank you."

"Anna," Bernard said, "get up—make us food to eat."

She rose from her mat seeking the out of doors to relieve herself. Bernard had already done so. One by one, they made their way around back until Bernard showed me the latrine.

We ate fruit and hard biscuits. The girls warmed to me. Smiles appeared, revealing teeth as white as their eyeballs.

"Where should we begin?" I asked Bernard.

"Tell us what is on that ship," he said.

Hesitating, I considered my options. "Hidden on the ship are valuables that belong to me. Those men know that. Further, the captain was my good friend until he committed suicide last night when the soldiers boarded the ship."

"Why did the captain kill himself?" Homer asked.

"Don't know."

"I would suggest," Homer continued, "that he played a part in your capture, and guilt overcame him."

That thought crossed my mind. "You think he betrayed me?" The word reminded me of the Bible on William's desk. Betrayal, I thought. The notes might provide explanation.

"Good chance," Bernard said. "Friends betray friends—Judas betrayed Jesus."

"Yes. Where can I go for help?"

"To the local constabulary," Homer said. "We must go first." In seconds, the men stood, moving about the hut preparing to leave. "You boys play around that ship. If you notice anything, come tell us. Act stupid like white men expect black children to act." James and Thaddeus ran off without a good-bye. "Let's be going," Homer said. "The day is wasting."

❦❧❦❧

Through the vegetation, I found a place to spy upon the harbor. A ship sailed around the horn toward The Sea Lion, flying an American flag. In a few moments, the crew tied alongside.

"Americans," I said out loud. "What are they doing, and why has England allowed them to use this harbor?"

"This harbor is abandoned," Bernard said. Homer and he stood behind me. "Any ship can use it. Why didn't your captain sail into Hamilton?"

"Don't know."

Homer took a step toward me. "Most ships sail into Hamilton."

"Betrayal," I said. "I am gravely disappointed."

"So was Jesus," Homer replied.

Standing, I peered back at the ships. "How will we know if they find the money?"

"So, it's money and not valuables?" Bernard asked.

"Money and a lot of it. If you help me, I will reward you."

"Going to the constable is a waste of time," Bernard said. "We must get to Hamilton to inform the English what happened here."

"How?"

"We can walk, which could take a day; or, maybe our friend, Ludwig, will sail us. He lives near Somerset."

"Let's go," I said.

I walked faster than either Bernard or Homer wanted to walk. They protested, but to no avail.

"Ludwig's boat is there," Homer said upon seeing the mast. Small and worse for the wear, I doubted its potential. "There he is."

Seeing a black man standing near a hut, I waved, realizing how desperate I must be. When Ludwig spotted us, he waved back, walking toward us.

"What a surprise," he said, shaking hands. Stepping back, he waited until Bernard introduced me. Once introduced, we asked the necessary questions. Ludwig confirmed it would take three hours to sail to Hamilton.

The trip went well, allowing us to arrive at the Hamilton constabulary by mid-afternoon. Hearing out account, the duty sergeant led us to the British Naval Office. Walking a quarter mile, we entered a white stucco building. After listening to the sergeant, a captain ushered me into his office. I explained the situation, short of giving the monetary details. I did include William's suicide. Two additional officers joined the meeting. The gold from The Bank of London heightened their regard for me. They decided that the next morning two British warships would leave Hamilton to intercept the American ship at Somerset. The captain asked me to remain in Hamilton to sail on one ship. I felt compelled to return with Ludwig, and so I did.

✞✞✞✞

James and Thaddeus returned with news the Americans had taken The Sea Lion apart plank by plank and had not found the treasure. Relieved, I dozed off and slept.

About five o'clock, James awakened me. Quietly, so as not to awaken the girls, the men and boys prepared for the day. A faint glow emanated from the eastern skies. They led me into reeds and vegetation from which we saw The Sea Lion and the unmarked ship.

"Wonder what they did with Captain Percival's crew," I said.

"In the warehouse in shackles," James whispered.

"I can get us on deck," Thaddeus said. "There's no guard dockside. We can walk onboard."

"Are you certain?" Bernard asked his son.

"Yes, sir. We watched till late last night. No one guards the ship."

"We should all go," Homer said.

Bernard stood. "The whole lot of us walking on board might not seem as strange as one or two creeping around." We moved toward the ships having no idea if anyone watched. Coming to the gangplank, we found it as the boys indicated: no guards and no crew milling about.

"Wait here," I said. "If I can see into the cabin, I will know if they found the gold." Bent over, walking up the plank, I raced toward the cabin door, which stood ajar. Enough light shone to indicate the floorboards remained in place. I returned to the others. "Let's go to our hiding place. We'll see what happens when the British arrive."

We scampered back to the vegetation where we remained for an hour. Crewmen began working on The Sea Lion's deck, a few voiding themselves over the side. While doing so, two crewmen caught sight of the British ships steaming into the Great Sound. An alarm bell rang bringing all hands on deck. In minutes, steam billowed from the American ship. Untied and loosed from The Sea Lion, it sailed, slipping between the British ships. One ship fired a warning across the American ship's bow. We watched as additional shots penetrated the American ship. Half an hour later, it keeled over and went down. Some sailors took to their lifeboats, while others jumped into the waters of the Atlantic.

Chapter 93

Amy Yardley

"Will you marry him?" I asked, gaining Stephanie's ear before George and I went upstairs.

"Plan to find out," she said as we stood at the entranceway to the hotel. "I love him; but, I question if I need him. I won't dishonor him or me," she smiled. "Don't take this wrong. I loved Drury and still love him. When we courted—when you and George courted—I needed sex. For whatever reason, I don't need sex. I need a strong, intelligent man. Doctor McAllister is intelligent. I have yet to discover if he is strong enough to meet my needs."

Giving Stephanie an intense hug, I whispered. "I love you. God bless you." George waited at the top of the stairs. Taking one last look at my friend, I went to him.

"Where's Celeste?" I heard Doctor McAllister ask at the front door.

"With Mr. Thomas," Patricia said.

"And where might Mr. Thomas be?" he asked.

Patricia looked upstairs at George. "In his hotel room."

Stephanie caught the meaning. "I'll be right back," she said. Running up the stairs, she knocked on Nathaniel's door.

"Who is it?" he asked.

"It is death if you have Celeste in there."

The door opened. Celeste smirked. "No need for killing. You're not the only woman around here allowed to talk to a man. Did someone appoint you our guardian angel?"

"No—I'm more inclined to guard Nathaniel."

Celeste turned toward Nathaniel. "Good night."

Before Celeste closed the door, Nathaniel got Stephanie's attention. "It started out as a good night until you showed up."

"You'll be glad I did," she said, closing the door. Taking Celeste by the arm, she marched her downstairs and outside to the carriage. George marched me into our room.

Chapter 94

Alexander Frey

"Mr. Frey," the captain of the British Admiralty said, sitting behind his desk, "I understand this is your gold, and it is intended for the Confederate States of America. If acceptable, my ships will sail you and your treasure to Savannah as soon as we transfer the money from The Sea Lion."

"Thank you," I said, "but why? Queen Victoria declared the Confederacy a belligerent."

"Appearances, that is all. The Crown speaks one thing and does another."

Arriving at The Sea Lion by carriage, I went to William's cabin, finding a mess. Papers and books strewn from one wall to the other revealed the scavenger hunt. My friend's life exposed the vestiges of war, greed, and betrayal. Out of respect, I gathered the papers one by one, examining each. Trying to provide organization, I stacked them according to either personal or naval content. Sadness filled me, seeing my friend's life in disarray. Then, I picked up an envelope now empty but with these words inscribed on the front, 'Open if chance encounter with Alexander Frey'. Putting it in my jacket pocket, I continued the task, until coming across a paper on which William had written biblical notes. Four times, my friend wrote, 'Betrayal requires the presence of Satan' and referenced Satan entering Judas Iscariot.

Then, I discovered the letter signed by Robert Tankard. William, I thought, why? How could war divide friends? Wanting to speak to him, to embrace him once more, to love him as a friend, I allowed tears of forgiveness to flow, thinking to myself, "Mr. Tankard, I wish to have the displeasure of meeting you. I wish to preside over your demise." Placing the letter in my pocket, I resumed what I considered an obligation. The very last paper contained one sentence, 'and Judas hanged himself—suicide.'

By noon the next day, the British Navy had transferred the gold, except one bag of British coinage, to the Trent, which had arrived in port overnight. The Admiralty thought better of sending a warship to Savannah when the Treant, a legitimate vessel flying legitimate insignias became available.

That morning, I made a slow walk to Bernard's hut. Thanking him, I presented the bag of gold. "I shall never forget what you did." Choking on my words, I went on. "Captain Percival did betray me as Judas betrayed Christ. In that, I lost a good friend. In you and your family I gained new friends. Thank you, again." I shook the men's hands and proceeded to embrace James and Thaddeus, thanking them for their help. Not wanting to omit a kindness, I followed with embraces for the girls and Anna. Before I left, Bernard delayed me, bowed his head, as did the others, and prayed a prayer of thanksgiving and safe journey.

Chapter 95

George Yardley

We awakened to a weather change. The wind ceased its incessant blowing, and the air felt warm. After breakfast, we began our journey. Arriving at the Snyder's farm by late afternoon, we enjoyed supper prepared by Mrs. Snyder. To make room for the ladies, Nathaniel, Rex, Bart, and I slept in the barn.

At dawn, Nathaniel and I awoke to a commotion—arguing coming from the house. Peering through a crack in the barn door, we saw twelve mounted Yankee soldiers.

Sitting tall in his saddle, Mr. Speakes shouted at Mr. Snyder. "I'm telling you," Speakes said, "your son, Rex, helped them."

"Quiet down," Mr. Snyder said. "We have female guests. There's no sense waking them with this useless dispute."

"What do we have?" Rex asked as Bart and he joined Nathaniel and me.

"Yankee soldiers accompanied by Mr. Speakes—your father's holding his own."

"Mr. Snyder," a lieutenant said, "two men will search your home while others search your barn and outbuildings. I know Rex is your son; but, we are at war. If you harbor him, I will hold you responsible."

"Search all you want," Mr. Snyder said. "You won't find anyone but the ladies."

Turning to Nathaniel, hoping he had devised a plan, I spoke. "We can either hide here or take them on. What do you want to do?"

Rex removed his pistol from its holster. "Fight it out. We have the element of surprise."

"Search the barn first," we heard the lieutenant say. He and nine others rode toward us.

"I'll take the lieutenant," I whispered. "Rex you take the one on the left. Bart, take the one on the right."

"Which one do you want me to take?" Nathaniel asked.

"The rest."

With our rifles aimed at the barn door, our pistols waiting, I saw that not one Yankee held his rifle or pistol in hand. When the door opened, I shouted, "Fire." Four men went down. With our pistols, we shot another volley. Ten men lay dead or wounded. Before I moved, we heard shots from inside the house.

"Oh, God," I said. "What have we done?" We raced to the house, Nathaniel and Bart to the front door, Rex and I to the back. "Come out with your hands up," I shouted. The door opened, revealing two soldiers. "Is anyone hurt in there?"

"Help, help," Mrs. Snyder screamed.

"Stay here—keep these men covered," I said to Rex. Passing the two soldiers on the front steps, I rushed into the parlor finding Nathaniel, Bart, and Mrs. Snyder bent over Mr. Snyder. Two puddles of blood showed themselves, one beneath the head and the other next to his right shoulder. "Amy," I shouted, "we need your help. It's all right to come out."

Doors opened on the second floor. Amy and Celeste rushed downstairs. "They shot Mr. Snyder—ten wounded or dead soldiers lay by the barn."

Amy went to Mr. Snyder while I rejoined Rex. "Tie those two up," I said. "Your father's shot. The ladies are tending him."

Something's wrong, I thought. Someone's missing. "Where's Speakes?"

Rex shook his head. Looking around, I yelled for Nathaniel and Bart. We ran to the barn. Giving a quick count, I found nine bodies. In the distance, I saw a lone horseman riding toward Manassas. "Nathaniel, saddle Winsome II—catch that bastard."

Patricia and Mary Ruth cared for two wounded Yankees. The others we found dead. Rex and Bart raced to their mother and father.

Amy Yardley

"Mrs. Snyder, I need your help. The head wound cut to the skull but is not serious. We must remove the ball from your husband's back. Heat water--bring it with clean linens."

Rex went with his mother while Bart helped me turn his father. Cutting away his shirt, I exposed a gaping wound next to his right shoulder blade.

"Hope that ball didn't hit his lung or heart," Celeste said.

"What can we dig it out with?" I asked. "We don't have instruments with us." Pausing, I turned to Bart. "Find your sharpest knife." He returned holding a thin blade. Inserting it in the wound, I felt the ball about an inch deep.

"Don't think it hit anything vital," Celeste said.

"If I dig that deep, I may kill him."

"Hope he remains unconscious," Celeste said as Rex carried a basin to my side.

"Will he live?" Mrs. Snyder asked.

"We'll know in a few minutes," I said. Wiping the knife with a cloth, dipping it in the water, I paused. "Here goes." As the knife entered the wound, I felt the ball move. Mr. Snyder stiffened, causing me to lose touch with the lead.

"Oh, my God," Mrs. Snyder screamed. "He's biting his tongue." Blood seeped from his mouth.

"Put a piece of linen between his teeth," I said.

Rex untied a leather strip from his holster, inserting it between his father's bloody teeth. Trying again, inserting the knife, I forced the ball to pop out, along with it a large clot. Soaking the wound with warm water, I applied pressure.

"He's in God's hands," Celeste said. "Let's put him to bed and pray he makes it."

Rex and Bart lifted their father's head and shoulders while George grabbed his feet, carrying him upstairs to his bed.

George Yardley

I asked Amy to walk with me to the barn. "It's hard to believe you can do what you just did. Wish I'd seen you work at Haymarket."

"Are they going to make it?" Amy asked Mary Ruth at the barn.

"Don't let me die," one soldier begged.

"We won't," Mary Ruth said. Looking at George, Mary Ruth continued, "These soldiers are mere boys—no more than sixteen or seventeen. Why are they here?"

Shrugging, I looked down, seeing the fear on the kid's face. "Don't know. Why are any of us here?"

Amy stooped over the boy, reassuring him. Patricia informed me the other one would not live.

In the distance, I saw Nathaniel returning with a second horse. "Found Speakes dead a mile up the road," he said, dismounting, guiding the horses into the barn. "What do we have?"

"Mr. Snyder fights for his life," Amy said. "This boy survived."

"What's the plan?" Nathaniel asked.

"Not sure, but I doubt we'll head to Fredericksburg today." I looked around. "If anything, the plan includes digging graves— ones no one can see from the road."

After burying the Yankees, I talked with the one wounded. To my amazement, he expressed a desire to join the Guard. Having lived in Maryland, his father, who served in the state legislature, was arrested along with seventeen other legislators, to prevent them from voting for secession. Lincoln ordered that those in Washington whose loyalties seemed questionable be detained without right of trial. Private Alton Cornthwaite believed he fought for the wrong side. The Snyders offered to keep him until spring.

Chapter 96

Alexander Frey

The Trent steamed toward Charleston. On board, James M. Mason and John Slidell, two Confederate envoys who had attempted to make diplomatic and economic inroads with The Crown, shadowed me the entire voyage. As we approached the coast, a Union clipper flying the stars and stripes closed, signaling The Trent to come to rest. The captain obeyed.

Making it known they intended a routine search, the American ship dispatched a boarding party. Sensing trouble, the captain hid me in his cabin behind a false bookshelf where he kept the gold. From there, I heard every word on deck. One voice belonged to Captain Charles Wilkes, who demanded information about Mr. Alexander Frey and a shipment of gold.

The Trent's captain denied knowledge of the gold or its owner. However, in the meantime, Captain Wilkes turned his attention to the two envoys. Informed of their Confederate leanings, Wilkes shackled them, returning them to his ship. Outraged, The Trent's captain argued, but to no avail. All the while the incident served as a distraction to my presence.

Additional Yankee warships blockaded Charleston harbor, but permitted us passage. I decided to disembark there rather than Savannah. Once safe on southern soil, I employed dock slaves to transport the gold to my company's bank in South Carolina. Watching the slaves, I felt depressed over their condition compared to Bernard's and Homer's. As a Confederacy, we had to find a way to free our slaves as England had. At the train station, I purchased a ticket for the next morning and sent a telegram to Sarah informing her of my pending arrival.

In my hotel room, I realized The Trent would return to England. Writing to Beatrice, I informed her of the events in Bermuda and my safe arrival in Charleston. In the morning, I went to the dock, thanked the captain, and placed the letter in his hands.

❧❧❧❧

As the train pulled into Atlanta, I saw Sarah alone on the platform. My concern over Amy's absence rivaled Sarah's concern over Beatrice's absence. We remained on the platform. With folded arms, Sarah's eyes penetrated mine. "Pregnant?"

"Have you not received mail?"

"None—for which I despaired—until realizing the naval blockades prevented delivery. Regardless, how could you leave your pregnant wife?"

"Beatrice understands my financial pledge to the South. I shall return to England within the month. Where is my daughter?" I listened but for a moment. "A field nurse? How—how could that happen?" We walked to the horse-drawn transport, owned by The Bank of Atlanta, which now held my baggage and gold.

"Yes, a field nurse and a good one," Sarah said. "Unfortunately, I know not her whereabouts, though her last letter indicated she resided in Front Royal, Virginia."

Studying the three large containers of gold on the wagon, I felt amused at how inconspicuous the crates appeared. No one could guess over five million dollars sat there. "How often do you receive mail from her?"

"It comes in bunches. I won't receive a letter for ten days to two weeks. Then, two or three arrive on the same day." She reflected for a second. Looking at the crates, she asked, "Is that what I think it is?"

"Could be; but, I'd prefer you not shout it from the mountaintops."

Horatio approached, Sarah having informed him of my arrival. Greetings exchanged, we made our way to the bank as Horatio informed me he had arranged a meeting in two days with Governor Brown, Vice-President Stephens, and Robert Toombs to determine the gold's fate.

Before returning to Sarah's, I had Horatio wire the families of James Mason and John Slidell to inform them of their captivity. The Trent's captain had wired England's ambassador to the Union, who in turn submitted formal charges against the United States, avowing that England regarded the atrocity as an act of war. Within the month, Secretary Seward released both men, issuing a formal apology less Britain enter the war on the Confederate side.

❧❧❧❧❧

Two days hence, I waited in my office for the leadership of the Confederate States of America. Jacob Goldman, my friend and business partner, arrived early.

"How goes it with the forge and boot factories?" I asked, standing at the door.

"Well, except the Confederacy fails to pay for the munitions and boots."

"Do they explain how we might function without payment?"

"No—Jefferson Davis thinks we owe him a favor."

"Being a Jew, I know you have estimates as to the operating costs for each factory."

"Thirty thousand dollars for the boot factory and twice that for the forge."

"If that's the case, I shall designate two hundred thousand dollars of my funds to provide the operating expenses."

Jacob's burly body seemed to twitch. "Jefferson won't like that."

"That's the way it shall be." I paused, thinking about another scenario. "Four and a half million dollars in gold remains. I shall give the Confederacy two million in January of 1862, divide the remainder equally, and give them half each January for the next two years."

Jacob sat. "He really won't like that. The leadership expects the entire amount now."

"It astounds me how men of political persuasion freely spend other men's money, especially when it costs politicians not one penny." Changing the subject, I guided Jacob into the office. "How are your sons?"

"Fine—two in Virginia and one in western Tennessee fight this war. I couldn't stop them, even though sentiment against Jews enlisting exists."

"I pray God keeps them safe."

"What about George and Amy? I hope you pray for them."

The front door opened. Horatio and Alexander Stephens entered. After we exchanged cordialities, I explained the formula for dispersing the gold.

"I agree," Stephens said. "Though I wish for a brief war, certain financial practices spun by our leadership alarm me. I will report your decision to the cabinet."

Having made his point, Stephens excused himself. Horatio and Jacob departed. Two complimentary emotions rushed over me: loneliness in that I missed Beatrice and concern for Amy. I decided if Sarah did not hear from my daughter within three days, I would go to Virginia. Walking home, I took in the sounds of carriages and church bells.

Sarah saw me coming. Standing on the porch, she shouted, "Hurry, Alexander, I have a surprise."

Hearing joy in her voice, I surmised a letter from Amy waited, but saw nothing in her hand as I climbed the steps. She opened the door. Amy rushed into my arms. The embrace lasted for what seemed forever, and I wished it so until I caught hold of my senses. "Wait a minute, young lady. You ran off into the midst of a war. What were you thinking?"

"To do what my father did by running off with his wife to a foreign country. And since I am my father's daughter, I expect your approval."

Smiling at her beauty and her candor, I spotted George in the dining room. "Why do you hide there?" He stepped toward me as I did toward him. Shaking hands and embracing, I felt the delight of life. "Do you lack control over the woman you married?"

"Yes, as you did."

"Agreed," I said, turning to Amy. "Why did you go to Virginia?"

"I love my husband," she said, looking at George.

"So it's your fault?"

"I choose not to take blame. She's your daughter."

"And," Amy said, "I understand I no longer hold the status as your only child?"

"After what you did—having neither regard for your own safety nor for anyone's feelings—God grants me the opportunity to raise a child less insolent and adventuresome."

She embraced me again. "Congratulations, Father."

"It may be time for juleps," George said, returning to the dining room where he had prepared the concoction.

Amy explained how she accidentally killed a major. The fact she took charge of the situation encouraged me. Before continuing, she remembered the Branners and referenced the family friendship. George served the drinks. "I remember old Mr. Branner, but for the most part, as children; our parents removed us from their social life."

Sarah stood. "I propose a toast." George took Amy's hand as I stood. "May this war end tonight and may we live happily hereafter."

We clanked our glasses. "Here's to my new sibling," Amy said.

"So you are the one?" I said to George.

He sipped his drink. "What one?"

"The one I read about in the London Times. The press mentioned a young captain who outflanked a Union army maneuver at Manassas, turning the battle's tide."

A look of admiration shot from Amy to George. "Father, what are your plans?"

"To return to England for my wife and I hope in time for my child's birth."

"Is it dangerous? From what you said, a naval blockade exists."

"That thought encompasses me. It behooves me to sail on either an English or Yankee ship. I could disguise myself and make my way to Philadelphia under an alias. If successful, I could gain passage to London."

"A horrible notion," Amy said. "I will not permit you to traipse into enemy territory. The Yankees want to capture you. What if you're caught?"

"I'll spend the remainder of the war in a Yankee prison."

The argument advanced for a few minutes as I thought of a way to gain safe passage. Traveling either to Charleston or Savannah to wait for an English ship crossed my mind. Otherwise, I realized the futility of discussing the matter.

At supper, I posed questions about George's plans. "I'd like to go to the farm tomorrow and spend a few days straightening it up. Then, I'll see Uncle Robert and Aunt Lillian. Afterwards, I'll bring Pearl here. If all goes well, I'll return Friday or Saturday."

"And after that?" I asked.

"Amy and I will spend the winter in Alpharetta." Amy nodded approval.

"And when the war resumes next spring?"

"The Guard shall return to Fredericksburg in March to reunite with General Lee's Army."

Sarah stood, clearing dishes. "I'm upset. George, you lead men into war. Amy cares for the wounded and dying. Alexander, you choose to sail the seven seas. Do my feelings matter? I sit here day after day waiting for a letter of doom." She moved toward the kitchen. "I'll serve dessert and coffee."

Standing, Amy gathered and clanked two plates. "I'll help Sarah."

My arms crossed on the table. "She fears the toll the war shall take on her family." Leaning further toward George, I whispered. "May Amy remain here with Sarah?"

Holding his fork, George tapped it once on the tablecloth. "She has a mind of her own. When you return to England, it's hard telling what she'll do."

"I depart this week, wishing to return to Atlanta with Beatrice before March. Would you encourage Amy to spend time with Sarah? I can't expect my sister to endure this war alone."

"They're probably engaged in the same conversation," George said. The kitchen door swung open. Sarah presented an apple pie while Amy carried a silver coffeepot.

"What do those smiles mean?" I asked as they set the coffee and dessert on the table. Each waited for the other to speak.

"They mean," Sarah said, "your daughter and sister have a secret, which we shall keep to ourselves. Ask all you want. We shall not reveal it."

"Young lady," I said, "you should not keep secrets from your husband—tell what you hide."

"I shall not, for I've crossed my heart and hope to die."

Leaning back, I eyed Amy. "When might you reveal your secret?"

"Possibly tomorrow evening at supper," Sarah said. "We wish you wouldn't bother us until then."

In an attempt to escape the dilemma, George turned to the pie and coffee. I intervened. "If you demanded submission from your wife as scripture teaches, she wouldn't keep secrets."

He swallowed. "Well, I keep secrets from her—guess we're even."

"What?" Amy said. "What secrets do you keep?"

"Many," he said. "If I tell you, they won't be secrets."

Sipping her coffee, Sarah turned to Amy. "He teases. George Yardley wouldn't keep a secret from his wife—no matter what—he's too truthful."

Amy peered at her husband, receiving a slight smile.

"Nice try," I said to my son-in-law.

಼

George remained in Atlanta an extra day. I, on the other hand, had business to finish. Gathering Horatio and my lawyer, Jonathan Grainger, we met at the club to establish the covenant regarding the gold. On January first, the Confederacy would receive two million dollars. Then, the second and third year, they would receive a million and a quarter dollars each year. Interest earned over the two years would keep the forge and boot factory working. Mr. Grainger requested my presence at his office the next morning to place my signature on the document.

"Fine," I said. "I return to England the day after tomorrow."

"Why so soon?" Mr. Grainger asked.

Horatio smirked. "He abandoned his pregnant wife there."

"Beatrice, pregnant?"

"Yes."

"Congratulations—I think," Jonathan said.

Chapter 97

Stephanie Stith

For two full days, we traveled. With warmer temperatures, the journey around the north end of the Massanutten Mountains to Strasburg took one day. There, we lodged for a night with Doctor McAllister's uncle, Elmer Tampkin.

Early the next morning, we set out on horseback up the valley. Therein, I learned a geographical lesson. The Shenandoah River flows north. For the locals, if traveling up the river, you travel south. If traveling down the river, you travel north. The river's winding beauty intensified with every bend as we rode the Valley Pike. Three times we came upon wild turkey, and I lost count of the whitetail deer we saw. Every leaf on every tree had fallen, but the surrounding gray countryside held a beauty and elegance the likes of which I had never witnessed. Arriving in Woodstock about mid-afternoon, William hurried me, that we might make the Mill by dark, which we did.

The Edinburg Mill stood three stories tall. Its grain bin rose ten feet above the roof line. Though white washed, the dust from milling made it appear light tan. The living quarters, located on the southeast side of the building, were comprised of a small parlor situated to the right and a large dining area to the left.

Beyond the dining area, the kitchen presented itself and beyond that, slave quarters, occupied by an elderly couple. Upstairs, Doctor McAllister showed me a large loft for females and a smaller one for males.

With William's presence, the entire family had returned home except his brother, Michael. His last correspondence indicated he served under General Johnston at Manassas. The family surmised Michael fought at Bull Run, but had not heard from him since the battle.

As Doctor McAllister and I listened, I pictured the countless soldiers buried in mass graves. William held his mother as he told her he doubted Michael survived. Breaking down, sobbing, she turned to her daughters for comfort. Overcome with grief, fainting, she remained in bed two weeks, save for the necessities of life. Becoming frail, sickly, refusing the medicines William offered, she died in her sorrow in mid-January.

When not tending his mother, William worked with his father, Jed, and his brother, Matt, milling and bagging flour. If a needy family appeared at the door with a sick child requesting Doctor McAllister's services, William refused remuneration. At times, he accepted a ham, roast, or jellies, whatever they could afford.

Contemplating the realities of war in Virginia compared to Georgia, I saw hardship in which weather and sickness took a morbid toll. Every aspect of life centered on preparations for the forthcoming spring battles. Wondering if Amy and George arrived home, I also wondered if they would return to Virginia.

At times, I attempted to help with the milling, but Mr. McAllister refused my assistance. Believing men and slaves performed such work, he'd send me back to the house, to the kitchen where I'd work with Gretchen and Dinah, William's sisters. When Mrs. McAllister died, both girls, as homely as William was handsome, latched onto me. They filled the void created by their mother's death with my strength and femininity. In the evening by candlelight, they taught me quilting.

At the end of January after a horrific cold spell, the valley warmed. William saddled two horses. We rode away for a picnic.

"Look at the Massanutten," he said, gesturing eastward as we rode north on the Valley Pike. "There's something I want you to see."

"What?"

"I can't explain it—trust me."

Turning east toward the Edinburg Gap, we climbed, coming to a spring from which flowed the coldest, clearest water I had ever tasted. Responding to the sun's warmth, we removed our wool jackets, storing them in satchels behind our saddles.

Continuing on, emotions I felt in the hospital tent at Haymarket sparked. "May we eat?" I asked with other motives in mind.

"One more mile," William said. By then, I thought, I'll have ripped off his clothes along with mine. The warmth, the horses, the ride increased my desire.

We entered a clearing. "I'm hungry." Our eyes met.

He looked up the slope. "Please give me five minutes. We're almost there."

He crested the mountain first. "Look," he said, as I rode next to him. "There's the other side of the Massanutten." In the distance, I saw another line of peaks encircling a valley.

"What is this? It looks like a giant basin."

"It is. We call it Fort Valley. Very few people know about it." Trees stretched downward and then upward as far as I could see. "There's not much to the south," he said, "but you can enter this valley from either New Market or Luray. It spreads out to the north where you can enter from Water Lick, halfway between Front Royal and Strasburg." Looking at each other, we dismounted. "Shall we eat?" Holding back for a moment, we embraced and kissed, the leafless trees our witnesses. For the first time, I knew I loved him and needed him.

Before our passion overcame us, I halted matters. Approaching my horse, I loosened the satchel containing the picnic and untied a blanket. With William's help, I spread it on dried leaves and unpacked the food. Four chicken legs, a couple biscuits and cakes quenched my hunger. The air chilled. Without a word, he removed the eating utensils from atop the blanket. Covering himself with one side, he descended upon me wrapping us together. We kissed.

"No more," I said. "I won't do this to you." Deep-set blue eyes proclaimed desire. "No—this will not happen until we're..."

Rising onto one arm, our eyes met. "Until we're what?"

"Nothing. I mean I..."

"I, what? Until what?" He knew my heart. "Until we're married?" he asked. Sitting up, I tried to apologize. "Is that what you meant to say? If so, I accept."

Not wanting to believe what I heard, I embraced him. "You are supposed to ask."

"Yes, but I couldn't take the chance that what I have wished for since the moment I saw you would escape my grasp." Without taking a breath, he asked, "When can we marry?"

"Tomorrow—let's find a clergyman before I dishonor you."

"Tomorrow it is," he said. "We must return to the mill before dark, lest we become lost. Without a moon, it is black as pitch."

Happy, smiling, we gathered utensils, the blanket, and retied the satchels to my saddle. Riding a few hundred feet, we heard horses. William pulled his rifle from the sheath as riders came into view.

"It's General Jackson," he said. "General Jackson, it is Captain McAllister." At least thirty cavalrymen and officers rode with him.

"Do I know you?" Jackson asked.

"Yes, I'm Doctor McAllister. I established the field hospital in Haymarket."

Jackson, looking puzzled, collected his thoughts. "Oh yes—I remember." His attention turned to me.

William, realizing the difficulty of the situation, didn't hesitate. "General Jackson, this is my wife, Stephanie." Jackson tipped his hat as I gasped, thinking that the first time I ever heard a southern gentleman story.

"I'm pleased to meet you, Mrs. McAllister," Jackson said.

"And, I you."

"What brings you here on a winter day?" William asked.

"Questions," Jackson said, sitting erect on his mount.

"We've enjoyed the warmth and a picnic," I said. "It is beautiful here—even more beautiful than Georgia."

"Georgia? Are you from there?"

"Yes, sir—from Atlanta."

"The Georgians at Bull Run fought well," he said. "The Milton Guards, under Major Yardley, saved our flank."

"My first husband served with Major Yardley before being killed in Cherokee, Georgia."

"My sympathies," General Jackson said, tipping his hat. "We scouted the Massanutten Valley to ascertain if it's a suitable place for refuge. I've been told an army quartered here could wreak havoc on the east and west. Please keep that between us."

"Yes, sir," William said. "Will you remain here overnight?"

"We make camp within the hour. Tomorrow, we ride to New Market gap and then, in a day return to Winchester through the north entrance at Water Lick."

"General," William said, "most people here refer to this basin as Fort Valley. Hearing how you intend to use it, one might conclude they named it appropriately."

He nodded. "We will see you in March at Front Royal."

"Yes sir," William said.

"Very nice to make your acquaintance, Mrs. McAllister."

"And yours—if you pass through Edinburg please stop at the mill." He nodded again, kicking his horse, to which the line of cavalry responded. William and I stayed put as they rode by, which allowed each man to eye me, mostly up and down.

"Let's go," William said. We trotted downward, the horses having a difficult time on the steeper slopes. Coming to a gradual incline, William stopped. "Do you feel badly toward me in that I lied?"

"Shocked."

"Please forgive me. That will never happen again. In trying to protect your honor, I dishonored myself before you and God."

"What do you mean, 'protect my honor'?"

"Well," he said as we rode, "I feared General Jackson would find fault in me if he discovered we picnicked alone and not married. He is a strict Presbyterian. Word has it, he spends two hours a day in prayer and study."

"In that case, I'm glad I'm not Presbyterian. Baptists preach judgment and damnation; but, once you're saved, you're on your own to worship on Sunday." I paused. "What do you think our chances were of coming face to face with General Jackson? Doesn't that strike you odd?"

"Hundred percent," he said. "Presbyterians believe God ordained the encounter."

"I believe God ordained it to demonstrate how far my future husband might go to protect his honor."

"No," he said. "Your honor was at stake."

Exhibiting a smile, I rode next to him. "Two lies in the same day?" I reached out with my left hand, grabbing his neck, drawing him close until our lips met. "This is fun. I married a military officer who didn't know how to lie, and now, I'm marrying a military doctor who doesn't know how to tell the truth." Laughing, shaking my head, I kicked my horse. "Race you home."

Unsaddling my horse, I turned to see William arrive at the mill. "I would have enjoyed the ride more if we had talked rather than raced."

"Race? If any slower, you would have missed our wedding tomorrow."

"What wedding?" Mr. McAllister, surrounded by Gretchen, Dinah, and Paul, asked from the porch.

"Ours," William said. "We marry tomorrow as soon as I can arrange it with a minister."

362

"Congratulations," Paul stated, smiling.

Standing, holding my saddle, I grew uncertain as to what to do. "Mr. McAllister," I said, "will you give us your blessing; or, should I re-saddle my horse?"

He glared, I think, never having been challenged by a female. Hesitating, he stepped off the porch and approached me. "You have my blessings." Taking the saddle, he carried it to the shed. Paul and the sisters walked toward me extending congratulations.

"Never seen father in such a state," Paul said.

Tomorrow did come along with winter's return and a ceremony at the mill.

Chapter 98

Amy Yardley

"And the surprise is what?" Father asked as we sat at supper the next night. Sarah sat across from her brother at the foot while George and I sat in the middle of the table.

"The surprise is," Sarah said, "your daughter and her husband, if he desires, and I will accompany you to England."

Father balked, but consented. "That would be wonderful."

"When do we depart?" I asked.

"The day after tomorrow—if that suits. We'll arrive the end of January, remain until the baby's birth, and return when Beatrice feels prepared to travel—by the end of April."

"A solid strategy," Sarah said. Then, to George. "Will you go?"

"Doubtful—I resume command of the Guard in February and must have them in Fredericksburg by March. The travel appears impossible."

"Well then," Father said, "we sail from Savannah in two days."

Chapter 99

Alexander Frey

A telegram from my Savannah office arrived the next afternoon as Horatio introduced me to James J. Andrews. Mr. Andrews infiltrated Atlanta society promising higher prices for cotton and rice to plantation owners burdened with the inflation of war. Such promises tickled the ear.

Horatio smelled a rat. Having met Mr. Andrews at social gatherings, and having heard his story, Horatio decided to introduce us. The meeting proved brief. After Andrews left, Horatio remained.

"Charming fellow," I said.

Horatio's hands found his hips. "Not so fast. Something's wrong."

"Something's wrong? What's wrong with paying fifty percent more for cotton and rice than I can pay? Rejoice for our plantation owners and farmers. They'll need extra income if the war lasts longer than expected."

Eye to eye, Horatio raised his index finger. "The New York papers quote prices a third to a half lower than Mr. Andrews promises. Alexander, I need your help and advice."

"Accept my apologies," I said. "Explain yourself."

"I believe Mr. Andrews and six friends, who make the same financial claims, are spies."

"Clarify your allegations."

"In two months, Andrews and his cohorts plan to fill a train with our excess cotton and rice from last year's harvest. Everyone who wants to sell at the higher price must deliver their goods to the Atlanta station on March Fifteenth. Andrews plans to issue bank drafts to each owner and ride away with their goods. I pleaded with our friends to request the drafts ahead of time to assure their validity. Everyone refused. Andrews charmed them and you. I believe the drafts worthless."

"What can we do?"

"Your associates in Virginia—contact them. Andrews contends he represents a conglomerate of Virginians who committed to pay these prices for the Confederate army."

"My agent in Norfolk—I will wire him. Amy met the son of an old family friend who practices medicine in Richmond. I'll dispatch a telegram to him also. We shall see if they have knowledge of Andrews. Meet me here tomorrow at mid-morning."

As Horatio and I stepped from my office, George met us, having informed Stephanie's parents about her relationship to Doctor McAllister. "George," Horatio said, "in Virginia did you hear tell of wealthy businessmen who sent agents to Georgia to buy our excess crops for the Confederate army?"

"No, sir," George said. "People in the Shenandoah Valley and south side of Virginia supply our soldiers. Why do you ask?" Horatio explained a shortened version of his theory. George shook his head. "If that was the case, I would have heard about it."

"I must send the telegraphs," I said, excusing myself.

Chapter 100

George Yardley

Watching as Alexander walked away, I saw two men duck down a side street. Mounting Splinter, racing with my revolver in my right hand, I turned the corner to find them drawing a bead on me with pistols. I shot twice. Getting down, kicking each man's chest with the point of my boot, I wondered who I killed.

"What's wrong?" Alexander said from behind me.

"Don't know—when I caught up to them, they pulled their guns. I shot first."

"You sure they're dead?" Alexander asked.

"Shot one through the eye and one through the heart. They're dead."

"Now what's going on?" Alexander asked.

"Don't know, but the sooner Amy, Sarah, and you set sail, the better I'll feel."

Horatio arrived with three constables. Alexander headed to the telegraph office. After explaining what happened, I headed to Sarah's, finding Sarah and Amy on the front porch. Alexander joined us as I completed the details of the shooting.

"One man I shot had a list of names. Your name," I said to Alexander, "was at the top of the list. What I said earlier still goes. The sooner you three board that ship, the better I'll feel."

Chapter 101

George Yardley

At ten o'clock, Sarah, Amy, and Alexander made a futile stop at the telegraph office. At eleven, they stepped on the train, leaving me with instructions to remain in Atlanta until word from Virginia arrived.

Watching the train pull away, I wondered if I would ever see Amy again. War might lead to my demise, as a ship sinking might lead to hers. Still on the platform, Horatio approached, appearing as if we lost the war.

"What's wrong?" I asked.

"Spies," he said. "We must stop James Andrews and his cohorts." He stared eastward at the tracks. "Is Alexander on that train?"

"Yes, but how do you know about these spies?"

He handed me a paper. "We received this from operatives in Washington."

Scribbled words read, "Infiltrators everywhere, especially in Georgia." My head bowed, staring at the message, contemplating its significance.

"You ridded us of two yesterday afternoon," Horatio said, making me look up, remembering the shooting.

"Did you come from the telegraph office?"

"Yes. I wanted Alexander to see this before I showed it to Governor Brown and Vice President Stephens."

"I'm heading to the telegraph office to inquire if either message Alexander expected arrived. If so, where can I meet you?"

"The club at noon." We shook hands, going our separate ways.

❧❧❧

The telegraph office smelled musty as if the operator never opened windows. Standing behind a desk, he handed me a telegram with the same readable scribbling as the one Horatio gave me. It read, "No such deal. Hoax. Doctor Branner."

The telegraph chattered. The operator, taking a seat, deciphered the message. "No knowledge of business association buying commodities. If I hear, will notify. L. Cooke."

Now what? I asked myself, leaving the office. Returning to Sarah's before meeting Horatio, I mounted Splinter, riding through Atlanta. My mind produced unfounded suspicions. Anger permeated my soul. The attribute of honor associated itself with war; but, spying on an enemy felt dishonorable—as I would feel if I dishonored Amy. Whatever James Andrews' purposes, I determined to do the honorable thing and kill him.

Chapter 102

Alexander Frey

Riding along, I wished the time away, hoping an English ship in port with a captain intending to set sail as soon as possible. At the tide's mercy, I long ago accepted my lack of control over such matters. Entering Savannah, I strained to see if masts rose at the dock, but saw none. Disappointed, I hid my emotion. Then, an emotion overcame me. What was I thinking? Why would I return to Savannah of all places with Amy and Sarah? What if a slave master or someone else recognized us? Rising, I left the car heading forward to the engine. Steam-pistons hissed; the metal wheels clanked against the tracks. I opened the door, pushing my way inside.

"Hey, what do you want?" the engineer hollered.

"Nothing, except to know if you continue to Charleston."

"Yes—in two hours."

Backing out the door, re-entering my coach, I seated myself next to Sarah. Amy sat two seats to the rear, resting her eyes. Putting my finger to my lips, I urged Sarah to refrain from disturbing my daughter. "I don't like being in Savannah," I said. "What if someone involved in the ruckus last year recognizes either you or Amy?" Sarah's brow furrowed. "This train travels to

Charleston in two hours. We can stay onboard or get off and take our chances here."

"Let's see if a ship is here," she said.

"Didn't see a mast at dock when we neared the water."

"We have two hours to decide," she said. I nodded, hoping the ship would arrive and depart within the day.

Loading our baggage, we rode a surrey to the hotel where I requested one room, having decided to spend the night but remain out of sight. Wasting no time, a slave led us to the second floor, opening the door to room 214.

I felt safe until the slave spoke. "Thank you, Miss Frey, for what you did on the dock."

Amy turned, her jaw dropped. "Were you there?"

"Yes, ma'am. You washed my brother's feet."

"What is your name?"

"Aaron."

"Aaron," she said, "you must do something. If a slave master discovers we're here, we fear they'll bring harm to us. Promise us you won't tell anyone."

"Yes, ma'am," he said, "but we wouldn't let harm come to you."

"We?" she asked.

"My people—they wouldn't let anything happen to you."

"Aaron," I said, "we appreciate that. These men are vicious—we're not certain you could protect us."

"We have ways. Don't worry."

He departed, closing the door. Amy and Sarah stood at the window, peering out on an empty harbor. Hour after hour passed. When I didn't pace, I stood rigid, staring, hoping, wishing to see a ship.

A knock alarmed us. Rushing to the door, I turned the latch with my left hand while pointing my derringer with my right. "Who's there?"

"Aaron."

Opening the door and stepping out, I made certain no danger lurked. "Everything's fine," he said. "If anyone tries to do you harm, they won't live to tell about it." We went inside. Aaron pointed toward the window. "Look there." In the distance, a ship made its way toward port. "That's The Trent."

"This may be our lucky day," I said. "The ship will dock in less than an hour. I'll wait until dusk, go to the dock, and book passage."

Aaron started for the door. "You won't have trouble—ain't many people leaving the country. Ship captains want passengers."

"Aaron," I said, "may we take supper in our room?"

"Yes, sir."

"Please return in an hour with our food and remain in the hallway while I go to the ship. I will reward."

"Do that anyway," Aaron said. "That is, I'm staying in the hallway all night with others. No need for reward. I'll bring supper."

"What others?" Sarah asked.

"Others who appreciate what you did." He left.

I collected both women, embracing them. "For some reason, I feel safer than I should. Whatever Aaron's up to, he has our best interests at heart."

✺ ❧ ✺ ❧

In an hour, a rap at the door startled us. I went through the same routine, drawing my derringer. Aaron presented a tray of food. Placing it on the bed, he set plates and utensils on a small cherry table next to the window.

"Mr. Frey," he said, "I'll be in the hallway. When you go to the ship, let me know. We'll see you safe there and keep the women safe."

"Thank you," I said.

Bowing, he departed, allowing us to dine. Though the tension subdued our appetite, the aroma of food whetted it.

Seated, I took Sarah's hand and then my daughter's, offering a blessing laced with prayers for safety and gratitude for Aaron.

Feeling refreshed, I opened the door. Before taking two steps, Aaron appeared. "What can I do for you?"

"Going to the ship."

"Fine," he said. "Follow me."

At the stairway, two slaves received instruction from Aaron to stand guard at our door while he escorted me downstairs. I listened, hoping them capable. "Walk to the docks," he said. "Others know you're coming."

A faint gray light illuminated the streets. People, white and Negro, milled about. No one paid me mind. Standing at The Trent's gangplank, I asked a crew member permission to see the captain. He tended to the task, returning, giving me directions to the cabin.

"Alexander Frey," the captain said, greeting me. We meet again." Cowering, I wondered if anyone on the docks heard his proclamation. "How may I help you?"

"I need three passages to England. My sister and daughter accompany me. If you remember, my wife in England expects a child."

"Fine," he said, "but we sail in the morning."

"I hoped so. May we have our cabins tonight?"

"If you desire."

"Thank you. How much is the passage?"

"Thirty dollars," he replied. I pulled my wallet from my jacket presenting the captain with a hundred dollar bill. "Don't worry about the change. Buy something you enjoy drinking."

Holding the bill in his fist, he shook it. "I will. Thank you."

Departing, I returned to the hotel acknowledging our good fortune. Aaron, standing in the hallway, overheard. "Master Frey," he said, tapping on the door, "I need to see you." He motioned for me to join him down the hall. "They know you're here and know Miss Amy's here. Safest place is on the ship. Let's get there fast." Lost in thought, Aaron found it necessary to snap me from my daydream. "What do you want to do?"

My shoulders shrugged. "I'm not certain."

"Get the women. I'll return shortly." He hopped down the stairs to the lobby. Before I moved, he came back. "A carriage waits at the back door."

Those words produced a response. Walking to the room, I hurried the women. Another slave waited at the door. Aaron and he carried the baggage down a back stairway as we followed. Exiting the hotel, we entered a dark alleyway in which the carriage waited.

"Let's be gone," Aaron said.

I helped Sarah, then Amy, into their seats. With the door closed, the driver snapped his whip. We jerked and lunged forward. Aaron and one slave stood on the back step while the driver and another slave sat on the front seat. Turning onto the main street leading to the docks, we heard someone holler fire. Looking toward the voice, a light drew my attention. On the second floor, flames shot through a window in the room 214.

"Don't stop," Aaron yelled. "Get them to the ship. We can't save that tinderbox."

The driver snapped his whip. From near the ship's stern, we gazed upon the second and third floors of the hotel engulfed in flames.

"That was meant for us," I said.

Aaron lifted a piece of baggage. "I know. Get you onboard before they discover you weren't there."

"I have a better idea. Let's make certain they think they killed us. After we're on the ship, go back and talk it up that Alexander Frey, his sister and daughter were burned in the fire. If they think we're dead, it'll quench their thirst for revenge."

Chapter 103

Amy Yardley

"Oh, my God," I said, reading the headlines and first paragraph of the article in the Savannah Journal the captain provided. "George will think we died in the fire."

Father took the paper, scanning it. "The ship can't turn around in this channel even if the captain agreed."

"What's wrong?" the captain asked, overhearing our conversation.

Standing, I explained the dilemma. "Is there anything we can do?"

"Not now. If we pass an incoming ship, we might get a message to its captain. Upon docking, he might send a telegram to your husband."

"It's a waiting game," Father said.

"I believe so."

We received permission to mill about the ship, but only in Father's company. At the bow, we began an ordeal of wishing. An hour passed when the wide expanse of the Atlantic Ocean presented itself. Something else presented itself. A ship in the distance circled toward us.

"Mr. Frey," the captain said, "retire to your quarters. That ship flies the stars and stripes."

Father stared outward and then at me. "We must go."

The captain nodded. "Don't worry. After the Slidell and Mason crisis, no American warship will stop and board an English vessel. You are safe."

"It seems," Father said, "God graced us with a slave and a sea captain."

The American ship sailed a semi-circle around us and headed away. In the cabin, I brooded over the message George would receive of our deaths.

Chapter 104

George Yardley

From the porch, I witnessed Horatio walking toward the house. Climbing the steps, standing before me, eyes filled with concern, he spoke. "Something terrible happened." Hesitating, his voice cracked. "The hotel in which Amy, Sarah, and Alexander stayed last night burned down. According to a slave, they died."

My memory recalled the smell of burning flesh at the Livingstones fire. "Come in," I said. "Were the bodies found?"

Horatio took a seat in the parlor. "Not that I know."

"Until I'm presented with proof, I shall not believe they are dead. Please do not think wrongly of me. If Amy were dead, I would know it."

Horatio stood, holding his hat. "I must depart. This tragedy incapacitates me."

"Would you go by the station and buy a ticket on the morning train to Savannah for me?"

He nodded and walked away, wiping a tear from his eye.

Chapter 105

George Yardley

Sleep proved impossible. Lying awake I drew two conclusions. Amy was alive, and I needed Nathaniel. Confirming the former required a trip to Savannah. Arranging for the latter appeared difficult, unless I rode to Alpharetta. At half past four in the morning, I mounted Splinter. Leaving Atlanta, I discovered the disparity of riding through the darkness of night with a partner and riding alone. Fear awakened my senses, especially hearing. I scrutinized every sound hoping Splinter saw better than I. Not having gone a couple miles, I realized my stupidity. Riding alone in the darkness, I thought, could either get me killed or scare me to death. Either way, one achieved the same outcome.

About the time I decided to turn around, I saw what I needed to see. Splinter lurched. Standing inside the tree line, my parents beckoned. Father's arm rested around Mother's shoulder, her hands prayerfully clutched at her chest. Splinter kept moving, but slowed. In a blink, the apparition vanished, but not its purpose. Amy's absence from the vision convinced me she lived.

Dawn emerged as I reached the Montross cabin. Light illuminated a window. "Who's there?" Howard shouted, startling Splinter and me.

"George Yardley—don't shoot."

"If I did, I'd shoot with my 'tallywhacker'. Give me a minute. I have to go." Finishing, Howard found me dismounted, standing on his porch. We shook hands. "What you doing out here at this hour?"

"Getting Nathaniel," I said, and then stated the reason. "Man, you stink."

"It's Friday. Most Fridays I smell worse. Come back tomorrow night, and I'll smell sweet as the sap from a Georgia pine."

"Doubtful." I said, turning toward Splinter.

Howard grabbed my arm. "You ain't going nowhere, until you have food to eat."

Hearing Hester rummaging inside, I relented. "No one's shot or struck by lightning, are they?" She said from the door.

Chuckling, I greeted her. "No, but you sure smell better than your husband."

"He's ill," she said, "and won't see a doctor. I'll need your help to bury him if he doesn't get better soon."

Peering at Howard the best I could, realizing the seriousness of Hester's comment, I challenged him. "Don't have a death wish, do you?"

"Nope, but if I'm gonna die, I'd just as soon die here and in God's good time rather than under the eye of a money grubbing doctor."

"Hester, if that's the case, Nathaniel and I will dig you a grave in a few days. That way, we can make Howard help us."

Howard opened the door. "Man shouldn't have to dig his own grave."

"If he's dumb enough not to get help to live, then he's dumb enough to dig his own grave. Besides, I have to leave."

Before reaching the ferry, I decided to cross on horseback. Giving Splinter a chance to shake dry, I put him into a fast trot, wanting to reach Uncle Robert's before nine o'clock.

Samantha spotted me first, screaming to the others. Lillian appeared on the porch followed by Nathaniel and Robert. Lillian had aged. Her hair revealed strands of gray. A few chiseled lines furrowed her brow.

Standing in the kitchen, I addressed Nathaniel. "I have bad news."

"What?" Lillian asked.

"News came to Atlanta yesterday that Amy, Alexander, and Sarah burned to death in a hotel in Savannah." Lillian gasped bringing both hands to her mouth as did Samantha.

"No," Nathaniel said.

"Nathaniel, I need help—get mounted. We're going to Savannah." I paused, as he started for the barn. "She's not dead. If she were, I'd know it. Besides, Mother and Father appeared to me without Amy on the road last night. She's alive." Robert and Lillian's expressions shot questions at me; but, they refused to speak. Nathaniel seemed paralyzed. "Get saddled."

"Hope you're right," Robert said.

Nathaniel returned, looking like a seasoned soldier, which served to put fear in Lillian's heart. "Do you see these gray hairs? You and George made me old before my time. All I do is work and worry." She banged a spoon against the table. "Did you hear me?"

"Why do you worry?" I said. "We did everything we could to get shot. It didn't happen."

"You're a liar, and you're both stupid," Lillian said, bursting into tears. "Stupidity will get you both killed. That's why I worry."

Putting my hand on her shoulder, I sought to comfort her. "I have to find out what happened. If we hurry, we can make the train to Savannah and be back in two days.

She pulled away. "The last time you went to Savannah, you created an incident that nearly started the war, and you did get shot at."

"Maybe it best you get on your way," Robert said.

Chapter 106

George Yardley

We pushed the horses hard, checking my watch from time to time, determined to make the train. Splinter broke the first sweat. We rested after crossing the river.

By half past ten, we entered Atlanta's north side, moving to the station. "It appears the steam engine awaits us," Nathaniel said.

After making our plight known to the ticket agent, slaves scurried about loading the horses and securing the gates on the livestock car. Nathaniel and I took seats as the whistle blew. The train strained forward. Within moments, I slept.

The smell of salt air awakened me. Repugnant, my nostrils verified our arrival in Savannah. Stirring, I caught a glimpse of a cloudy, misty day. The smoldering remains of the Savannah Hotel received a light rain on the charred planks and boards. I considered the possibility Amy's body lay in the destruction.

Nathaniel stood, stretching. "Can't imagine the agony you feel."

Stepping off the train, I saw James Andrews stepping onto the platform from the next car. If I counted right, at least seven men accompanied him. Not wanting to enter into frivolous conversation, I pretended not to notice him.

WISH IS MY MASTER

"Mr. Yardley," he called, approaching, reaching to shake hands. "Mr. Yardley, whatever are you doing here?"

"Here on sad business. Received word my wife and her family were in the fire."

Andrews gasped. "My sympathies—anything I can do?"

"No," I said wanting to rid myself of the scum. "My cousin and I plan to investigate the matter. If you don't mind, we must go." James Andrews tipped his hat.

Nathaniel and I walked toward the cattle car. "If in Virginia, I'd have shot Andrews on the spot."

Drawn to the hotel, we walked the horses through the streets until we stood before the burned ruins. More drizzle fell, causing us to don our oil cloths. What I smelled confirmed my suspicion. The smell of burning flesh seared into my memory from the Livingstone fire failed to present itself.

Nathaniel, having seen enough, asked a passerby where we might board. Receiving directions to a Miss Jacquelyn Bruce's establishment, we rode six blocks from the harbor until we came to a large gray house. Nathaniel approached the front door, pulling a bell-rope. The door opened. A plump woman with a smiling round face greeted him. After chatting, Nathaniel returned, directing me around back to a small stable where we brushed the horses.

"You going to talk to me during this trip?" Nathaniel asked.

"I apologize. Seeing the hotel set my mind wandering. Also, James Andrews—he's trouble."

Finished with the horses, we approached the back door. Miss Bruce opened it, encouraging us to call her Jackie. "No baggage?" she asked, while showing us to the stairs.

"No," Nathaniel said. "We don't expect to stay long." He paused. "My cousin was told his wife died in the hotel fire."

Miss Bruce sighed, turning toward George. "My sympathies."

"Have you heard reports about the fire?" I asked.

"The fire started in your wife's room," she said. "They didn't escape."

"Were their bodies found?" Nathaniel asked.

"No—they burned up." She groaned, I think realizing the severity of what she said.

"Glad they didn't find remains—gives me hope. Flesh burns. Bones don't."

"Maybe so."

"Maybe so," I repeated. "Do you know the people who owned the hotel or anyone who worked there? We stayed there once. Slaves tended to the clientele."

"True—you might find the slaves in the slave quarters at the docks. As to the owners, I'll ask if anyone knows their whereabouts. Let's get you to your room."

"Room?" Nathaniel said. "Any chance you have two rooms?"

"Certainly, if you'll pay for two."

"George wants to pay for two. Give the lady four dollars, Confederate."

"You men don't like sleeping in the same room?"

"True," Nathaniel said as we started upstairs. "He's restless and snores—keeps me up."

❧❧❧❧

"They're rooming in a boarding house about a half mile from here," one of James Andrews' cohorts reported to him after following George and Nathaniel. Andrews absorbed the news while considering the bad luck that Alexander Frey's son-in-law had shown in Savannah.

"He seemed suspicious of me at the train depot," Andrews replied to the messenger and the other five men with him. The seventh man remained posted outside the boarding house.

"He's a good-for-nothing traitor too big for his britches," one stated.

"We're all traitors," Andrews mused, while wondering what to do. They stood at the bar in a tavern, waiting word as to when and where they would rendezvous with their informants. The tavern owner, a Yankee sympathizer named Richard Grove, had made his business and connections available to Andrews.

"You'd best be careful how you're thinking," Grove said, responding to the comment. "Mr. Yardley has proved himself time and time again, and that cousin of his isn't too shabby. The best way to get killed is to think your enemy isn't worthy. Either man will shoot you lickety-split if you give him cause." He walked behind the bar allowing his comments to sink in while pausing to see if anyone wanted a drink. No one made a request.

They heard a noise from beneath them. Grove went to a table in the corner of the tavern, setting it aside about five feet and then removing a worn throw rug on which the table sat. Placing his index finger in a small hole, he lifted a trap door through which five men emerged: three white and two Negroes. Quick greetings were exchanged amongst the whites, while the two Negroes faded off into a corner near the bar.

"What's the news?" Andrews asked waiting for a reply.

"Tell them, Aaron," one man ordered the slave.

"Ah, well," Aaron stammered. "Mr. Frey's on The Trent with his daughter and sister."

"How did they escape?" Andrews demanded.

"No one knows," Aaron said. "But they had help."

"So, Mr. Frey is on his way to England while his son-in-law is in Savannah," Andrews said. Aaron caught himself before gasping at what he heard. "Mr. Yardley doesn't know his wife is alive. We don't know how much money Mr. Frey plans to bring from England."

"What difference does that make?" Grove asked from behind the bar.

"A lot," Andrews said. "Mr. Yardley and his cousin killed some of our best spies—one named Speakes—and set the town of Dumfries on fire, killing others situated to help our side. After that, they turned the tide at Manassas Junction giving the rebels a victory they didn't deserve. While in my sites, I may put them six feet under."

৵৵৵৵

"Wonder where she's going?" I said as I watched through the window. Miss Jacquelyn Bruce walked in a quick pace up the street disappearing around a corner. From the other room, I heard Nathaniel's breathing, indicating he slept. Even though I felt imprisoned, I knew better than to make my way to the slave quarters by the docks alone. Understanding if any slave master caught a glimpse of me, he would shoot on sight, I had to stay put.

Miss Bruce reappeared walking toward the house. Suspicious, I hoped she hadn't informed anyone of our presence. What if she knew of my last visit to Savannah? After strapping on my belt and holster, I awakened Nathaniel.

"How do you want to play this?" he asked, sitting on his bed.

"I want to find out if Miss Bruce is for us or against us. Get ready—let's go downstairs."

Nathaniel pulled on his boots, then strapped on his holster. Giving each other one last look, we descended the steps, entering the dining room where we saw bowls of steaming vegetables and biscuits on the table.

Miss Bruce came through the kitchen door carrying a platter of ham. "Hope you're hungry. Since war broke out, I've not had much business—feels good to prepare a hardy meal."

Nathaniel took a seat. "We're much obliged." She gestured offering me a chair. Returning to the kitchen, she brought a pot of coffee and a pitcher of water. Seating herself, she asked Nathaniel if he would offer a blessing, which he did.

Nathaniel and Miss Bruce conversed regarding our war experiences in Virginia while I remained silent listening to empty words and for sounds of impending danger. Halfway through the meal, we heard a knock on the back door. Nathaniel and I exchanged a strained look.

Miss Bruce stood. "That must be Joshua. I went to where he lives while you rested and asked him to run an errand." She placed her napkin next to her plate and excused herself. We drew our weapons hiding them under the table. "Come with me," we heard Miss Bruce order and watched as the swinging door between the kitchen and dining room opened. Before us stood a youthful Negro accompanied by a slave, who held his hat with both hands in front of him.

"Mr. Yardley," she said, gesturing toward Nathaniel, "Mr. Thomas, this boy is Joshua—a slave owned by the Richman family around the corner. And, this is Aaron—a slave who worked in the hotel and worked the night of the fire."

"You did?" I asked.

"Yes, sir," Aaron said. "Trouble awaits you."

"Trouble?" Miss Bruce said. "What do you mean?"

"This afternoon, I met with a Mister Andrews who's awful interested in you—heard him say he wants you dead."

"What else did he say?" Nathaniel asked.

"Seemed concern you two killed people in a place called Dumfries. Those people were important to him. He wants to stop you, Mister Yardley. You killed a spy named, Speakes."

I couldn't wait any longer. "Do you know what happened in that fire? Was my wife, Amy Yardley, there?"

"Yes, sir, but me and friends took them to a ship—got them onboard before the hotel burned."

"They're safe?"

"Yes, sir."

"Who started the fire?" Nathaniel asked.

"The slave masters you offended."

Nathaniel turned to me. "What will we do about that?"

"Nothing—go home in the morning." Thinking for a moment, I turned my attention to Aaron and Miss Bruce. "I owe you both. Why did you help me?"

"Cause the best thing the Confederacy could do is set all the slaves free," she said. "No one deserves to be treated the way they're treated. What you and your wife did for them left a deep impression. The least I could do is help you find news about Mrs. Yardley."

"I'm much obliged. And, Aaron, thank you for coming tonight. I hope it didn't put you in danger."

"Don't think so," Aaron replied. "Pleased to help."

I wanted to reach in my wallet to give Aaron a reward, but felt the gesture would demean the Negro; so, I didn't. A shot rang out. Window glass crashed to the floor. Aaron collapsed. Rushing to Aaron's side, hearing Miss Bruce's screams, seeing Nathaniel race to the front door, I saw Aaron breathe his last.

"Two men—running for their lives down the street," Nathaniel said. "There's nothing we can do for him. Let's find the killers."

With pistols drawn, I wanted nothing to do with a chase in a strange city. "In the morning, we'll see this man gets a proper burial. Tonight, we'll make certain Joshua gets home. When our work is done, we'll head to Atlanta. We have a war to fight."

Nathaniel returned his pistol to its holster. "What honor is there in that? A man died for you tonight. Will you abandon him—his family? What if he had abandoned you?"

My heart sank. My head shook. "Honor—maybe I don't have any honor left in me."

Nathaniel stared. "God, I wish you hadn't said that. But, wishing is all I ever do."

ACKNOWLEDGEMENTS

One joy in life is to come face to face with someone who has your best interest at heart. Last summer, near Dumfries, Virginia, over a cup of coffee, I sat across from Rebecca Ferrell. Within seconds, I experienced that joy. Having read, The Honor of Love, she expressed amazement, intrigue, and happiness at what she learned from the book. Most importantly, at least for me, she began to do what she does best, teach; and, teach she did. For the past nine months, I have benefited from her patience and knowledge, as she taught me what I believe is the true meaning of editing: to inspire an author to continue to seek the pleasure of writing. I would hope that in every author's life, there is a Becky.

Another joy approached me in the autumn of 2010. Anita Hampson, a retired teacher, offered to read and edit the manuscript. During that process, if I had to guess, she wished she had foregone the privilege—so to speak. However, Anita's insights and encouragement moved me forward in a wonderful way.

I especially wish to express my gratitude to Marion for the reading, editing, and motivation she continually provides, and to Frank Weaver for the manner in which he so easily goes about publishing a book.

Our hope was to publish The Honor of War by March, 2011. As many of you know, my brother, Bill, died shortly after Thanksgiving. Marion's mother, Barbara Brown, died in January. Both passings delayed publication. Then, on April 5, 2011, we received word that our two-year granddaughter, Finn, was diagnosed with what the doctors suspected was a malignant tumor of the liver. On Palm Sunday, April 17th, doctors informed us the tumor was benign. And so, I offer this work in memory of Bill and Babs, and in gratitude for the blessing God bestowed upon us in Finn.